The Impossible Takes a Little Longer

By

Eric Edis

ISBN: 978-1-4092-0301-8

Acknowledgements

This book could never have been written but for the help of my good friend Elaine Burrell of Chingford, who unscrambled and put on computer every word of my handwritten scribble, turning it into a legibly readable manuscript.

My thanks to Michael Learner for scrutinizing the manuscript for any missing words, commas, or full stops etc., and for his input on ocean-going oil tankers.

Thanks to my long-suffering daughters, Carolyn and Wendy, who listened, without complaint, to my endless ramblings whilst I read passages from the manuscript to them

The photographs for this book were kindly scanned and prepared for publication by Fred Harmer.

This book is dedicated to my dear wife, Betty, who suffered my absence whilst bringing up our daughter for far longer than had been planned. The expedition took twice as long to complete than could reasonably have been envisaged.

Please note that the photos in the book were taken nearly fifty years ago so any low quality is solely due to age.

Foreword

The Impossible Takes a Little Longer is the story of an adventure-packed overland journey made by an inexperienced group of young men and women. These intrepid young people set out to drive across the world to Australia and back in two old motor vehicles. The chosen route would take us, through the bandit-infested areas of the famous Burma Ledo road, en route to Singapore, where, hopefully, the plan was to work our passage across to Australia by ship.

Many problems, disappointments, and mistakes were to arise during the early planning stages of the expedition. The Foreign Office refused to support an application to the Burmese Embassy in London for transit visas through their country saying that it was too dangerous. The Burmese themselves also refused my direct approach for permission. They informed me that due to the unstable political situation, insurgent activity, and appalling road conditions, its borders with India had been closed to outsiders since the end of World War II. Without Burmese visas, the trip would have been dead in the water. However, I couldn't accept that my long-term dream to become the first person to traverse both directions through of that benighted country to and from Singapore, with an added trek across Australia's Nullarbor Plain, was doomed to failure before it had even begun. I would take my chances and sort the Burma problem out when we arrived in Calcutta.

This journey was made on a very limited budget, and all our equipment was basic. The vehicles we used had certainly seen better days, and sponsors were few and far between. There was no winch on the Land Rover □ we couldn't afford one □ so had to rely on man, women, and animal power to pull to us from the swamps. There was much sickness on the return half of the journey, which included malaria, jungle foot, hookworm, fever, guinea worm, a hand infection, and dysentery.

Although there were no guidelines to work on, it was reckoned that the whole journey would take about nine months. That was grossly underestimated; in fact, it took twice as long. The delay in leaving Australia, which was due to a hold up with shipping bound for Singapore, resulted in our late arrival in Thailand and Burma, where we ran smack into a monsoon and suffered all the delays and hold-ups associated with it.

The complete journey (London – Singapore – Australia – Singapore – London) covered a road distance of 40,000 miles. Over 5,000 miles of those were in Australia.

On the return journey we towed a small trailer to carry some of our equipment and free up space in the vehicle. On the surface it seemed like a good idea at the time, but it didn't take long to realize it was a big mistake. It caused nothing but problem after problem and was always in need of some kind of repair. However,

I wasn't about to give up on it. So against my better judgement, we suffered it and dragged it all the way back to England. For the last 1,000 miles its steel body had to be supported and was propped up with thick bamboo canes.

We were helped along the way by many people I choose to call my friends, and I give a special thanks to the staff at a number of our embassies, who very kindly gave us accommodation, facilities for repairing the vehicle, and medical attention from their own doctor.

Why did we go? This is a question that is frequently trotted out; I suppose the answer must be, because I wanted to. I had talked about it for years before deciding to put my money where my mouth was. Whether it was a complete success would be for the reader to judge. For myself, I have had a world of travel and adventure, and seen places I could once only dream of. I accomplished almost everything that I set out to do. Even down to working my passage aboard ship, which, I had been told, was impossible.

Introduction

Ever since I was a boy at school I have always been enthralled by stories of travel and adventure, and usually found it hard to resist a dare made to me by my school chums. This lingering thirst for excitement was to remain with me into my adult life. It was, therefore, no surprise to friends and others who knew me when I made up my mind to chase my long-term dream and take up the challenge of leading an expedition overland to Singapore. From there, taking my vehicle with me, I planned to work my passage aboard ship to Australia for a short respite, before driving back home again from Singapore.

The early planning for this journey was thought out and written on scraps of paper during a prolonged spell in a hospital bed, and it soon became clear that there were many problems to overcome. Currency regulations were in force and those travelling abroad in the late fifties were allowed to take no more than £40 per person out of the country. Although many letters were written to companies seeking sponsorship, apart from Castrol, who very kindly supplied all our oil along the route, and Kraft Cheese, who gave us special discounts on their products, very little else was forthcoming. Money was tight all round and everything was organized on a shoestring budget.

I advertised in the *London Weekly Advertiser* for suitable like-minded people with a spirit of adventure to join me. Soon the letters started to flow in with each one making their pitch to convince me they were the people I was looking for. But sadly, in most cases, they weren't. Finding people with the right motivation wasn't easy. The expedition was looked at by some as nothing more than a glorified long holiday.

My original intention had been to make the journey with six people using one vehicle, a long wheelbase Land Rover. However, because of the severe currency restrictions and the need to generate more income that could legally be taken out of the country, the only way I could see around this problem was to increase the size of the party. This was a big mistake that I was later to regret.

I purchased a second vehicle, a Ford 15-cwt truck, for £50 at a government surplus auction of military vehicles in the north of England. Seemingly things were beginning to shape up, and against my better judgement, I settled on a party of fifteen, ten men, which included me, and five women. Their ages ranged from seventeen to thirty-six. Of these people, some were accepted solely on their ability to raise the necessary contributions, but I couldn't help my nagging doubts about whether all the members of the group had the necessary grit to stay the course.

How long that course would take I had no real idea. The best assessment I could arrive at was to be back home in England within nine months. That prediction turned out to be wildly optimistic. There was no yardstick from which I could take guidance as nobody had ever completed a trip overland to Singapore and back again, with a journey across the Australian desert thrown in as an added extra.

When the International Vehicle Carnet was applied for, the AA informed us that travel visas through Burma were unobtainable. I sought the help of the Foreign Office in support of my application to the Burmese Consulate for overland travel visas. Their response was uncompromising. "It is impossible and we would never recommend it. Permission would never be granted. Burma is a dangerous place! Sorry, but we can't help." I then applied directly to the Burmese Consulate, who confirmed that their land borders to and from India had been closed to road traffic since the end of World War II. This was a major setback to my aspirations of achieving something that had never been done before.

However, I wasn't ready to buckle or throw in the towel and accept that my dream was over. I knew the odds were stacked very much against me, and I realized that without being able to penetrate the jungles of Burma's no-go area, the natural barrier to Singapore, it would have spelt the death knell of the trip and left us pondering in Calcutta. That was a problem that would have to be overcome when we arrived there.

When we left England I could never in my wildest dreams have envisaged a situation where I would be rescued by the Mujahideen from the frozen hell of an Afghan winter, or be saved from walking into a minefield by a notice board that I couldn't read. I was also to rescue a trapped and injured Afghan driver from a crashed Russian tanker spilling fuel. It was never on the cards that our vehicle would be pulled from jungle swamps by an elephant, and that I would be struck down by malaria, or that the girls would suffer from guinea worm and athlete's foot. When I doctored our Burmese visas, I never thought they would be so convincing as to be authenticated by the Burmese immigration officials, who would then drag us from the river into that benighted country using an old British Bren-Gun carrier. Although I knew that the Naga's had a culture as head-hunters, we never expected to find ourselves dancing with them round a fire in their village.

Upon my return, I received many letters from other would-be expeditionists wishing to follow my route to, or from, Singapore only for them to be thwarted by the Burma factor.

Three army officers once approached me from the Pegasus Overland Expedition seeking information on how I was able to enter that forbidden land. Although willing to help in other ways, information about my entry into Burma was excluded. I had gained entry by using all my ingenuity and initiative, which had not been without great risk, so it was my philosophy that it would be a fitting test of their own inventiveness to do likewise. Although it was no surprise to me, I could understand their frustration when I learned some months later that they too had been denied entry.

It had never been my intention to write of my travel experiences, but browsing through my diaries rekindled the events of those bygone days, prompting me to take up the pen and relive my overland adventures from the comfort of my armchair. As my journeys had in the main taken me twice through the same countries, it would be repetitive to write about the same places a second time. So, I have chosen to begin my story from Singapore, after arriving there on the first leg of the journey out of England.

However, as events on the outward journey through Turkey and especially Burma had played such a significant part in the ultimate success of the expedition, I have, therefore, highlighted some of the problems encountered along the way, together with a description of my chosen routes.

Highlights Of The Outward Journey

It was the morning of October 28th 1957 when the two trucks headed towards Dover on the outward journey to Singapore. I couldn't help suffering from twinges of anxiety about how my group of individuals, previously unknown to each other, would cope on such a long journey about which so little was known.

We crossed the Channel to Boulogne and headed straight for Paris, where we had our first taste of pitching the tents for our night's camp. The journey across Europe, apart from a puncture, was fairly straightforward and took us through Switzerland and Italy to Yugoslavia, where we were held up by an army patrol who prodded us with their rifles whilst they examined our travel documents.

We skipped through Greece and crossed the border into the European side of Turkey. By the time we reached Istanbul it became apparent that the party had divided itself into two distinct groups. I was stunned by the news that seven members had decided they wanted to leave the main party and head for Africa instead. At length we waved goodbye to the seven deserters as they drove away in the 15-cwt truck. We were to lose two more members: nineteen-year-old Steve, who was homesick, followed a few days later by Dick, also nineteen, who was missing his girlfriend. That reduced the group to six. They were: Pat, a twenty-three-year-old typist from London who was the first applicant to join the trip; Roger, a seventeen-year-old student from St Ives in Cornwall who was 'God willing' hoping to join his mother who was living in Singapore; Margaret, a twenty-two-year-old Australian from Melbourne who was returning home after a holiday in the UK; Elmore, a twenty-three-year-old Jamaican-American who wanted to visit Australia before returning to his native US, and whose passion was playing cricket; Norman, a twenty-one-year-old hairdresser from London who was seeking adventure and joined the trip looking like a big game hunter complete with rifle and a tiger-skin band round his hat. I completed the six.

Since leaving London we had covered just over three thousand miles. Our next lap was to take us into Iraq and on to the small town of Zakho just over the border and close to where the frontiers of Turkey, Syria and Iraq all meet. Then onto the RAF base at Habbaniyah, where we could all expect a hot bath and to rest up for a few days. We were expected at the airbase where my brother-in-law was stationed, and the C/O had cleared it for us to have the Land Rover overhauled and serviced.

At that time Iraq was in turmoil, a new regime had taken over and they wanted the British out and the base closed down. Although we already had our Iraqi visas, which had been issued in London, we had no way of knowing if the current situation would affect us in any way. This latest trouble had been brewing since we left the UK three weeks before. We knew it wouldn't be easy for the expedition to leave Turkey at the border town of Cizre, near where the River Tigris meets the Euphrates, and enter directly into Iraq as there was no official crossing at that point. We heard through the grapevine, however, that it was possible to cross, but it meant taking risks.

We drove into Cizre at 2.30 p.m., and I wandered through the hot, smelly and muddy streets with grimy open-fronted shops to find the police station. I came across a butcher's shop where three goats were hanging outside. They had been skinned but still had their heads on and they appeared to be covered with a black coating of something or other. On closer inspection I found that the carcasses were completely covered by thousands of flies enjoying a free lunch. I was determined at that point not to eat any more meat whatsoever while in Turkey.

I found the police station just around the corner from the butcher's shop. It was a fairly small room with two iron-barred cages. A tall bearded man with no shoes occupied one. There were two scruffy brown-uniformed policemen sitting at a small wooden table eating a meal. A bare light bulb hung from the ceiling and there was a small oil lamp on the wooden table. One of the policemen stood up, still trying to finish his last morsel of food, before he spoke. He wiped his mouth with the back of his hand and said something in Turkish. I had no idea what it was.

Placing my hand on my chest I said, "English."

He turned to his colleague and said, "Ingleezy."

I said slowly, "I go to Zakho."

The other policeman then stood up, raised his head towards the ceiling and pursing his lips said, "Yok, Zakho, you go Mardin."

I repeated, "I go Zahko."

At this he looked angry and turned to his friend, they talked for a while, then turned to me saying, "Kaimakam," and pulling a chair beckoned me to sit down. One man left the room, returning a few minutes later with bread, goats' cheese and some yoghurt milk. I thought this sudden bout of hospitality was a sign of good things ahead. As I started to eat the food one of the policemen put on his black leather coat and left the room. I heard an engine start up and a vehicle moved off. My awareness of the prisoner in the cage became more intense as he watched me eating my bread and cheese from behind the bars. I had very uneasy feeling that he was hungry himself.

I made a gesture to the remaining policeman of my desire to pass some of my food through the bars to the prisoner. This was met with a swift and determined rebuff. At this he raised both hands to emphasize 'under no circumstances'. I asked with my hand gestures what the prisoner had done. The policeman put his hand up to his head as though he was looking into the distance indicating that the prisoner was a spy. He then raised his arms as though he was holding a rifle; I understood he was to be shot.

The vehicle returned with the policeman accompanied by

another man who was quite smartly dressed, I assumed that this was the Kaimakam, a kind of governor of the province.

He shook me by the hand and said in faltering English, "Why do you come to Cizre?"

I explained our desire to cross the border to Zakho. He just smiled and said this wasn't possible as the border was closed. It seemed nobody was allowed to cross and that we had to stay there for the night before going to Mardin the following day. Our hopes had taken a nosedive, but the original plans still lingered in my mind.

Margaret and Pat were invited to stay for the night at the home of the Kaimakam. We were a bit doubtful about agreeing to this, but once we had met his wife and daughter we weren't so worried. We boys booked into a small hotel not far from the police station, but as the beds were a bit grotty we used our own sleeping bags.

In the morning we discussed the situation and decided to drive down to the frontier and reconnoitre the area. I thought it best that I went with just one other member of the party rather than have everybody go.

Norman and I made our way through the thick scrubland towards the river. I noticed a small hand-operated vehicle ferry in the distance. I told Norman to wait where he was while I went down for a closer look. I manoeuvred myself through some barbed wire fencing and after a few yards I saw a notice written in red letters. This worried me a little as I couldn't read what it said, but I decided to proceed no farther and went back to where I had left Norman.

I heard a soft nervous voice say, "Is that you, Eric?" Then all hell broke loose and we were suddenly surrounded by soldiers pointing guns at us. They escorted us to a camp of large bell tents where they separated us. Norman was taken to one tent and I was helped into another with a flat-handed push in the back from one of the soldiers. An officer walked into the tent and demanded to see my passport. He inspected my Turkish visa thoroughly, handed it back to me and with a strong voice shouted, "Where you go, Ingleezy?"

"I go Zakho," I said. That was a name he certainly didn't want to hear. He opened his mouth in anger, exposing a perfect set of white teeth contrasted by his long black moustache.

"Yok! Zakho, you go Mardin," he said and crashed his fist onto a portable table, causing a mug to fall to the ground. He then went on to emphasize the danger of trying to cross there. He shouted, "I Cap-pit-tan, I go Zakho." He then took the stance of a machine gunner and tried to imitate the sound of its rattle. Then he shouted, "You Ingleezy, you go Zakho."

He then went through the machine-gun routine all over again. I got the message.

I was given a stool to sit on while the captain opened a map and pointed to the wire fence I had crossed earlier. He walked two fingers across the paper, stopped for a second and went, "Boom, boom!" I realized then that I had walked into a minefield. That red sign I had seen earlier was probably my guardian angel. My mind flashed back to the police station and I wondered if that prisoner was going to have company in the next cage. It had been foolhardy and irresponsible given the situation we found ourselves in, but sometimes the desire to succeed can override one's better judgement.

We were allowed to continue our journey through the good auspices of the Kaimakam. We never did get that hot bath in Habbaniyah or know the fate of the prisoner, and I couldn't rule out the possibility of many similar experiences along the way, but the morrow was another day.

The border incident at Cizre made it necessary to make a diversion of over 700 miles in order to leave Turkey and reach the border town of Maku in Iran. We ran into heavy snow on the way and sometimes had to dig our way through snowdrifts. Norman and Roger, our seventeen-year-old, were both suffering from a bout of dysentery and to make matters worse we had trouble with the radiator freezing up.

Our numbers were further reduced in Teheran when Norman decided to call it a day and fly back home.

The five remaining members of the expedition headed out across the South Persian Desert via the holy city of Qum, then through Yazd, Kerman, Bam, and Zehedan into Pakistan, and on to the North-West Frontier town of Quetta.

After spending a number of very cold nights camping in the loneliness of the desert during the 1,587-mile drive from Teheran, we were pleased to accept the hospitality of Abdual Rauf, proprietor of the Imperial Bakery in the town. We met this gentleman whilst looking for a hotel and he very kindly offered us the use of a room in the back of his bakery in which to rest up for a few days.

Getting the Land Rover on a 'ferry' to cross the Ganges was no mean feat.

On leaving Quetta, we picked up a good asphalt surface through the Bolan Pass, which continued on for most of the way through Jacobabad, Sukkar and Multan to Lahore. A two-day stopover there was necessary for servicing and repairs to the vehicle. We crossed the border into India for an hour's drive to Amritsar and into the Punjab, and then joined the grand trunk road to Delhi. Thence by way of Agra, Cawnpore (Kanpur), Lucknow and Gorakkpur. We then turned off onto some very bad roads and passed through Siwan to Sonepur, where we boarded a country boat for the two-hour crossing of the Ganges to Patna, where due to a map-reading error we misrouted for eighty-two miles to Purnia and had to double back. We then crossed the river again to Bhagalpur for the three-day run to Calcutta.

We had reached the most crucial stage of the whole journey; if the travel ban through Burma couldn't be overcome in Calcutta, the whole purpose of the expedition would be lost and it would result in failure. We holed up at the Salvation Army hostel while we tackled this most pressing problem. The British Consulate advised we give up the idea as the Burmese were not about to change their minds. I had no intention of giving up and at the time had no reason to be optimistic either. I knew that there was no point in asking the Burmese for land-route visas so I tried a different approach. I asked them for visas to visit Rangoon, saying that we were travelling by boat or by air. No mention was made of motor vehicles. They said it was possible providing we obtained a letter of confirmation from the airline or shipping company from whom we booked our passage. This was a setback, but not the end of the world.

We went along to the shipping office to try and get a letter of confirmation, but there was no sailing for a month, so we went on to the airline office. I gave them some spiel about us spending a week in Calcutta sightseeing before flying out, but that we needed to organize our visas first. They gave us the letter confirming that we had booked our flights on the understanding that we paid for our tickets three days before flying out. This arrangement suited us fine and was the first chink of light in the chain of events that was to follow.

Armed with our letter and passports we returned to the Burmese Consulate, who agreed to issue us with tourist visas that we could collect two days later. The two male clerks in the visa section were quite friendly towards us and obviously enjoyed chatting to Margaret and Pat. This was something we were to use later to our advantage.

We stopped for a break at a city teahouse and a Chinese guy who had seen our Land Rover standing outside got into conversation with us. We mentioned to him of our plans to travel through Burma and he told us about the different armed factions operating within the country, and he pointed out the problems we could face. He offered to provide a document that would help us should we run into difficulties with any communist insurgent groups. Although this seemed a bit far-fetched, I agreed to meet him again to pick up the so-called document. True to his word he returned to the teahouse a day later and handed me an ordinary sheet of lined paper with a message written in Burmese and franked in red with the hammer and sickle.

Our slightly worn communist document

The British Consulate deemed the paper to be genuine and made copies of it, but it has always remained a mystery to us as to why the name on the paper bore no resemblance to mine.

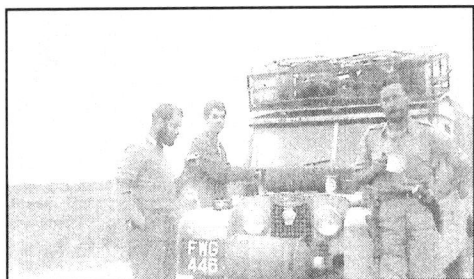

Roger, Barry (one of our hitchhikers) and myself

It was during our stay at the Salvation Army hostel that we met Ken and Barry, our two hitchhikers. They had heard we were planning to drive through Burma en route to Singapore and asked if they might join us. The idea of extra muscle at that time was just what was needed. Ken and Barry hadn't exactly been without problems of their own. Barry had originally set out from England to travel to India on his motor scooter, and from there ship to Australia. Unfortunately, his scooter was stolen in Cairo and he hitchhiked the rest of the way to Calcutta. Ken had set out from the UK with four friends to cycle to India, but the group had fallen out and they had all gone their separate ways. Ken had continued the journey to Calcutta alone.

On our return to the Burmese Consulate to pick up the visas we were shell-shocked to find they had been stamped in red with the words 'Not valid for entry into Burma by land route.' Although this was a massive blow, we couldn't openly show our disappointment for fear of making our true intentions known. My brain immediately went into overdrive on how those nine words could be eliminated from our passports.

The visa section was a long narrow office with a counter all down one side; a bit like a post office but with no grill. Amongst other items displayed on the counter was a large tray containing all kinds of office paraphernalia with franking stamps and inkpads etc., but what caught my eye in the tray was a small stack of white cardboard labels edged in blue with the words 'Burmese Consulate General Calcutta' printed on them. I realized at once how these could be used, so with the connivance of Roger and without being observed, we were able to pick up some of these labels and take them with us.

Back at the hostel we were delighted to find the labels fitted perfectly, blotting out those nine words stamped on the visas. I began to feel that my determination to beat the system had been given an unexpected boost, but that wasn't the end of the problem. The labels needed to be authenticated, which meant we had to return to the visa office and somehow 'borrow' their franking stamp to frank them ourselves. This was a tricky operation and success depended entirely on whether the office materials on the counter were still in place.

The following day, accompanied by Margaret, Pat, Roger, and Elmore and with everybody's passport in my possession we returned to the consulate. Our excuse for going back was to ask if they had any maps of Rangoon they could let us have.

The two visa clerks were again soon happily chattering to our girls, who had been briefed to keep them occupied in conversation for as long as possible. In the meantime I surreptitiously made my way farther along the counter to where the tray was. Thankfully the franking stamps and inkpads were still there. Roger had quietly strolled down to join me and stood by my side shielding my movements. I removed the largest and most impressive looking round stamp from the tray. I had no idea what the wording was as it was all in Burmese. With the girls' diversionary tactics in full swing, the passports were stamped in about forty-five heart-in-the-mouth seconds. We thanked the two visa guys for the map and I, for one, couldn't wait to get out of that office.

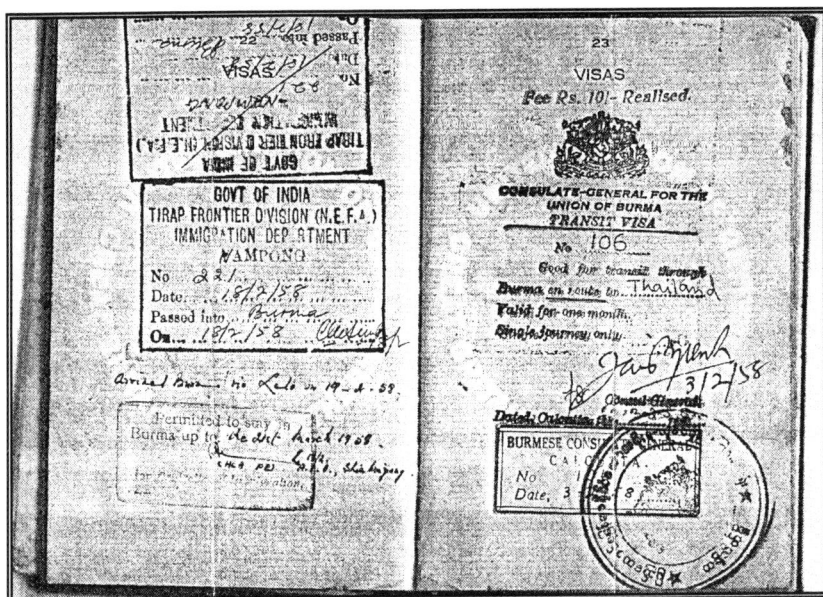

My passport with the infamous label

Armed with our reconstituted visas we lost no time preparing to leave Calcutta for the long haul to the India/Burma border. My upbeat mood was soon to be shattered, however, when reluctantly we had to say goodbye to Margaret and Elmore who, rather than travel through Burma, decided to leave us and go to Rangoon by air. Of the original party, only three of us now remained.

After our worst night trying to fight off the mosquitoes we left Calcutta on the 2nd of February 1958. Barry and Ken, the two hitchhikers, soon settled into our routine and were a great help with the number of punctures we had to deal with.

We crossed, by ferry, a number of small rivers between Calcutta and Dhulian Ghat, followed by a two-hour crossing of the Ganges to Khajuria Ghat. Inadvertently we strayed over the border into East Pakistan (now Bangladesh) and it was only when confronted by a soldier who was trying to pull his trousers on and wave us to stop at the same time that we realized our mistake.

Just one of our many Ganges crossings

Three more rivers were crossed before entering Siliguri and on to Dhubri, where we crossed into Assam. We joined the Assam trunk road to Jogighopa Ghat and crossed the wide expanse of the

Brahmaputra by ferry to Goalpara. After passing through Guwahati, Dibrugarh and Margherita to the end of the Assam trunk road, we arrived in the village of Ledo, which became famous by virtue of its location as a command post for the allied armies in World War II. We had now reached a most critical stage of our journey and realized that the moment of truth had arrived.

A photo opportunity in Assam

We soon became aware of the surprise that our arrival had caused due to the number of villagers and officials that surrounded our vehicle; we were seen as alien to the norm. We were met and informed by the district officer that to pass through to the tribal territories a special permit had to be obtained from the Governor of Assam in Shillong, some 200 miles away. A valid Burmese visa must accompany that permit; even then there was no guarantee it would be granted. That word 'valid' really hit home when we were asked to hand over our passports for scrutiny. They were not returned to us for over an hour and we were convinced that our dodgy visas had been rumbled. It was only when a smiling district officer returned and said our visas were in order that we breathed a huge sigh of relief.

There was nothing more we could do but drop anchor and wait for a reply to a telegram that had been sent to the governor seeking permission for us to cross the inner line into the tribal areas, which could take up to three days. Although it was so far so good, our fate hung solely in the hands of the decision of the governor.

During the wait and with freedom of movement I was able to keep my eyes open and work on formulating a plan that might be possible to use should entry be denied us. It was the afternoon of the second day when all those devious thoughts were cast from my mind. A telephone message from the governor's office in Shillong confirmed that we could continue our journey through to Burma.

I was absolutely delighted with the news that at last we were free to enter that forbidden land and travel along its forgotten road. The district officer made it clear that it was his duty to escort our vehicle to the border and emphasized that under no circumstances were we permitted to stop along the way.

We followed their jeep out of Ledo for the hour-long drive along a track that was the Stilwell Road. The only indication of our arrival at the international frontier was by way of a simple yellow-painted sign that said, 'India-Burma'. We thanked our escort, who wished us a safe journey. They then turned and headed back to Ledo.

The total recorded mileage of our journey through Burma from Ledo down to Rangoon, then to Tachilek at the Thai border was 2,322 miles; this included backtracking eighty miles after taking a wrong turn. The journey wasn't without incident, however, as during our first day in the country we were about to board a small ferry when a jeep with Customs and Immigration officers on board skidded to a halt by the ferry and asked to see our passports. They had been chasing us for twenty-five miles. I thought we had been rumbled, but apparently we had driven though an unmanned checkpoint without realizing it, and all they wanted was to check and stamp our passports and visas.

Road conditions in many places were very challenging and we struggled to make headway. Driving south to Rangoon we passed through Myitkyina, Bhamo, Namkam, Goteik Gorge, Mandalay and Pyinmana. In Rangoon urgent repairs were carried out on the Land Rover in the garage of the British Embassy. We were debriefed by Colonel F.G.W. Walsh, the military attaché, who was amazed at the way we had entered the country, and pointed out that even they weren't allowed to visit that part of Burma, so it was essential for him to glean as much information from us as possible on everything that we had observed. He thought it was a 'damn good show' but a little foolhardy.

Meeting some rather dangerous-looking natives on the Stilwell Road in Burma

One of Burma's terrorist groups had been busy trying to disrupt life in the capital again by blowing up Rangoon's water supply. We left Rangoon after three days and headed out on the long trek to the Thai border. We were driving in the darkness one night on the road to Meiktila when we came upon a bush fire. Trees and bushes were ablaze all down one side of the track like flaming torches; it was all rather eerie and a bit of a white knuckle drive for nearly a mile not knowing if one of those blazing trees might topple.

As we passed through Meiktila and Thazi on the way to Loilem we heard an explosion in the distance, and shortly afterwards we came to a culvert in the road that had been blown up by a band of dacoits. A group of villagers were at the scene filling in the hole and laid planks across, allowing us to continue.

Villagers repairing the damage done by the dacoits

Through Loilem we arrived at the Salween cable ferry at Takaw only to find it out of order. Three small boats were lashed together with a bamboo platform over the top so that we could be rowed across. The fast-flowing current made it impossible to land at the normal landing point; all we could do was land farther downstream and remove the vehicle from the platform the best way we could onto a rocky shore and find our way back to the track.

The mountainous jungle-clad road to Kengtung made progress very slow. For five miles we climbed, twisted and turned as darkness closed in around us. After rounding a small downhill bend our headlights picked up three men with rifles levelled at the vehicle. Different thoughts darted around my brain. Was this the ambush we had always feared? What was I to do next? I had my gun strapped on so I would be able to put up a defence if necessary, but as no shots had been fired, and with no wish to exacerbate the situation, I chose a wait and see approach. Leaving my headlights on and my gun in the Land Rover, I walked down the beam of light towards the men with no idea what I was walking into. I was greatly relieved to see that they were soldiers from a Burmese Army unit who thought we were insurgents fleeing from the fire. So instead of bullets it was tea and handshakes all round.

At a repair garage on the outskirts of Kengtung an officer from the Immigration Department escorted us to his office to check our travel documents. As we didn't have the required 'special permit' that allowed us to carry on the journey to the Thailand border, we were instructed to remain in Kengtung until clearance could be sought from Rangoon with permission for us to leave, but due to our precarious situation, waiting was certainly not an option. We undertook to return back to immigration the next day, but under the cover of darkness we moved out and headed for the Thai border. Having been warned in Kengtung that dacoits had been active in the area, the two-day drive to the border was a bit of a strain on the nerves, but apart from a small bridge that had been blown up we had no serious problems.

At the border Burmese immigration never mentioned anything about any special permit we were supposed to have to leave the country. Our passports were stamped and after removing the fan belt and extending the exhaust pipe of the Land Rover, we forded the deep waters of the Mae-sai River into Thailand at Tachilek.

By way of Chiang Rai, Payo, and Tak we arrived in Bangkok. At the British Embassy I was debriefed by Colonel Potter, the military attaché, who had our Burmese exploits passed on to him from his counterpart in Rangoon. Our exploits had caused us to become hot property with the Australian and British Intelligence Services. After more repairs to the vehicle at the Land Rover agents, we left Bangkok and headed south for the 900-mile drive towards the Malayan border.

Blow out of our last tyre, between Ranong and Taguapa

The road from Ranong to Taguapa was nothing but jungle track and we suffered puncture after puncture along its 110-mile stretch. Our tyres were in a bad state, but it was a case of make do and mend; our financial position wasn't healthy enough to afford new ones. We needed to conserve what little money was left for the last few hundred miles to Singapore. By the time we reached the Thai border we had been 'blessed' with a further seven punctures and one complete blow out. All of our vulcanising repair patches had been used and in order to keep moving we had no choice but to purchase a dubious, but cheap, second-hand tyre of a larger size. In addition, cracks had appeared in some of the leaves in our springs.

Burma 1958, having crossed the river at Takaw, driving across this part of the country cost us three vehicle springs.

We crossed the border into Malaya at Changlun; Malaya was the last country before we reached Singapore. It was a treat to drive on good asphalt roads again. After passing through Alor Star we were frequently stopped at police checkpoints and by British Army patrols on the look out for communist terrorists. Although warned to be on our guard we were twice refused permission by the army to be allowed to stay overnight in their camp; it was, as they reminded us, against regulations. It didn't seem to matter much that we were all British. They had their orders!

By way of Taiping, Kuala Lumpur and Segamet, the journey through Malaya took us four days.

Arrival In Singapore

It was the 27th of March when we headed towards the causeway for our final run to Singapore. It was a wonderful feeling to think we were actually going to arrive in a city that for so long had been a distant dream to all of us. We had been on the road for five months and travelled nearly 16,000 miles since leaving England. Although we had three broken front springs in the Land Rover, I couldn't resist putting my foot down a bit more than usual. Everybody was in high spirits and we were nearing the end of the journey for Barry and Ken, our two hitchhikers who were bound for Australia. Roger was staying on in Singapore to spend time with his mother, who had a bungalow near the Changi RAF base. Roger had actually left us the day before when we were held up in KL with tyre trouble. He had hitchhiked the rest of the way to Singapore rather than wait another day while we sorted out the tyre problems. Who could blame him? His desire to see his mother must have been most compelling.

We stopped at the beginning of the causeway to take a picture and reflected that our 'Malaysian Adventures' were now over. It had been a gruelling drive to reach this point of the journey, fighting bureaucracy, breakdowns, punctures, deserts, jungle fires and swamps. You name it, we had endured it! If only that were the end of our problems, I was acutely aware, however, of my financial situation. I was reduced to my last twenty pounds! Also, Pat had already confessed that she was virtually broke. We still had one of the most difficult parts of the journey to do - reaching Australia. We often talked of the possibility of working our passage from Singapore, but that was a pipe dream: we knew really that this was a non-starter and a thing of bygone days.

We arrived in cosmopolitan Singapore and headed straight for Changi Village. It was piddling with rain all the way. It seemed a bit of an anticlimax; nobody knew we were coming or that we had arrived. We felt like shouting from the housetops. "We're here, open up the champagne!" If only we had had a welcoming committee who were eagerly awaiting our arrival, but we had to be content with inflating our own egos.

We dropped off Roger's luggage at his mother's bungalow and were grateful to be invited in for a meal and be waited on by Roger. It seemed very strange to see him looking so neat and tidy, and for once not covered in mud as we all usually were. We took our leave of Roger, but not without a tinge of sadness. Pat, Roger and myself had been together for five months so life without him would be a new experience for us.

We drove down to the airbase to look for a place to camp and were stopped by the RAF police. However, after a few minutes chat, they took us to a quiet place at the side of the base, it was an old building that wasn't used anymore.

The next morning Ken and Barry had an early start. Ken was busy moving all his cycle parts from the top of the Land Rover for reassembly, while Barry sorted out and discarded all his unwanted bits and pieces. Pat and I rearranged and cleared the back of the vehicle. Ken cycled away after saying his goodbyes. Pat wasn't at all sorry to see the back of him; she often referred to him as a loudmouth know-it-all. Barry took leave of us a couple of hours later; he thought he would have a better chance of getting work if he was on his own. He confided in me that if I was to have any chance of working my passage I should do the same.

Whereas a ship's captain might be inclined to take on a man on his own, he was less likely to do so if that man was accompanied by a woman, but I couldn't subscribe to those sentiments. When the expedition left London, everybody knew it was their own responsibility to make arrangements for continuing on from Singapore, and this was completely understood. However, not in my wildest dreams did I envisage a situation would develop where so few of the original party would survive the journey to Singapore. Now that there were only two of us left, there was no way I could leave Pat, who had been such a loyal member of our group, on her own. I couldn't help feeling just a little bit responsible for her; could anybody leave a young woman, who had shared all our experiences and adventures for five months, alone on the other side of the world with no money?

We left Changi Village and returned to Singapore to challenge that impossible dream of finding a ship with an understanding captain who would allow us to work our passage to Oz. Our first port of call was to see the manager of Mansfields, the Blue Funnel Line agent. He very nearly shattered our hopes at the start.

"Working a passage is a thing of the past," he said. (Where had I heard that before?)

"I have been in shipping for many years and working a passage is just impossible."

Any encouragement there flew right out of his open window, helped along by the fan over his desk. The word 'impossible' didn't trip easily from my lips. It might be impossible for him, but as for me, I've always found that the impossible just takes a little longer. I certainly have no room for it in my limited vocabulary. If I had, on leaving London I would have got no farther than the Old Kent Road!

Next we went to the office of the big Inter-Ocean Lines. They offered us sympathy, without the tea to go with it, but the end product was the same. We decided to find somewhere to sleep while we still had some daylight left. We tried the YMCA, but although it was cheap, it was still too expensive for us. We needed to keep what little money we had for food. We saw Barry at the YMCA so decided to park up for the night in their car park and sleep in the Land Rover. Sleep didn't come easily; there were too many mosquitoes on the rampage. We crawled out of our sleeping bags in the morning. Although it had been a hot sticky night the bags did give us some protection against the mosquitoes, and it was the lesser of the two evils. Thankfully, the YMCA allowed us to use their washing facilities without charge.

As we prepared to leave the car park we found another flat in one of the front tyres; we badly needed a new set of tyres. We drove slowly out of the car park to a garage round the corner where we proceeded to mend the puncture. The garage man looked on with interest and soon appeared with two Pepsi Colas. Before we could get the wheel back on a big thunderstorm broke so we took cover in the garage until the storm passed about an hour later.

The garage man had enjoyed our company and he invited us for a meal, which we were only too pleased to accept. We went by taxi to a classy Chinese restaurant a little way out of town. The restaurant did us proud, as our beer glasses emptied so they were refilled time and time again, and our stomachs felt happier than they had for a long time.

We returned to the garage feeling rather pickled; I put the wheel back on with a little more difficulty than usual. We thanked our host for his hospitality, returned to the car park and slept the sleep of the just.

We continued our quest, concentrating on some of the smaller companies, but the answers were always the same. We tried the Wakefield Oil Company, thinking they might have a tanker going to Australia. The manager was, like most of the others, sympathetic, but apart from offering us a free service for our vehicle, which we gladly accepted, there was nothing we could test our sea legs on. However, he did tell us to keep in touch.

We met up with Barry again. He had had no luck either and decided, with Ken, to book passage for a sailing in two days time. The fare was £53.00 each. They decided to stay in the YM until the ship sailed, this information left Pat and I a little pissed off; a ship to Australia and we couldn't be on it. Anyway, we said good luck to Ken and Barry.

We went along to the NAAFI club, where I had to convince the doorman I was in the Merchant Navy. I couldn't say the RAF as I was wearing a beard. We had fish and chips and talked to some of the swaddies who were stationed there and who offered all kinds of advice and suggestions. We then talked to the manager, hoping he might have a few connections. He was surprisingly sympathetic and made a few phone calls on our behalf, one being to the publicity officer at Changi RAF base, who suggested he might be able to help in exchange for some sort of story about our trip. We were to see him the following day. Our imaginations ran a bit wild at the thought and our hopes went up a few notches. Could this be the breakthrough we were looking for?

I told Pat I was going to Changi on my own as it might change our luck. Not a bit of it, it was a complete waste of time and petrol. Why he suggested a meeting in the first place I will never know. He was all geared up with regulations 'old boy' and all that. Hell, all I wanted was a lift to Australia with my Land Rover; it was not much to ask! Having spent nearly five years in the RAF myself, making my own small contribution to the defence of the realm, I was already well versed with regulations. I had a meeting later in the day with a Captain Locke at the GHQ in Orchard Road; he was an intelligence officer. A meeting between us had been arranged by the military attaché at our embassy in Bangkok for me to be debriefed. I spent some time with the captain, a typical British Army officer, tall, straight backed, with a well-trimmed moustache. I continued to be surprised at the interest my unauthorised trek through Burma had caused. That was the third time I had been debriefed since India, with another to take place by the Australian military forces in Melbourne. I did wonder if we would ever reach Melbourne.

We settled down in the vehicle for our night's sleep, I was stretched out across the three front seats and Pat was in the back. I heard a voice outside say, "London to Australia." Somebody was reading the sides of our filthy vehicle. I sat up and got into conversation with a chap who said he was something to do with the church. He wanted to do an overland trip to somewhere or the other and wanted to talk to us about it, so he invited us to dinner at the YMCA the following evening.

At ten that morning we visited Mr Tom Wall, the Singapore representative for the Rover Company. Over a cup of tea we told him the story of our trip using one of their vehicles. We also told him of the urgent need of a major overhaul for our vehicle. He said in view of the extensive advertising we had given the Land Rover, he would write to the parent company in England for permission for our repairs to be carried out free of charge. We then went on to Champion Motors, the Rover Agents in Orchard Road, where we were introduced to Mr Clerks, the manager. Tom Walls told him of our mammoth drive from London and Mr Clerks invited us to stay at his home for a few days while he looked over our vehicle. We were delighted, a real bed at last seemed too good to be true.

Mr Clerks lived alone in a big house with a Malay servant whose name was Fatima. We were very comfortable there but realised we couldn't stay too long and encroach too much on Mr Clerks' hospitality. When Fatima had a day off Pat was asked to do the cooking for lunch. Mr Clerks, a Dutchman, produced some meaty bones and Pat concocted a stew by adding an assortment of vegetables. I think she enjoyed the challenge; it made a change to cook without having to use our petrol burners.

We kept our dinner date at the YMCA with Mr Constanto, the man from the church. He was accompanied by another couple, a Mr & Mrs Adkinson, who were on the committee of the 'World Council of Churches'. We talked 'overland trips' for a couple of hours and Pat was able to answer all the girlie questions thrown at her. I think some of our photographs may have caused them to rethink some of their plans. Afterwards, we returned to Mr Clerks wondering what the morrow would have in store for us.

We wandered around Kepple Harbour talking to ships' crews, asking where they were bound for, but nobody mentioned Australia. We had an offer from one captain who was willing to take us to Japan; this was the first positive offer we had had since we arrived in Singapore. If the offer had been taken up, we wouldn't have been in any better position than we were already.

The Land Rover, with the map of our route from London painted on its side, became a familiar sight around Singapore. Whenever we stopped people would gather round in wonderment asking if we really had driven all the way from London. Those who didn't speak the lingo just looked on with wide-eyed interest. We had so many invitations it was impossible to accept them all. Although always readily available to receive hospitality, it sometimes made us feel a little like beggars, even though it was always generously offered.

I went along to the office of the Australian High Commission enquiring if it was possible to travel to Australia by way of an assisted passage, as was currently being offered from the UK to help swell the population of Australia. Again it was a no-go situation. Unfortunately, we were told assisted passages were only possible directly from the UK. We seemed to be thwarted at every turn of the coin; perhaps the guy at the Blue Funnel Line was right, it was impossible.

We returned to Mr Clerks' house and retired to our beds. I tossed and turned, sleep wouldn't come easily. I lay there cursing the world, when God made Heaven and Earth why the hell couldn't he have joined Singapore to Australia and saved me from all this anxiety? My thoughts drifted back to Barry and Ken, who were now well on their way. Would they reach Australia before we had even left? We had now been in Singapore for eight days, visited innumerable offices, agencies, High Commissions, consulates and that was apart from tramping the harbours and uttering the odd prayer, but we had still come up with nothing. Our options were becoming fewer and fewer as the days went on.

Tom Wall invited us for a night out at the Princes Hotel with Mr Clerks, an occasion that called for an examination of our few presentable togs that hadn't been used or unpacked since we left London. I felt I had entered the civilised world again; white shirt, tie, blazer and clean shoes instead of looking like an overland saddle tramp. Pat had recaptured her femininity having discarded her travel-worn garments for a pretty, flowered dress and black high-heeled shoes.

We started with drinks in the exclusive little bar with white-coated waiters in attendance and dined under the soft lights to the sound of a good band. I devoured a perfectly cooked porterhouse steak with all the trimmings. Pat went one better and wrestled with a huge T-bone steak nearly as big as herself.

Tom Wall, with an air of reluctance, broke the news that the parent company in the UK had turned down his request for funding to repair our travel-worn vehicle, irrespective of all the propitious advertising we had given to this vehicle. We were naturally disappointed but not altogether surprised, this new turn down fitted in perfectly with all the other setbacks we had suffered here. It crossed my mind that our special night out was perhaps a consolation prize to soften the blow. We will always be grateful to Tom for all his efforts on our behalf and for all the hospitality shown to us. At least our stomachs had been well serviced that night.

During the next couple of days we re-doubled our efforts by visiting some of the many export companies and made further trips to the docks. We had heard of the possibility that a Norwegian tanker might be coming into Singapore in the next few days then continuing on to Australia. This seemed more speculation than fact, but as this was 'Australia' we wanted to believe it to be true. We resolved to go down to the harbour every morning to seek more information and felt a little excited at the prospect.

We hadn't seen a lot of the highlights of Singapore since our arrival so we went on a visit to Singapore's notorious Changi jail where most of the British troops were imprisoned when Singapore fell to the Japanese in World War II on the 15th of February 1942. We were escorted round the prison by the chief warden. We visited the little chapel and saw the beautifully painted murals covering the walls, One couldn't help but be moved by the thought that these emaciated men, who had been treated with such barbarous cruelty by the Japanese, had had the will to produce such marvellous work. We had tea at the jail and later went to the home of the prison governor, Lt. Martin, and his wife for drinks.

Next day we returned to the harbour and received confirmation that a tanker was in fact arriving in two days bound for Australia. Our hopes went into orbit and reached childish proportions, we were speculating on everything and assuming this and assuming that, as if we had already been accepted as crewmembers. Tom was clearly delighted with our news and promptly invited us to join him on a sightseeing tour the next day, which we gratefully accepted. We were on a high for the rest of that day, wanting the time to go quickly while awaiting the arrival of the tanker.

On Saturday morning Tom Wall picked us up from Mr Clerks' after breakfast at about 10.30 a.m. He invited me to drive his new car; it was a Rover, of course, and a dream to drive on good tarmac roads. It made life seem normal again, no rivers to ford, and no punctures to mend. However, life was far from normal for us; all we had were possibilities to look forward to that might come to nothing.

We stopped for a leisurely lunch and did a little more sightseeing before heavy rain set in. As it continued for some time we went to the swimming club, remaining there for tea later on. We thanked Tom for our lovely day out and returned to Mr Clerks'. For the rest of the evening, with the help of Fatima, we caught up on our washing and prepared for when we moved out. In any case we had decided that whatever happened in the next few days, we would leave Mr Clerks' house. I wasn't prepared to wear out our welcome and take advantage of his generous hospitality any longer.

We arose early next morning, ironed the washing from the previous night and generally made ready for our fifteen-minute drive to the docks. Once there we walked around for a while and saw a long line of ships anchored by the quayside. We passed seven or eight of them and suddenly stopped in our tracks as there was the most beautiful of all the sights we had seen in Singapore. There she was, the tanker that had occupied our thoughts over the last few days: the *Polykarp*. I felt my heart pounding against my frame with nervous excitement.

The gangplank was down with a piece of rope across its entrance, we just stood there and stared for a while, my mind flashed back to our arrival in Singapore and Barry's comment that a skipper might take a man on his own but not accompanied by a woman. I asked Pat to remain on the quayside while I ventured on board to see the captain. I had already made my mind up that we either both went or nobody did.

I was invited to the captain's cabin and offered a seat. He was drinking coffee and poured one for me.

"How can I help?" he said.

I entered into great detail about our journey from England, the search for a ship, plus our financial position. I also mentioned that there were two of us. He leaned back in his chair and commented that his crew was three under strength.

"I may take you, but at the moment I can promise nothing. I have to go to the Norwegian High Commission this afternoon, come back tomorrow morning and we will talk again, and bring your friend with you," he said.

We shook hands and his parting words to me were that he thought it should be all right. They were truly golden words, I felt

I had one foot in the door. However, we still had mixed feelings for the rest of the day, elation at the thought we were now in with a chance, but fear of what could go wrong.

We returned the next morning to find Captain Jacobson waiting. I introduced Pat; he looked surprised to see a woman but didn't comment. He asked me to accompany him to the High Commission Office, if their doctor found me medically fit he would take me on as a crewmember, for which I would be paid wages, but he said nothing about Pat.

The doctor found me medically acceptable and we returned to the *Polykarp*. The captain agreed to take Pat but was not able to offer her a job as a crewmember as there was no such provision on board, therefore she couldn't be paid. That was absolutely the least of our problems, we were sailing to Australia and that was all that mattered.

As our departure was only thirty-six hours away, Captain Jacobson suggested we return with our Land Rover and luggage as soon as possible. We didn't need any prompting, we returned to Mr Clerks', loaded our belongings straight away, thanking him and Fatima for their generous hospitality, then we went on to see Tom Wall to say our goodbyes.

Boarding *Polykarp*

We were back at the docks in two hours; we couldn't wait to get on board. As I looked with some trepidation at the Land Rover being lifted aboard by the ship's gear, it all seemed like a dream I was yet to awaken from instead of another chapter in my life about to begin. The Land Rover had to remain on deck during the voyage, exposed to the sea spray, so I was provided with timber to construct a rough shelter to afford some protection.

The captain showed me to a large spacious cabin saying, "This is where you will live for the voyage." I was very surprised to be given such luxurious quarters boasting two beds, en suite bathroom, two portholes, table and chairs and mats on the floor. The captain informed me that it was the ship's owner's cabin, also used by the pilot when necessary. A few days earlier we would have been prepared to accept sleeping anywhere on any ship as long as it was Australia bound. Pat was shown to a cabin behind the wheelhouse.

We left Singapore on the afternoon of April 12th 1958. It was difficult to explain our feelings as we pulled away from the shore. A mixture of excitement and deliverance flowed over us; the built-up tension and the uncertainty of the last two weeks just melted away. Europe and Asia were now behind us and at last we were on our way to Australia. To my surprise we learnt that we were not sailing directly to Australia after all, but to Borneo first to fill up with oil.

My watches on board consisted of four hours on and eight hours off. I was surprised when I was taken to the bridge and given some instruction on how to steer the vessel, use the ship's compass and stay on the correct course. It didn't seem too difficult to begin with, but after the tanker had been filled with oil and was low in the water it was a different story. Thousands of tons of extra weight made the vessel slower to respond to any adjustment of the wheel. Thinking I hadn't adjusted enough I would add more, which only made matters worse, so I would repeat the process in the opposite direction.

On my first day with the tanker loaded the captain came in laughing, saying that I had steered a beautiful 's'. At least I had provided some light-hearted entertainment for the captain and the officers. I think this reminded him that I was, after all, only a landlubber; but after a bit more practice I got the hang of it.

My two-hour stint at the wheel was followed by two hours as lookout on the fo'c's'le where there was a large bell to clang to signal the bridge if another ship was sighted or wreckage was seen in the water. Three clangs for dead ahead, two for the starboard side and one for the port side. If there was no response from the bridge, the process had to be repeated.

Sometimes during the voyage my workload varied; instead of

working on the bridge or fo'c's'le, I would do two hours of painting. This was a continuous operation throughout the voyage and most of the crew took turns at splashing on the white paint covering up all the brown patches that always seemed to reappear after a few days.

Pat was given a job, unpaid, as a mess girl for the officers. She would carry containerised food from the galley along the catwalk to the captain's mess. Invariably, when the sea was choppy, she would get a bit of a soaking when the odd wave washed over the catwalk, and this was a source of amusement for the officers.

Although our excitement and anticipation increased as the days slipped by, old worries remained. Our vehicle was badly in need of repair and our finances were at rock bottom. We could only hope that my wages from the tanker would be enough for the approximately 700-mile drive from the Geelong Oil Terminal near Melbourne to Sydney.

Captain Jacobson gave Pat a present one morning, some flying fish he had picked up on deck, and suggested she had them cooked for breakfast. He told us we would be arriving at our destination in two days and I should start thinking about removing the shroud over my Land Rover. I wondered how I was to get my vehicle ashore as this hadn't been mentioned yet. I thought that maybe he was going to surprise me.

We had our first glimpse of the Australian shoreline on the 2nd of May 1958, twenty days after leaving Singapore. The pilot joined us on board for the remainder of the voyage to anchorage; he would share my cabin till then. The *Polykarp* would discharge her cargo of oil from its anchorage three miles or so off shore by underwater pipeline raised from the seabed.

I awoke the next morning aware we were no longer moving and I realised this was our big day. The tanker was climbing higher and higher in the water as the oil flowed its three miles to the storage tanks on shore. The captain had organised a tug to take the vehicle ashore as soon as the discharge of oil was completed. It was quite surprising how much the tanker had raised itself out of the water, like some oversized whale coming up for air. We were visited by the Customs and Immigration officers, who inspected our vehicle and passports. The captain paid me my dues, which, after stoppages, amounted to twelve pounds eleven shillings and tuppence halfpenny, and handed me my Norwegian Seaman's Certificate. I felt it was my graduation day, from landlubber to seaman; I had arrived.

The time I spent on the tanker was an experience I wouldn't have wanted to miss. It was always on my mind when organising this trip from the UK that I would like to arrive in Australia by sea in an unorthodox fashion. Being on a Norwegian tanker with a professional crew, an excellent captain, plus being paid for it was a bonus beyond my wildest dreams. Since joining the *Polykarp* we had grown to love the old tub. The atmosphere, the friendliness of the officers and crew, the work we did, and the excellent food. Even old man Poseidon played his part. My skills as a painter might keep me in good stead for the future if I ever needed to work my passage again. Perhaps I'd get by next time without my steering becoming a joke with the captain. There was a tinge of sadness when we left.

Landing In Australia

The tug pulled alongside for the lowering of the vehicle with the ship's gear. We gave our grateful thanks to the captain and crew for all the kindness shown to us during the voyage. As the vehicle was lowered it was discovered that it was too long (109″ wheelbase) to fit lengthways, so after much deliberation it was decided to place it crosswise with the front and rear overhanging each side of the tug.

As we were now so high in the water, the ladder down to the tug had a shortfall of nearly six feet. I was forced to go hand over hand for the last few rungs until my feet had a safe base. Pat's somewhat precarious descent, tempered with disapproving squeaks, reached its climax when she found there were no more rungs of the ladder on which to place her feet. I went to her aid by hanging on to the last rung, enabling her to lower herself by placing her legs tightly around my neck. Then with the help of the tug men, we were able to lower her into the tug.

This exercise caused enormous entertainment for the crew watching from above shouting all kinds of humorous advice. I bet they had never had such an amusing trip as this one. The tug turned and headed for the shore.

The harbour master expressed his regret that a charge would have to be made for the hire of the tug. Although this was fair, it was an expense we hadn't reckoned with. After explaining our financial difficulties he agreed to postpone payment until we reached Sydney and found work. I was asked to write a letter explaining our trip from England. As a result a reduction in the cost of the hire might be arranged. This was a very generous gesture and I wondered how many travellers have hired a tug on such easy terms.

I delayed the drive to Sydney to make an unplanned stopover in Melbourne to visit an old aunt living in Spring Street. I had never met her before and it made a nice two-day break. I parked the vehicle in front of the station and got a right old rollicking from the parking attendant, he called me everything but a 'pommy bastard'.

The drive to Sydney was a slow one as we had to consider the state of the vehicle, especially the broken springs. It took three days and we slept overnight in the Land Rover. The sight of Sydney Harbour Bridge, a symbol of this great city, really hammered home to us that we had actually arrived. For Pat, this was journey's end, her dream had been realised. For me it was just an interlude, I had the journey to do all over again. If I succeeded this would be the first time this had ever been accomplished. I needed to start organising at once. Getting a new party together, finding a job to pay for repairs to the vehicle, and be ready to arrive back in Singapore before the start of the monsoon season began. This was the start of a whole new challenge.

Preparing For The Journey Home

During my preparation for the journey home it would have been easy to say everything went smoothly and according to plan, but far from it, as well as the best times, there were the disasters. I had been lucky to be able to stay with my brother in Wahroonga, a few miles out from Sydney; he had emigrated out from England with his wife and children after the war.

I virtually took the first job that came along, driving a truck delivering sand and gravel. This was to lead to my first disaster. On the fourth day on the job, whilst I was removing a bag of cement from the top of a high stack of bags in the storage shed the whole stash toppled over on to me, with one of the bags breaking open across my face. Having breathed in a quantity of the powder I finished up in the hospital for over a week, and every time I coughed I expected to spit up a ready-made cement block.

My main worry wasn't so much the accident but the possible delay it would cause to my eventual departure. I had started writing letters in earnest, and sought sponsorship from various firms, inserting advertisements in newspapers inviting applications from interested parties who wished to join me. Then, out of the blue, came an offer I couldn't refuse. I was invited to appear on a television programme entitled *Meet the People* to tell my story. This couldn't have come at a better time; at last I could start to refurbish my coffers.

The feedback from the programme was very encouraging. I no longer had to worry about advertising in newspapers as a steady flow of letters from would-be overlanders had begun to arrive. There was, of course, the usual timewasters whose only interest was curiosity. Surprisingly, however, more applications came from women than men.

My thoughts drifted back to the forming of the party that started from England where I had made many mistakes in selecting the people who were to join me and had lived to regret it. So I was determined this would not happen again. It was important to realise that the people I accepted as being suitable must also be happy that I was suitable and acceptable to them; it was a double-edged sword. The fact that I had already completed the outward trip, however, did help with their confidence in me.

The first letter I opened stimulated my interest. It was from John Bookluck, a civil engineering draftsman and a member of the Sydney Bush Walkers Club. John was a keen photographer and wanted to join the trip to save him from marriage and boredom. He bubbled over with enthusiasm and had a terrific sense of humour. He introduced me to another friend from the Bush Walkers. Lynette Baber, aged twenty-three, who worked as an artist for the Sydney-based *Women's Day* magazine. Lyn had a smile as big as her enthusiasm to join the trip. The activities of bush walkers told me enough about them to realize that they would be the types not to buckle at the sight of a snake, or if they got their feet muddy.

Lyn invited me home for a meal and to meet her family. Her father was in the Sydney Police Force. I was asked if I liked chook, as that was what we were having for dinner. I remarked, "What's chook? I've never heard of it." He explained that it was chicken. During our travels Lyn mentioned about my visit to her home and of her father's remark when I left.

"Bloody Pommy, didn't know what a chook was so how the bloody hell did he find his way here?"

Things were now beginning to shape up and I had found my last three applicants to join the group. They were Bruce Russell, a twenty-three-year-old architect from New Zealand who had served in the NZ Air Force. Louise Whitfield, a secretary, and Angela McMahon, a ceramist. That completed the party of six.

I was very pleased to receive some offers of sponsorship. Boots the Chemist very kindly supplied to us all our medical and hygiene requirements with advice and recommendations from their own doctor. This was an invaluable contribution and greatly appreciated. Other donations of tinned fruit, vegetables, cereals and sweets were gratefully received.

A visit to Sydney one morning proved to be another disaster. I parked my vehicle in Macquarie Street, the Harley Street of Sydney, only to find on my return it had been towed away by the police. None of my explanations convinced them to release my vehicle until the statutory fee had been paid. So much for some of the funds starting to flow into my coffers. However, I managed to secure another job with an American cosmetics company, which went very well, so much so that after a few weeks in the job I was offered a permanent position with the company. Unfortunately, a secure job wasn't part of my plan. With my wages I purchased a small trailer for added comfort on the journey back, as it would give us more room in the vehicle. Whether this would be an asset or an encumbrance only time would tell; but for the moment it seemed like a good idea; although I'd never heard of a trailer being dragged that kind of distance before, maybe it would be a first.

The Land Rover at last went in for those long-awaited repairs, it would be great to drive with a complete set of new springs and new tyres again, although there were still a hundred and one other repairs still to be carried out. I was delighted to be able to settle my account with the harbour master at the Geelong Oil Terminal; it was very satisfying to know he had been prepared to trust us.

Booking a passage from Sydney was to prove more difficult than we thought. Ships to Singapore were few and far between and the only one available to suit our proposed departure date was the Blue Funnel Line Ship the *Charon*, which was sailing from Broome in Northern Australia on 27th October. This would involve another 4,500-mile drive, adding an extra quarter to our overall journey. This was an unexpected blow and not something I had contemplated. It would mean leaving Sydney at least three weeks earlier to allow for any problems we might run up against. We couldn't risk, as one might say, missing the boat.

We made a tentative booking on the *Charon* to be confirmed and paid for when we reached Perth. The situation having been forced on us, we soon became resigned to the new challenge. The 'usual experts' came out of the woodwork and offered advice and filtered stories to warn and discourage us from making the drive across the arid Australian desert where all kinds of things might happen to us. We could run out of water, break down with no help, or run out of petrol and get lost. All those stories were mostly from people who had never travelled much farther than the bottom of their garden! We noted their concern, but when you have cut your teeth on the Burma road and had plenty of practice extracting yourself from the sands of the South Persian Desert, you knew you would face the drive to Broome with the same determination as usual.

Nothing motivates me more than to be told it is too risky; it has just the opposite effect. It was a fact of life that on the trip we would run into trouble somewhere along the line, we always did. Our formula for this was, as it had always been, make a cup of tea and reflect a while on our next move (our teapot worked overtime on many occasions). This system seemed to work eventually. The remaining few weeks in the shadow of the 'Coathanger Bridge' were spent looking up relations I had never met.

In Blacktown and Concorde, as in Singapore, the Land Rover with all its route markings painted on the sides became a familiar sight around Sydney. People would ask us when we were starting our drive back to England. One guy actually asked for my autograph. Well, you have got to start somewhere; I could almost feel my head swelling up. Such is the power of television.

We had a dress rehearsal in the bush on the run up to our departure to christen our new baby, the trailer. Bruce christened it 'Wi-kiki-kanga' and named the Land Rover 'Tessa'. We then checked our equipment to make sure we hadn't forgotten the tin opener, but most importantly it was a chance for the new team to gel. It had taken nearly five months to prepare for the journey, but I now felt everything that needed to be done had been done, and I had great hopes and confidence in the new party. I hoped they had the same confidence in me.

I couldn't start my return journey without first saying goodbye to Pat, who had contributed so much to the success of the outward journey. We had a farewell dinner together in Sydney, where she confessed to wishing that she was making the return journey with me and added that the trip for her had been the journey of a lifetime. She had taken a job in Sydney as a typist for a travel agent and called it a huge anticlimax.

Journey Across Australia

We left Sydney on 30th September amid the picturesque setting of Circular Quay, surrounded by the brilliant blue of the most beautiful harbour in the world. Saying goodbye to Sydney, my brother and his family wasn't easy. I made up my mind there and then that one day I would come back. The *Women's Day* magazine photographed our departure and then we were on our way.

We headed out towards Western Australia, passing through the beautiful Blue Mountains at Katoomba, where we stopped to admire that well-known landmark The Three Sisters. The excitement and preparation of that day had left us all feeling a little drained. We had covered just 148 miles when we called it a day. We made camp by the river at Evans Plain Creek, about six miles outside Bathhurst. The girls soon got cracking preparing a meal of chops, chips and onions, followed by fruit salad. I had my doubts that we were going to see many meals like that.

Our first night's camp together went very well. Our system of packing before we went made setting up camp quick and easy. John and I showed our appreciation to the girls for cooking the meal the night before by taking them a cup of tea in bed that morning.

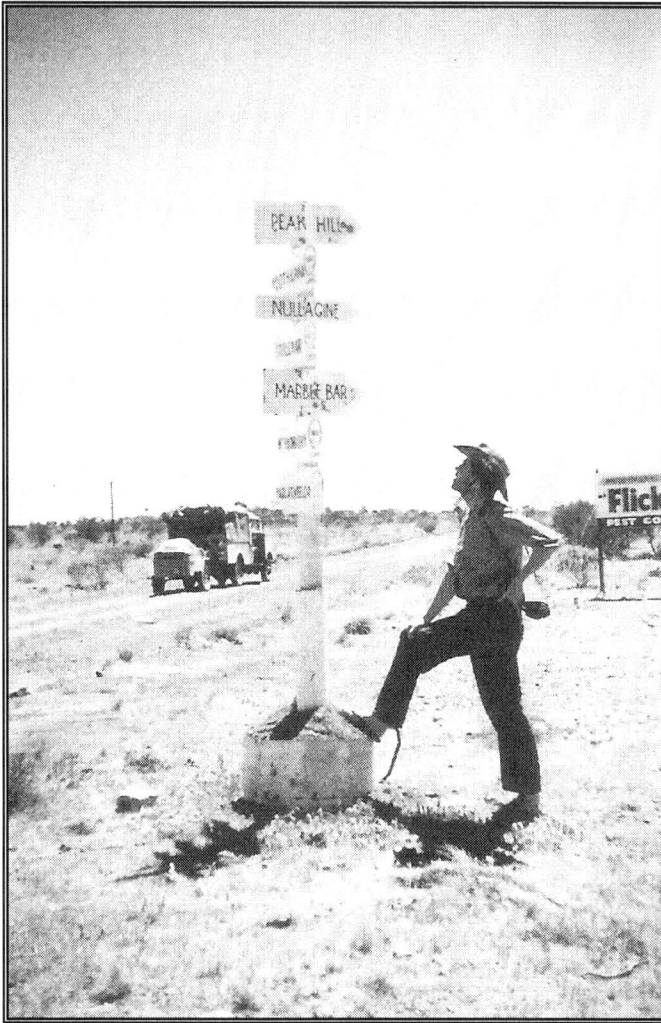

Finding our way in the Outback

We joined the Mitchell Highway passing through Orange, Wellington, and Dubbo, where we saw the first sign of wildlife. Life might not be the appropriate word as there were six dead wallabies which had apparently been knocked down by passing vehicles.

We hit the Barrier Highway at Nyngon, where six miles out

the road deteriorated. The asphalt gave way to a dirt and dust surface which steadily worsened between Hermidale and Cobar. Disaster struck a few miles outside Cobar as the trailer broke away from the tow bar and overturned, causing damage to the axle and one of the wheels. It was a stroke of luck we were near to Cobar and able to get repairs at the one and only workshop.

Our beloved trailer after it had overturned.

Earlier we had manoeuvred the Land Rover and trailer up a bank and across the railway line. As there was no special crossing place for vehicles you just picked your own spot and bounced over the line the best way you were able. The trailer breaking away had contributed to our woes. The enforced stop, however, enabled John, Bruce and I to struggle with a glass of the local beer while the girls did some shopping. Before we moved out I was able to purchase 100 rounds of .22 ammunition for my rifle.

One of the many railway lines to be crossed on our journey across Australia

We left Cobar at 1.00 p.m. and were surprised and saddened to see more dead animals along the route. This time it was kangaroos. It wasn't clear how they had met their fate. The farther we travelled more and more wildlife became evident. The dry open plains gave a feeling that cannot be readily explained. You could travel for hours without the sight of another human being and the solitude and tranquillity of the desert made us feel as if we were all alone in the world.

We had our first puncture four miles out from Wilcannia. Trying to use a jack in soft sand and dust was a waste of time. Unless you have a strong firm base on which to stand the jack, the weight of the vehicle sinks the jack down into the sand. To overcome that problem we dug out the sand from under the wheel. When the wheel could be freely turned it was removed, while the rest of the team supported the weight, preventing the vehicle from toppling.

We made camp that night beside the River Darling. As rivers in the outback are few and far between, we took full advantage of the unrestricted supply of water to have a good bath. Instead of erecting the tent we bivouacked round a fire, as it gets quite cold at night in the desert. The first one to wake up in the morning would put the billycans in the embers then creep back into their sleeping bag until the billies boiled for tea and breakfast.

Teaching the girls to shoot in the Outback of Australia

Before we left that morning I thought it a good idea to spend a little time showing my friends how to load and fire the rifle, so we used some of the newly purchased ammunition to shoot at an empty cheese tin as our practice target. After expending nearly 25% of my new ammo supply, I came to the firm conclusion that it would have been considerably safer standing behind the cheese tin than anywhere else. Louise was the only one of the five that actually hit the target, so more practice was on the agenda before we entered more hostile areas.

We passed through Wilcannia for the 125-mile drive to Broken Hill arriving at midday. Driving into this old mining town wasn't only an experience but a surprise. The dust of the desert was blowing down the wide main street with tumbleweed bounding towards us in stops and starts. There was the customary corrugated metal and wooden buildings on both sides of the street with horses tethered to some of the larger buildings; we assumed they were the pubs. One could be forgiven for thinking we had inadvertently wandered into a Hollywood film set and John Wayne would soon appear to tell us that 'this town ain't big enough for both of us'.

Whilst having an oil change at the local garage it was discovered that one of the bolts that connected a main spring had sheared. Being the weekend the Land Rover agents were closed so we, the boys, went to one of the pubs. There was one on most corners so we had plenty of choice. The girls, however, couldn't join us as men and women didn't share the same bar. The ladies congregated in a room of their own. We pondered the reasons for the segregation and wondered if it was a case that the men wouldn't have to be too choosy in their choice of words, or they could possibly lie more easily to their wives about how much they had had to drink.

The local reporter from the *Barrier Minor* had got wind of

our arrival in town and came to interview us in the pub, where else? It hardly mattered what we told him as he printed his own account of things, which was quite different from ours. He even changed the name of John from Bookluck to 'Booknick'. From then on the name stuck with John throughout the trip. The reporter was helpful to us in as much as he took us to the home of the foreman of the Land Rover agents, who not only opened up for us but also fitted a new bolt to the affected spring: total cost £1.00. We shared a few yarns with the locals, who educated us on local history.

Broken Hill evolved in the late 1880s. A guy called Charles Rasp, who was employed to repair boundary fences, discovered a rich source of minerals which included lead, silver and zinc and went on to form a syndicate which eventually became Broken Hill Proprietary Company, Australia's largest public company. The four Australians in our group thoroughly enjoyed discovering their own country, having never ventured into the outback before. We were all intrigued at the sight of the hundreds of beautifully coloured birds and wildlife that ran free.

We took our leave of Broken Hill driving the thirty-odd miles to Coburn, where we crossed into South Australia, which boasted an area of over 308,000 square miles. We made good progress towards Port Augusta driving adjacent to the railway line, but the bull dust gave us hell that day. The vehicle being a soft top and open at the back acted like a vacuum, sucking in the dust which covered everybody and everything in the back.

A few miles before Peterborough we once again had to bump the vehicle and trailer across the railway line. Being mindful of what happened a few days earlier, we kept our fingers crossed. The trailer never looked happy when that manoeuvre was carried out. Although it was early days I had begun to wonder whether the tow bar was robust enough for the job that it had to do.

Everybody, with the exception of John, who couldn't drive, took a turn behind the wheel. It was a good day for them to test their driving skills and get a feel for the vehicle. They didn't have to worry about traffic as there wasn't any. A couple of emus, mother and baby, ran in the path of our vehicle and continued to run dead ahead as though we were in pursuit. Mother suddenly swerved into the bush, but baby kept going on ahead not knowing which way to go. It suddenly slipped over in front of the vehicle, which caused us to take evasive action, giving the three in the back a bit of a shake up. However, baby lived to squawk the tale and all ended well with mother and baby reunited. Frequently kangaroos would run alongside the vehicle, seemingly unable to decide where they wanted to go, or they zigzagged out in front causing many near misses.

Mindful of the fact we still had a hell of a way to go we stopped in Port Augusta just long enough to buy fresh food and petrol. After joining the Ayre Highway we passed through Limba and Cedtuna to Penang, where we started the crossing of the desolate Nullarbor Plains, which curve around the Great Australian Bight and skirt the Southern Ocean, whose blue waters cover the continental shelf.

It had been heavy going that day, but having covered a good mileage we made camp a bit earlier than usual to clean off all the dirt and dust of the day before starting to cook our evening meal.

Water was always a problem as we were rather limited on how much we could carry so we needed to be economical on how much we used. A five-gallon container was stashed in the space between the front bumper and the radiator grill. In addition to that most of the group carried a personal water bottle. I didn't carry one myself as, strange as it may seem, I didn't drink water from any source.

On my journey out from the UK I stopped drinking water after leaving Europe and entering Turkey. From then on I always waited until we stopped for our breaks, then when we had a good brew up I would fill up with one, two, or even three large mugs of tea. As we normally stopped three times in the course of the day, my liquid intake of tea was sufficient for my needs.

Since our departure from Sydney we had covered over 1,500 miles, and according to calculations we had another 1,400 miles before we reached Perth. Apart from a few setbacks we had managed to keep to a reasonable schedule.

The temperature in the Nullarbor was becoming increasingly hotter, fluctuating between 104°F and 114°F some days. The steering wheel was so hot at times it became unbearable to touch, necessitating the use of a piece of rag in order to steer.

We came across a two-foot long iguana sitting by the

roadside, I tried to photograph it but it took off like Dan Dare's rocket. For a bit of banter I chased after it, much to the amusement of the others. These lizard-like creatures have amazing speed and it left me standing.

The dust was again exceptional and the three in the back were covered from head to foot. They had the appearance of three statues painted grey, with two holes for the eyes and big grins on their faces. They looked so funny I just had to take a photo for posterity.

After that we tried a different system, instead of travelling with the back open we closed the back and rolled up the sides, thereby eliminating the vacuum effect. It was very effective and reduced our dust intake by about 80%, making the rest of the desert crossing more tolerable.

Bruce, Lyn and Angela in the back of 'Tessa' covered in the dust of the Nullarbor Plain, Australia.

We stopped in Norseman for petrol, water and whatever fresh food was available, then went on to Coolgardie, where we joined the Great Eastern Highway. To speed up our arrival in Broome we embarked on an occasional night drive to boost our daily mileage. This wasn't without its problems. Kangaroos appeared regularly in the beam of our headlights, they pricked up their ears at the sound of our engine, stopped and stared at the light as though they were mesmerised, causing us to slow right down and sometimes stop completely before they leapt and bounded away. It was easy to understand why we found so many wallaby and kangaroo causalities when we started the desert crossing.

On the night drives four of us would rest in the back while the driver and co-driver swapped positions every two hours, after five hours we would stop for a meal prepared by the drivers who would then wake up those resting in the back. On those occasions we used our emergency supplies of food as it was impossible to keep fresh food for any length of time in the temperatures in which we travelled. We carried a reasonable quantity of dried and tinned foods, Vesta beef curry was one of the favourites and we were dab hands at preparing those. We always cooked extra rice and with what was left over we made dessert by adding powdered milk with sugar and mixing it with the rice; hence we had rice pudding. We finished the meal with a wedge of Kraft cheese from a twelve-ounce tin. Preparing a meal late into the night when it was cool was much more agreeable than in the heat of the day. The most difficult part was waking those in the back to get up and eat it.

Having made good progress over the last few days before our arrival in Perth, we took time out to give ourselves a bit of a grooming. The dust had certainly taken its toll on everybody's hair and it was certainly a case of 'I can't do a thing with it', it was a tangled mess where the sweat had mixed with the dust and caked together. We also caught up on some washing. Drying it was never a problem, we just dangled it out of the window as we drove along and it dried in no time. At least we could now arrive in Perth looking almost human again.

We drove into Perth, the capital of Western Australia on the 30th of October. It is the gateway to Australia's great west where the wide expanse of the Swan River meanders through this beautiful city. Although it was good to mingle with the civilised world again and relax a little, there was still much to be done before the last leg of the journey to Broome.

We delayed confirming our booking on the *Charon* as we had heard of a Japanese ship that was due to sail in the next few days. It would save us the last 1,400-mile drive to Broome but unfortunately this wasn't to be. Only two berths for two persons were available so that was a non-starter. Another possibility we looked into was a cargo boat going to Singapore with a shipment of manganese. We were offered a very attractive deal, but it would mean a wait of two weeks, so without further ado we confirmed our bookings with the Blue Funnel Line.

After all the dust we had eaten getting there we spent the next few days sightseeing like normal tourists, taking in some of the historic sights along the banks of the Swan River. We visited Fremantle, a few miles from Perth, a place thousands of British immigrants will remember when they disembarked from there after sailing from England to start a new life after the end of the Second World War, for which they paid the princely sum of £10 each. My brother was one of them. As previously mentioned, he and his family had settled in Sydney.

We mixed our sightseeing with maintenance and servicing of the vehicle. The usual suspects were soon at it again raising their heads above the parapet to warn us of the dangers ahead. This time they added stories of vehicles that had broken down with the occupants dying while walking in the scorching heat to get help then losing themselves in the desert. I realised that those good people only had our best interests at heart and their local knowledge was far superior to ours. We thanked them for that. But in our case there was little choice.

I was pleased to provide the Shell Company in Perth with an information sheet on the route I had taken from England for anyone wishing to follow my journey.

We left Perth after four days, joining the Great Northern Highway heading towards Mt. Magnet. We soon became aware of the changing colour of the sand from a brownie hint of red to a much deeper red. It made you feel that you were on another planet. After about 300 miles we saw a tin sign full of bullet holes saying 'Paynes Find'. We passed three huts with corrugated tin roofs with some aboriginals standing on one of the verandas. We assumed we were on the outskirts of Paynes Find. It was only after driving many more miles that we realised that was Paynes Find!

We passed an old building that had been taken over by the desert. It had no roof, doors or window frames, but the inside was three-quarters full of deep sand and soon to be completely consumed and buried forever. Could this be the remains of an early settler's house living in complete isolation and a reminder of bygone days? If a settler's wife had lived there, what on earth would she have done without a vacuum cleaner?

A house soon to be overrun by the desert

We saw more wildlife as the days went by. Beautiful tall eucalyptus trees filled with parakeets on every branch with a background of clear blue skies; a perfect setting for the artist's brush. So that none of this magnificent scenery was missed we would sometimes stand on the running board at the back of the Land Rover looking over the top of its canopy for the perfect view.

Getting a good view of the wildlife

We met a very interesting old-timer mounted on an old horse. He had a little black and white dog sitting in front of him across the saddle. He said he was a drover, seventy-three years old and had been roaming the outback since the 1914-1918 war. He delighted in telling us his old horse was the sister to the horse that had won the Melbourne Cup twice. He kept us entertained with his yarns and outback stories for a couple of hours. He seemed a bit overdressed for the heat of the day, which was around 118°F, maybe he knew something we didn't.

He was very pleased to join us for one of our tea-drinking

sessions and we found a few titbits for his little dog. After drinking tea in that kind of heat the sweat oozes from the pores of the body and eventually gives a cooling effect. In my case, as previously explained, not being a water drinker I needed to drink enough tea, not just as a refreshment beverage but also to actually quench my thirst, which could mean three large mugs or more. The sweat could then be quite intense at times as though I had just stepped out of a hot bath so I always kept a towel handy at tea times.

The scenery changed at lunchtime from the desert to hilly green shrub with varieties of native plants growing in the red sand. Louise and I climbed a very high hill that had captured our interest. There was a large cave at the top frequented by kangaroos and we found the body of a baby kangaroo near the entrance. The number of kangaroos in the area had increased immensely, and whatever direction you looked there they were; whenever the vegetation increased so did the wildlife.

We reached civilisation again that day at Mundawindi, the home of a very large cattle station. It had a petrol pump, a workshop and a rather cute homestead erected in 1890. We were told the station covered two and a quarter million acres and there had been no rainfall for eight years. The drought had caused the death of 16,000 head of cattle over the previous two years alone. The bodies were either blown over and partly covered by sand or had been eaten by millions of ants. It only took a couple of weeks for them to lay bare the bones of one of these unfortunate creatures. We had earlier seen a number of dead steers lying by the roadside, with others on their last legs dying from thirst. Although there was a windmill water pump, the water it produced was just a pittance of what was required to fill the water holes. We felt distraught to see all that suffering around and unable to do anything about it. Before we left the homestead we were each given a bottle of ice-cold ginger beer to drink to wash away the dust. It seemed ironic for us to enjoy such luxury amid so much suffering.

The water supply at the cattle station at Mundawindi

The journey to Nullagine was very heavy going. We ran into deep sand and the four-wheel drive had to be used for long periods to make any headway. We pulled into Nullagine at 6.30 p.m. It was a very small one-horse town typical of the outback, one store sold everything, it had to, there weren't any others, and of course there was a pub. We bought some fresh food as Louise and Lyn had promised to cook something special for dinner.

We headed into the trees just outside town, made camp and soon had a good fire going. The girls put their money where their mouth was and produced a meal of chips, boiled onions, and breakfast sausage. John complained that the chips weren't done. I made my contribution to the meal; I opened two tins of creamed rice. We had only been in camp three hours and had already made three billies of tea. We then all settled down to write diaries and letters, except John. He wasn't wearing any trousers, just a raincoat to cover his dignity. He had a toothbrush in one hand and was poking the fire with the other. He looked like a real sex symbol. We tried not to compare him with the proverbial dirty old man wearing a raincoat.

Before leaving Nullagine we filled up with beer, well, one glass anyway, and had a yarn with the locals in the bar about the road ahead. We were very amused by a notice hanging over the bar that showed a list of fines for dirty deeds and bad habits. It read, 'Being sick on the bar floor 2/6-, swearing 6d to 2/6-, being sick on the veranda 2/-, breaking a glass 2/6-, corny jokes 2/-.' All the cash went to a local health fund. I bet the swearing bit collected the most.

Petrol there was the dearest so far, 6/4d a gallon. Marble Bar was much the same as other outback stops: one hotel, two shops and dust blowing up the main street from one end to the other. We had lunch in the pub garden and bought some bread made by one of the locals, it cost 2/6- a loaf. It was good bread even if it was expensive. The publican's wife was very anxious to talk with us whilst out of earshot of her dearly beloved husband. She said she was 'blo-o-ody' pissed off with this dusty place. She had been there for eight 'blo-o-ody' years and couldn't wait to get out. She said, "I want to do something like you people and travel. I want him to sell up and get out, if you had room for me, I would pack up and join you."

She made us a pot of tea on the house; Louise poured it out and put salt in the cups instead of sugar. We also had a long chat with a school inspector who explained all the difficulties of children's education in the small isolated outback hamlets. The children were educated by correspondence teaching and by radio programmes. His job was to mark the papers of the correspondence lessons and his impression on the whole was that the children weren't interested in this method of teaching and thought they needed to be competitive with other children. Many of the kids were sent away to the large towns to be educated.

Over the last couple of hundred miles we had heard from locals of the existence of herds of wild horses and camels. On the way to Broome we saw the first small herd nestling in the shade of the mountains and our unwelcome arrival sent them galloping away to seek more undisturbed pastures. Again, it was like a scene from a Wild West cowboy film.

We understood there was talk of eventually putting a hard surface road through to Port Headland. Although it would be difficult to turn the tide of progress, it would be a great shame if all the wildlife we saw were denied to others by driving them inland as the area was opened up. What one hears or reads about the outback might capture the imagination of what it is like but all your preconceptions are dashed when you arrive, as it has a uniqueness all of its own. Strangers who waved to us after their vehicles emerged from a cloud of dust would sometimes stop for a chat. One guy commented, "You're the only thing I've seen with wheels for two days."

We drove the last forty miles to Port Headland in the dark and made our way to the nearest hotel for a beer and information. We all looked a little worse for wear covered in the usual dust. As we entered the bar all went quiet. Bruce looked a little worse than the rest of us. He was dressed in shorts, a short-sleeved shirt and his digger hat complete with NZ Air Force wings and matted hair full of dust, with a beard of many colours that matched all the coloured dust mixed together. The look on the face of the locals said it all. I bet they were thinking *Good God, whatever is this coming in?* Although, that day had been hot, around 110°, the beer was cold and delicious.

The locals directed us to a campsite on the caravan park

where we polished off a thick steak sandwich each, followed by coffee. A local couple invited us over to their caravan for a cup of tea and to find out a little about us. Bruce told them I was the greatest tea drinker in Australia (if it had been some other drink I don't think it would have been mentioned). We all had a long-awaited shower by torch light in a corrugated tin partition. The cold-water pipe oozed water that you could be forgiven for thinking had come from a hot tap. It was a rare luxury just the same. We didn't bother putting up the tent; we just bivouacked around the Land Rover.

As we had made good time to Port Headland with only about 370 miles left to Broome, we decided to stay a while and try for a spot of work to augment the freight charges of the Land Rover to Singapore. We contacted the foreman of a manganese transport company who engaged casual labour to drive lorry loads of manganese for delivery 250 miles away. They paid £17.50p per load and you could do as many loads as you wished. We reckoned that two of us could have done two runs each during our short stay and earn £70.00.

We entered a very disorganised transport yard with piles of rusty old iron and lorry bits all over the place and enquired about the possibility of getting some work. The foreman asked us how long we could work for. I told him about three to four days, or enough to do a couple of runs.

"Three to four days is no blo-o-ody good to me," he said. "Sorry, I can't help. G'day."

We tried the local government office, but the answer was the same, nothing. We were, however, offered a job painting the front of a shop. That would only take about four hours so we turned it down and decided to carry on to Broome and try our luck there.

There was no petrol to be had between Port Headland and Broome so we took on an extra twenty-six gallons, hoping we wouldn't have to use our four-wheel drive too much. About fifty miles out of Port Headland we ran into a small bush fire just burning at a steady pace. A little breeze was all that was needed to fan the flames and create a blazing inferno that could spread and burn for days. We spent a little time trying to douse the flames by chucking the red dust at it with some success.

While dozing in the back with Louise and Angela I was suddenly aware of the vehicle being driven through water. I heard Lyn cheering from the front; there was no mistaking it, we were actually in a large pool of water. We were soon wide-awake, out of the vehicle and found ourselves in all that was left of a salt river. We were soon dancing in the water like a load of kids on their first visit to the seaside. It was the first riverbed in nearly 4,000 miles that wasn't completely dried up. I thought the gods were smiling on us. First a shower, then a riverbed that actually had water in it. What more could we have asked for. We lingered for an hour, boiled a billycan, and then pressed on. As the sun went down and the temperature dropped we decided on a night drive to Broome, as it had been about 114° in the shade.

We were suffering with brake problems. They didn't work

and we had to rely on the dust and sand to stop us. It had been quite effective and saved us using the handbrake. One of the leaf springs in the front had broken two days earlier for the umpteenth time. As a temporary measure I wedged a block of wood under the affected spring to take some of the weight away. This helped prevent any of the other leaves from breaking; a practice I had used before as it works as a stopgap. We needed to keep the speed down as the Land Rover was swinging all over the place due to the deep bull sand which made steering difficult. Many times we nearly went off the road.

We could hear the sea as we hit the 80-mile beach, with the gentle waves of the Indian Ocean licking the edges of the wide stretches of white sands only yards away in places.

As our stomachs cried out for food, we decided to look for a suitable pit stop to make a fire. There were times when we were reluctant to use petrol for our cooking burners as we couldn't always be sure when and where further supplies would become available. The burners used a significant amount of petrol when cooking a main meal for six of us so conservation was a priority. We treated our water supplies in much the same way, topping up our containers at every available opportunity. Liquid intake was important in those very hot climates and we were all aware of the dangers of dehydration.

Clumps of trees or bushes never seem to be around when you needed them. It was another two hours before we noticed a dark patch of vegetation well off the road across the sands. With my broken spring in mind, I asked Bruce to guide me over as a precaution. We had a good fire going in a matter of minutes. The chops we bought from Port Headland were soon sizzling on our open fire. Being nearly twelve o'clock our meal was truly a midnight feast. After an hour and a half we ploughed through the bull sand back to the road, just missing some kangaroos as they hopped in front of us.

We changed drivers a couple of times, but were all feeling a bit lethargic so as it started to get light we stopped for breakfast, and all went down to the beach to freshen up. We thought about having a swim but chickened out when someone mentioned the word 'sharks', and we settled for washing our feet and sluicing our faces.

Louise drove the last leg into Broome. I had expected to find a bigger place; it seemed very quiet, as if it had been asleep for years. We had been told that this was once a boomtown, but I couldn't see much boom going on at that moment. We pulled in at a little shop for a drink, served by a half-caste aboriginal girl with lovely eyes and a nice smile, who directed us to the post office, where we picked up our mail. We then made our way to the beach and found a suitable spot to make camp.

We ran into a chap there who said his name was Johnny McQueen, a short thickset chap who was as brown as a berry. He showed us a small tin dwelling he had built on the beach complete with a veranda. He worked on loading the boats with meat from the cold storage plant, and lived all alone, but he was quite happy.

He looked at us with envious eyes as he told us of the great shortage of women in Broome; therefore, our girls were already making quite a hit. Many of the white men were married to aboriginal girls, while others just went around with them. It was a great honour in Broome for an aboriginal girl to have a white boyfriend. As one girl coolly remarked, "I have a white man now."

Many aboriginal girls had babies, the fathers of whom they didn't know. One girl we heard of sued a white man for maintenance for her child. The man appeared before the judge with three witnesses, all of whom said they had spent nights with the girl. His aim was to prove the girl didn't know who the father was. The judge had a very good sense of humour and made an order for all four men to pay £2.00 a week each, remarking that as they had all admitted to possibly fathering the child they must all pay for it. Even Solomon would have been proud of this judgement.

Most of Broome's population of 1,800 were men. Pearl diving was a very large thriving industry in Broome with a fleet of luggers crewed by Malays and Japanese divers. Only recently a pearl farm had been created to increase the production of shell for Mother of Pearl; buttons made of this grace many of the garments we wear. Work was hard to come by in Broome. The big meat cold storage plant employed casual labour, but was only open for six months of the year.

After a visit to the local pub for some ice-cold beer

(guaranteed in Australia), we were invited to a party at the home of a police sergeant. It would appear the word had spread around that girls had arrived in town and we were in no doubt that it was they who were the main attraction for the invitation. The men hung around them like bees round a honey pot, with the girls clearly enjoying their celebrity status. John, Bruce and I were quite convinced that we had only been invited because of our female companions. Nevertheless, it gave us the opportunity to let our hair down a bit and have a few beers to wash away all that bull dust clogging our gullets.

We were all offered accommodation from different people in different places. It crossed my mind that in a town of men hungry for women it was wiser if we all stayed together.

We left the party after midnight and I must confess the process of unclogging my gullet was a bit overdone. Bruce being less inebriated than the rest of us drove us back to our camp on the beach and Louise very kindly made my bed for me. We asked around in the morning about the possibility of two or three days work but without success, so we then went along to the Broome Meat & Cold Storage Company that Johnny McQueen had mentioned. The foreman was only too pleased to give us a few days work starting the next day. So pleased in fact it made me wonder why with such a shortage of work in Broome there weren't more queuing for jobs.

We were engaged for two seventeen-hour shifts starting at 5.30 p.m. and working through the night, finishing at 10.30 a.m.

We were advised to wrap up as warm as possible because no special clothing was provided except for a pair of gloves. We rummaged through our limited wardrobes for the warmest gear we could find. I donned a vest, two pairs of pants, a pair of pyjamas, a shirt, short and long-sleeved pullovers, short and long socks plus my lamb's wool jeep coat, not forgetting my digger hat.

We made our way down the railway line to the meat works and wondered what we had let ourselves in for. The girls had rushed around to cook a meal before we left and appeared quite worried about our frozen meat escapade. I felt a little concerned about leaving them to their own devices in a tent on the beach, especially as they had already been invited to another party; I secretly hoped they would give it a miss.

The foreman handed us our gloves and informed us we would be in the freezer with two other guys. We entered through a small oblong door about 3' x 2½' there was meat everywhere. Carcasses wrapped in sacking and weighing about 190lbs apiece. The smell was more likely to make me search for the door that says 'Vegetarian'. We soon felt very cold, the temperature was about ten degrees below, and our hats had frozen up. We soon realised that this was bloody hard work. The first few carcasses we threw down the chute were very weighty, but as we got more into the rhythm of things they seemed to get lighter. Bruce and I worked as a pair, whilst John worked with another guy. Although he found the going tough, I was surprised at the way he stuck with it.

We soon understood why there was always work to be had at the freezer centre. It wasn't the kind of job one could stand for more than a few days at a time. The freezer rooms were about 125' x 100' and the temperatures varied from ten degrees below zero in some rooms to lower temperatures in others. We threw the carcasses into a chute to be taken off by one of the outside gangs at the bottom. They were then loaded onto trains to be carried to the jetty for loading on to the ships.

Our first few hours in the freezer made us feel very tired until we became acclimatised. We were allowed to leave the freezer for ten minutes after each hour. We all looked forward to that and couldn't wait to leave our frozen tomb; they called these ten-minute breaks 'a dry smoke-o', and after every second hour break it was called 'a wet smoke-o' (in other words a cup of tea, a sandwich and a smoke). Each time we emerged our beards would soon unfreeze and a cloud of steam would rise from our cloths as we thawed out. At midnight we had an hour-and-a-half break with a meal being provided at a local café. With time to spare we returned to our camp to check on the girls, they were out to the world in their sleeping bags.

Our shift finished at 10.30 a.m. The girls had erected the other tent so we could sleep without being disturbed. Although the heat of the day prevented much sleep, as we had more than a twenty-four-hour interlude before the start of our final shift we took advantage of the warm waters of the Indian Ocean for plenty of swimming. It was strange that in such hot weather there were no other swimmers on the beach, and we had it all to ourselves. The next day was much the same, no other swimmers on the beach. Late in the afternoon a guy walking along the beach came up to us.

"You wouldn't get any of the locals swimming here," he said.

"What's the problem?" I replied.

"Bloody sharks," came a swift reply, followed by stories of shark attacks along this beach.

"The locals swim two miles farther along in a safe roped of area."

The guy was surprised that nobody had warned us of the danger.

Our last shift was no different from the first, but the pace was beginning to tell a little as we were working slower than the previous night. The thought of the money boosted our morale a lot. As this shift ran over into a Sunday we had visions of double time for Sunday work. We worked out our pay would be about £28.00 each, so we were happy.

The *Charon* was due to sail at 9.30 a.m. the next day and we would be working on loading the ship in which we were to sail. John couldn't quite make the entire seventeen-hour shift. He called it a day four hours earlier, but Bruce and I made it to the end okay. Our wages were paid by cheque and we were shocked by the paltry amount we received, £14.18.3d each after stoppages, John's was a little less. Apparently there is no such thing as double time, or time and a half, for extraordinary hours. We had learnt a hard lesson and a bloody cold one, but at least we had a few extra bob in our pockets. Even if half of our expectations were frozen!

Aboard The *Charon*

The propeller of the *Charon;* taken at low tide

The girls had done an excellent job of breaking camp and packing the Land Rover and trailer. The *Charon* had already docked beside the jetty, looking very much like a stranded whale stuck in the mud with the tide out. We would be boarding when the tide came back in. John and the girls had already boarded earlier and gone straight to their cabins. We boarded a little later after seeing the vehicle hoisted aboard, plus the loading of 800 sheep bound for the Singapore market. They were housed in the hold for the six-day crossing. Because of the heat large flexible air ducts were installed to ensure a continuous airflow into the hold.

The captain had informed the passengers that an expedition would be joining the ship at Broome and they had already begun to line the rails to watch us embark. They were in for a bit of a shock. Bruce and I were still wearing the same clothes we had been wearing when we left the meat works. Our hair was long and hanging down from under our digger hats. We hadn't had a chance to wash and had very little sleep in the previous twenty-four hours, and we were about to meet our fellow first-class passengers. We pulled our hats down more over our eyes, hoping the ostrich routine would work for us, and strutted up the gangplank.

The *Charon* in the mud at low tide

We heard the gong sound; I said to Bruce that we might as well go the whole hog and have some tea! So in all our dirt and glory we headed towards the sound of the gong. We sat down at the nearest table hoping the smell of the meat works hadn't followed us too closely.

A couple of old dowagers seated at the table next to us nearly swallowed their cups when they saw us. They went into a huddle, probably discussing what we were, man or beast. We cleared two large pots of tea and every cake and biscuit on the table □ we hadn't eaten for ages □ and then we asked for more. We all also made very good use of the showers and looked forward to sleeping in the very comfortable looking beds with the white sheets and coloured bedspreads.

All the passengers had dressed for dinner: our girls made as good an effort as their limited resources would allow, and us boys wore rather loud shirts, mine being a brightly coloured one that I had bought in Singapore. I also wore Chinese sandals, which flapped up and down when I walked, and no socks. The ladies, as you would expect in first-class accommodation, were dressed up to the nines, all vying to keep up with each other, or go one better. One thing we were sure about, they certainly couldn't keep up with us. When we entered the dining room some of the passengers were highly amused and started to laugh, others, however, just glared. We were expecting to sit together, but that wasn't to be. One of the girls sat at the captain's table, John and Bruce sat with the two old dowagers and the doctor. I was seated with three other girls at another table. One introduced herself and said that us boys were the most sensibly dressed of everybody for this type of weather and thought the other men must envy us. Apparently some of the women and girls on board were bored as there were twice as many women as men, and only three of those were single.

I had a word with the captain asking if he would make an announcement to our fellow passengers for us regarding our dress. He agreed and made the following announcement:

"You are already aware of the very interesting expedition group that have joined us. They have asked me if we would kindly bear with them regarding their dress. They are not able to carry the type of clothes appropriate for all occasions while on an overland trek."

Our 9.30 a.m. departure from Broome didn't pass without a tinge of sadness that our Australian adventures were now over and another chapter of our journey was about to begin.

It was four weeks since we had left Sydney. Our travel-worn Land Rover had taken us more than 4,400 miles over arid desert where scenery and colour changed with the day, and where we could choose to wander free as the air without restriction. Where troops of kangaroos hopped in their thousands. Herds of wild horses and camels could be seen living their lives in freedom. Large varieties of reptiles, their type unknown to me, were scurrying around, and emus with their young running for cover. This was the 'Outback', the great outdoors.

Camping under the stars had a special delight all of its own in this vast unspoiled campsite, where you could listen to the howls of the dingoes breaking the silence of the night. The great iron bark trees were covered with cockatoos, finches, parrots and many more birds, while eagles circled slowly overhead.

The isolated little townships whose pubs were a mine of information, where a yarn or story was always on tap. You might even pick up a swear word you didn't know already. Although crossing this great continent was never part of my plan, it was a journey that could never be envisaged, only experienced.

We soon settled down to enjoy our few days of luxury aboard the *Charon* taking full advantage of the excellent food and facilities available, especially the laundry service. We were keen to rid our clothes of the obnoxious smells of the meat works. Drinks on board were very cheap and all duty free. Our popularity soon increased immensely with the other passengers when they discovered Bruce could play the piano.

While aboard the *Charon* we didn't entirely spend the time kicking our heels. There was much planning and preparation still to be done before we reached Singapore. I had left the final inspection and servicing of the vehicle to be done there. It would be much cheaper and there were far better facilities available than in Broome.

Throughout our short time together the group had been a

happy and united party working well as a team. Although I had already discussed with them before our departure from Australia that the conditions in some parts of Southeast Asia would be far worse than anything they had yet experienced. I thought that while we were in such a relaxed atmosphere it was a golden opportunity to paint a much clearer picture for them on what to expect when we hit parts of Thailand and the Burma road.

At that point in time there was absolutely no guarantee that we would be driving into Burma at all. We had already been refused land-route visas for Burma in Australia. All we had been able to obtain was a tourist visa to visit Rangoon, the capital. At least that was a start, and had given me something to work on. My biggest worry was that if I pulled the same stunt again going back into Burma, I might be recognised as the guy who had entered illegally a few months earlier on doctored visas, especially if the same border officials were on duty. The cards were very much stacked against me being able to pull off the same audacious deception a second time around and get away with it. I tried to derive a little comfort from the thought that there has to be a first time for everything. The Burmese government wasn't a regime to fall foul of. I tried not to think of the consequences if things were to go wrong as I didn't want to cause a diplomatic incident.

Much of our time on board the *Charon* was spent answering the 1001 questions from passengers about our travels. They wanted to know where we were going. Where did we start from? What happened if we got sick? Wasn't it dangerous? If we had already done it once, why do it all over again? And why do people do such crazy things? That was a very good question, and one I had often asked myself. Since I was a boy at school I could never resist a challenge. My old headmaster's punishment book was full of the results of some challenge or another of mine. I used to have the marks on my arse to prove it. In any case, I had never been a person to leave a job half done.

When I left home many people were sceptical of my chances of success. I think if you mix a little guts, stir in some determination with a pinch of luck, that can sometimes be a winning formula. It was that pinch of luck that was sometimes hard to find.

On our last day on board ship we were invited to the captain's cocktail party where we shared a few moments of hilarity at the manner in which we had joined the *Charon* at Broome. The captain commented that it had been an exciting and unusual experience, one which he said he had enjoyed immensely. Just as well for us they didn't have a steerage class in those days. The evening was celebrated with a farewell dance on deck. As it was our last night we took full advantage of the festivities and had a few extra drinks. For the boys' part, we certainly hadn't gone short of dance partners with so many unaccompanied ladies on board.

On our last morning at breakfast, we had to face up to the fact that it was the last time we would enjoy the excellent food we had been given for the six days we were on board. We ate rather more than usual to fill us up for the rest of the day.

Return To Singapore

When we docked at Singapore the sheep were the first to leave the ship by their own special exit. One of the ship's crew walked up the gangplank with a ewe on a lead. He turned around at the top and walked back down again with the ewe in tow, then the rest of the sheep followed. Having seen it with my own eyes I could now appreciate the saying 'They followed like a load of sheep.'

We said our farewells to the captain, crew and our shipboard friends as they disembarked, while we waited patiently for the unloading of the Land Rover and trailer.

It had only been seven months earlier that Pat and I had felt trapped in Singapore. I thought we would never get out of the place. Now I was pleased to be back with my new party, preparing for the trek home to England.

We found a cheap hotel to use as a base and booked one large room that all six of us shared, this helped to keep the cost down, and we used our own sleeping bags.

As it was their first visit to Singapore, my five companions started their sightseeing with a visit to the famous 'Haw Par Villa', off the Pasir Panjang Road, on the western section of the island, whilst I made my first port of call to the Land Rover agents in Orchard Road for repairs and servicing.

Striking a pose in Singapore

I was pleased to see Mr Clerks again, who had been so kind to Pat and I when I passed through on my last visit. I was sorry to hear that Tom Wall was on vacation, which meant it wouldn't be possible for me to see him again before we left.

The Royal Thai Consulate in Singapore took two days to process our transit visas through Thailand. So while we waited we made another application to the Burmese Consulate for land-route visas through their country. That was again turned down with the emphasis that land-route travel was not possible. That latest knock back was no surprise as we had already been refused in Sydney, Australia. The only chance we had now was to try again in Bangkok, which would be the last chance saloon.

We visited a place called 'Change Alley', the Singapore money market, where you could barter for the best exchange rates just as you could haggle for anything else. We did the rounds of the little chain of shops down Change Alley and wrote down all the best prices on offer of the currencies in which we were interested, then returned to the shop that offered the best deal and made our purchase. I found that in most of the countries I had visited in Southeast Asia pounds and dollars were always sought after. People would stop you wherever you were and ask, "You have dollar?" or "You have pounds?" They would always change your money for you at a much higher rate than that which was given by the banks.

I visited the British Consulate and met with the military attaché to collect ammunition for my Colt .45. Disappointingly, none was available but arrangements had been made for me to pick some up in Penang. I was also asked to meet the naval attaché for a chat. He informed me that a team of naval ratings would like to follow my route on an expedition of their own to the UK. Although I was happy to help with any information I could give; I made it clear that my expedition was completely independent and not attached to any official or government body. It was, therefore, easy for me to bend the rules and be as unorthodox as I needed to be. However, with an official naval backed expedition they would have to follow the 'paths of righteousness'. I also mentioned the refusal of the Burmese to grant us visas whilst in Singapore and asked if their guys were also refused would they still press on and be prepared to explore more dubious methods of gaining entry. I left him with those thoughts to ponder.

We went along to the Land Rover agents to pick up our vehicle, plus a few extra spares costing a total of £20.00. We had made a list for our final round of shopping as it was going to be our last opportunity until we reached Kuala Lumpur.

The bloodhounds of the press had followed their noses to our hotel for another story (I had given them one on the way out) for their paper *The Straits Times*. A Singapore radio station asked us for an interview and details of our departure times.

Before leaving Singapore I went to see Roger at Changi. It was good to see him again. I introduced the new group and we all had a meal together. We certainly had a lot of news to catch up on.

Roger knew we had arrived back in Singapore as he had seen the article in *The Straits Times*. Since his arrival in Singapore he had been working as a waiter, saving for his return journey back to the UK. He was quite prepared to drop everything and join us if only the room had been available on the vehicle. I told him that with all our problems on the journey out he was certainly a glutton for punishment. I would have been most happy for Roger to have joined us again.

We left Singapore via Birkit Timah Road at 3.30 on the afternoon of the 8th of November 1958 and headed for the causeway. We were surprised at the number of people, both young and old, that were lining up to wave us off. Like Roger it appeared they had also read *The Straits Times*, or listened to the radio. People were tooting their car horns at us. They opened their windows and frantically waved their hands. From that farewell we certainly understood what real celebrities must feel like and drove on with our heads slightly increasing in size.

About two miles from the causeway we were held up by the police, who were stopping all traffic. We were told that the King of Malaya was passing through Johore Bahru, just over the causeway. Our ignorance was highlighted by the fact that none of us knew that there was a 'King of Malaya'. The hold up lasted about twenty minutes, during which time the police had a marvellous time dashing around on their motorbikes stopping everything and everybody that moved.

Entering Malaya

As we crossed the mile-long causeway into the Federation of Malaya I couldn't help feeling a slight quiver of excitement that I was now heading for home. Customs and Immigration paid little attention to our arrival and soon stamped our passports, welcoming us to Malaya. They were much more concerned with other vehicles which were thoroughly searched and bags opened. Although the political situation had eased a little since my outward journey the state of emergency still remained in force with some regulations being vigorously implemented. Vehicles making long journeys were forbidden to carry foodstuffs through terrorist areas for fear it could fall into the wrong hands. Although this was understandable, my problem was that I had half of a trailer full of foodstuffs which had been donated to the expedition in Australia. We hadn't actually been asked if we were carrying foodstuffs but other vehicles were being searched for it. I wasn't prepared to risk having all our supplies confiscated so I decided to bend the rules again and say nothing and left with all our food supplies intact. As the old saying goes, 'A still tongue keeps a wise head'.

Whilst on the road to Batu Pahat heading towards the Malayan capital, Kuala Lumpa, a coach overtook our vehicle. An

Indian boy was sitting in the back and began waving to us. We politely returned his wave, but he continued to wave for some twenty miles. He then started making gestures with his hands which we couldn't understand. I gave him a final wave and tilted my head sideways resting it in my hands, indicating that we were going to find somewhere to sleep and gestured goodbye.

As the coach stopped in the small town of Ayer Hitan, the boy jumped out and ran up to our vehicle. He spoke good English and said, "You have no accommodation tonight? You must stay at my sister's house." This was twenty-five miles away. He then jumped into the Land Rover and introduced himself as Muhtu. He told us he was twenty-one and a student. He had seen a report about the expedition in the Singapore papers and was very excited about meeting us. His sister's home was a bit of a diversion off our route, and I pondered whether the extra mileage was worth more delay, but the disappointed look on his face when he thought we weren't going with him settled the matter. Although his poor sister was unaware that she was about to have six complete strangers dumped on her by her brother, at least we had made him happy. On the way to his sister's we ran into very heavy rain. It fell in torrents and visibility was down to zero. We couldn't see a bloody thing!

We eventually arrived at Muhtu's sister's place, which was just outside the town at 7.00 p.m. It was a typical medium-sized Malay house with a thatched roof perched on short stilts. It had a little garden with pot plants scattered around. We were shown up a flight of wooden stairs to a small bare room overlooking the road. Muhtu's sister eventually appeared looking very attractive, wearing a green Sari patterned in gold, overhung by her long black shining hair. She welcomed us to her home and told her brother to take us to an Indian eating-house a short distance away, 'as we must be very hungry'. We asked our friend if he would order for us as our own efforts were getting us nowhere. He took our request very seriously and ordered the food like there was no tomorrow. We hadn't reckoned on a banquet. Much of the food remained untouched. We decided that from then on, regardless of how many cock-ups we made, we would order for ourselves in the future. It would be much cheaper.

Back at the house my five friends tucked down for the night in their sleeping bags in the bare room. I had decided to sleep in the Land Rover parked outside the house. That was a big mistake. All the local dogs in the area had somehow been alerted that a stranger was sleeping in the vehicle and decided to show their disapproval, taking it in turns to bark the night away. By the morning I was thoroughly fed up as I had had very little sleep. I left the vehicle and sat in the garden of the house, waiting for the others to appear.

Muhtu's sister had very kindly arranged breakfast of bread and jam, with tea in glasses. We bade farewell to Muhtu and his sister and thanked them for their kindness.

We headed towards the ferry crossing at Batu Pahat. We were told the fare was three dollars fifty, but after our usual bit of bargaining the price was reduced to three dollars. We thought we had done well; only to learn later that the actual fare for the crossing should have been only two dollars fifty. I had learnt during my travels in many similar circumstances the trick was for the operator to quote a higher price fare to start with as they expected travellers like ourselves to bargain the price down. In the main they would always try it on with foreign travellers who looked a bit gullible, probably like us.

We carried on for another thirty-two miles along the coast road of the Malacca Straits and then crossed on another small ferry to the small town of Muar. We actually paid the correct fare on this occasion, two dollars fifty.

We continued on along the coast road to Malacca and headed inland via Aldr Gajah before joining the Kuala Lumpur road. We had a quick lunch of tinned fish, tomato and a brew up before reaching Sereban.

As we continued our journey we were slowed down by a heavy storm that lasted about half an hour. Louise took over the driving for a spell, but it wasn't up to her usual standard; she was driving much too fast for the conditions, and I had to ask her to slow down a little.

We met a group of young Malay girls along the way who were returning to their village. We decided to take some photographs of them. They were very wary of us first of all and very shy and reluctant to come forward when we asked them. Eventually one sweet little girl, who was probably about seven years old, walked towards us and had her picture taken. We gave her a few cents for being so brave. She then rewarded us with a big smile. The rest of the group were now more relaxed, and two more walked over to us holding hands. I persuaded them to sit on the Land Rover and we had a picture taken together. Then they all went on their way giggling about their great adventure.

The road to Kuala Lumpur, me with two Malaysian beauties

We drove into Kuala Lumpur, the Malayan capital, in the late afternoon. I visited the offices of the *Malaya Mail* to get a copy of an article they had published about my arrival in Malaya on my outward journey.

On returning to the vehicle there was the usual crowd of sightseers gathered around trying to satisfy their curiosity. One Malay man, who introduced himself as Mr Chin, took us along to the Roman Catholic Church of Saint Anthony to enquire if we could bed down in the local school hall for the night. Father Edmond, the priest and administrator of the school, welcomed us and we were readily given permission to stay. But he had lowered his voice almost to a whisper whilst explaining that the toilets were in a very bad state, and probably not like we were used to.

I smiled at him and said, "Father, whatever the state of the toilets, it won't be a problem for us!" During my travels I had probably seen far worse.

Father Edmond shared a few jokes with us whilst in the meantime our new friend, Mr Chin, had taken over the organising of the moving of the desks to make space for the setting out of our sleeping bags. He was determined that we were to be made as comfortable as possible before he left.

Word soon spread of our arrival at the school and we were very pleased that we had been able to speak to some of the teachers. The school had over 800 pupils who each paid ten dollars a month for their tuition. In sterling terms this was about 22/- shillings (£1.10p).

We were informed that Malay children were only educated up to the age of eleven years in government schools, after which they had to leave or pay for further education. We had the pleasure of speaking to many of the children; I don't use the word pleasure lightly. These kids were so polite and respectful, spoke good English and were so keen to be educated; I couldn't help but contrast them with some of the children I had come into contact with back home in England. English was, we were told, the only language taught in the schools and all other subjects were from an English syllabus.

Medical treatment was free for all who needed it in Malaya, but this would be accompanied by a long wait in a queue. Those able to afford it could take advantage of private medicine.

Before tucking into our sleeping bags that night I made us all a cup of cocoa. The first cocoa we'd had on the trip.

We left the school early next morning. The intention was to clock up a good mileage, but that idea soon went out of the window. The vehicle started to play up before we even left town, which gave me little choice but to strip down the carburettor in the main road, watched by a crowd that had soon gathered around to see what was going on. We had wasted over an hour before we were able to get moving again. Apart from our engine problem, everybody wanted to talk with us, and we always felt obliged to try to answer any questions put to us.

Thanks to the good tarmac roads we were able to cover the next 200 miles passing through Selanger, Butang Padang, Kuala Kaangsar and on to Taiping without further problems. Bruce had wanted to look up a friend of his in Taiping who was stationed there, serving with the New Zealand Army as a dental officer. Unfortunately, he wasn't there at the time, but a colleague of his invited us to the officers' mess for a beer, which turned out to be many beers.

Later we were all extended a further invitation to join the officers for dinner. I must say, we didn't have to think too long about accepting. There were only five of them in all as it was a small active service unit carrying out jungle patrols to root out the communist terrorists. We learned a lot about the terrorist situation in Malaya from the officers, who were convinced that they now had the communist terrorists on the run and that they now had ceased to be an effective force. They reckoned that only about 800 were still fighting. For any of these bandits, as they were sometimes called, that were handed over by a civilian, a reward of around 6000 Malay dollars was given by the authorities. If it was an important CT a reward of up to 25,000 Malay dollars could be awarded. This was around £600 sterling. Our group joked about catching one for ourselves.

They had a stuffed kiwi in the mess, which was the C/O's pride and joy. He used to keep a very close eye on it with his routine inspection. We were all invited to stroke it before we left.

We spent the night at their sports field on the veranda of the pavilion, but the bloody mosquitoes had given us hell. Bruce and I seemed to be bitten more than the others. We had even tried lighting a mosquito coil but being in the open this didn't help very much.

After a good breakfast in the mess we watched the departure of a squad of soldiers, clad in their jungle green outfits, going off into the jungle on another terrorist pursuit operation. After wishing them good luck, we said our goodbyes to our friends, not forgetting the kiwi, and headed off to Butterworth, about sixty miles away. Bruce never did catch up with his friend.

We arrived at the airfield at twelve noon, where we set about trying to find my contact F/LT Smith, who we were informed had gone to Penang, but we were met by a F/Lt Keith Price, who had been made aware of our arrival. I was given instructions to meet with F/LT Smith in Penang, where he had been given the label of 'Temporary Housing Officer'. Keith gave me Smithy's phone number to contact him on our arrival on the island.

We crossed over on the Penang-Butterworth ferry, landing at the Church Street Pier and headed straight into George Town via Church Street, Ghaut. We drove around for a while trying to find our bearings. We were in Beach Street, near the clock tower when two ladies driving a big black car hailed us to stop. They got out of the car and came over to us. They said they were from Sydney, Australia and had noticed our English and Australian flags on the land Rover and had wondered whether we were the group mentioned in the *Strait Times* (our news story had certainly got around). After the usual chat, the girls were invited to stay with them, an invitation they gratefully accepted. I had a sneaking suspicion that the girls welcomed this opportunity of a break from us boys to catch up on some purely feminine chitchat.

After the girls had left in the car with the two Sydney ladies, I gave Smithy a call. He said, "I've been expecting you, there's six of you I believe."

"No," I said. "Only three." I then explained about the girls and the ladies from Sydney. "We need some accommodation for ourselves," I said.

"That's already taken care of," he replied. "I've got a house for you, and something else you're expecting." I knew what he meant.

We met up at a place called the 'Sydney Bar' for lunch and a drink. We were then taken by Smithy to a large house. "This is where you'll be staying," he quipped.

I was surprised, it was quite modern with electric lights, a cooker and it was well furnished. The rooms were so large that a person sitting at the other end of one of the rooms looked small. I thought, *Smithy, you have done us proud!* As he left us to settle in, he handed me a package and said if we needed anything, just to call him. The package was the ammunition I had been promised since leaving Sydney.

John and Bruce joined me for a visit up to Fort Auchey, an army depot, to see Jeanne and Peter West, the couple Pat, Roger and I had stayed with on the way out. On the way up to the fort we ran into torrential rain, which had caused flash flooding; the water was ankle-deep in places. Some of the vehicles had been caught and were being pushed out of the water. One stretch of water we hit too fast sent a sheet of water right over the top of the land rover. Fortunately, we weren't towing the trailer! I had left that at the house.

Peter and Jeanne were not surprised by our visit; they were expecting it. The *Strait Times* was well read in Penang (I thought the world and his brother must both read it). Jeanne introduced us to five army wives who were at the fort. Their husbands were away on army exercises somewhere. Peter and Jeanne invited us to stay with them again, but I explained about the house Smithy had given us.

When we returned to the house, the girls were waiting for us. They had come back to collect some of their things. As the time was getting on they stayed long enough to share some baked beans on toast with us. We had it in real style, on china plates, sitting up to the table with knives and forks, and real china cups and saucers for our tea instead of the usual mugs.

An air force officer had joined us at the house. He said he was the official photographer of the Australian Air Force, and after the girls had left us to return to their digs near the Island Nightclub, we spent the rest of the evening discussing the current political situation in Southeast Asia with him.

We intended to have a service done on the Land Rover before we left the island so we went along to see Jim Maher, the Castrol agent. Jim had received a letter from Singapore advising him of our impending arrival so a service had already been organized. He took us to see the manager of Borneo Motors, who was to carry out the service on behalf of Castrol. While this was in progress, Jim took us along to his club at The Eastern Oriental Hotel for a few Carlsberg beers.

A phone call came to the club while we were enjoying our drinks with a message to say our prop shaft was loose and asking if we wanted it tightened. We collected the Land Rover just after two p.m. and were told by Borneo Motors that there was nothing to pay. Castrol had paid the bill for the whole service, plus the adjustments made to the prop shaft.

I gave Smithy a call and told him we were moving out. I said to the others that we'd had a pleasant break, and made some new friends, but all good things had to come to an end! We collected our gear, hitched up the trailer and were gone within the hour, catching the first ferry back to Butterworth.

We headed immediately towards Changloon, the Malay /Thailand border, eighty-five miles away via Alor Star hoping to cross the border by nightfall, but we were thirty minutes too late. The border closed at six p.m. A little hut was made available for us by the Customs and Immigration Department, so we spent another night on Malayan soil. We were back to the old routine of curling up in our sleeping bags once more.

Louise and I ambled back to the village. We had hoped to buy some Thai ticals for when we crossed the border the next morning, but we were out of luck, none were available. We stayed in the village just long enough to have a chat with one of the locals, and then returned to the hut and bed.

As we intended to make a quick start that morning, we had a hurried breakfast and whilst the others packed the vehicle, I wandered to the Customs and Immigration shed and started the ball rolling to get our clearance underway. The officers were very friendly and helpful. They were keen to have their photographs taken with us in front of their office with the Changloon border sign in the picture.

We passed into no man's land for the eight-mile drive to Sadow, the Thai border. We had been given a stark warning that we must not stop on the road under any circumstances, as bandits were known to be over the border. I said to the others, "Let's hope that we don't have a puncture or a breakdown on this stretch."

To be on the safe side, I had my Colt .45 on hand, and suggested to the girls that it might be safer if they were to keep out of sight in the back of the Land Rover.

Thailand

We checked in at the customs shed just inside the border. Their first concern was how many cameras we had. To be on the safe side we only declared three just in case there were some new regulations we hadn't yet heard about that might have come into force. We were then directed to another office, two miles away, where our passports were stamped and we filled in forms about our personal particulars. We were asked to pay a charge of fourteen ticals for some kind of stamp duty. I questioned that, as it seemed a bit unusual. The officer said he would pay it himself out of his own pocket. Although this was a kind gesture, I didn't accept that this was something he should do. As we had no Thai ticals, he was pleased to accept two Malay dollars in lieu. We were then passed on to a second customs office where the carnet was stamped and his portion removed.

On our departure from Sadow we were asked to report to the police station to have our vehicle registered. As we entered I saw two cages at the top of some wooden stairs. One contained a safe, which could be seen by all and sundry through the stout iron bars, and looked as secure as the crown jewels in the Tower of London. The second cage was strategically placed next to the first one. It measured about 7'x6'x6' and contained five prisoners, all squatted on the floor of the cage. A guard was seated close by with a shotgun firmly placed under his arm. We were told that they were terrorists. I thought the word terrorist was rather ambiguous. Using the word terrorist one can easily slip into a well-known tract. A terrorist by any other name can give an entirely different meaning. It's really a political term, a meaningless expression with so many connotations. What type of 'terrorist'? Were they the same ones as those mentioned to us on the Malayan border, or were they of another brand of criminal? Whoever they were, it seemed ironic placing them in full view of the safe. It was akin to locking up a thirsty man with a dripping tap just out of his reach!

After we left the police station we joined the only road that headed north towards the capital, Bangkok. We passed through many of the sprawling rubber plantations before we arrived in the small town of Haad-Yai. We had a letter of introduction to the Castrol agent there from the agent in Penang asking him to supply us with any oil that we might require. The agent introduced himself as Pinyo Wattakorn, and after he offered us coffee, he was very keen to show us his excellent collection of colour slides. This was followed by an invitation out for a wonderful Thai meal. The variety of food in the restaurant was superb. We tucked into fried rice, eggs, and pieces of pork on wooden sticks which were dipped in excellent prawn soup. There was hot liver curry with side dishes of cucumber salad followed by more soup, and then by wonderful tasting lotus nuts in sweet syrup and finally prawn crisps and coffee.

We all chatted for about an hour over our meal. All the time we were in the restaurant we had been closely observed by the lovely Thai waitresses, who seemed to have great charm and character written in their faces. They held their lovely figured bodies very upright and would have graced any of the catwalks of the London or Paris fashion houses.

We left Haad-Yai at 2.30 p.m. to the amiable waves and shouts of 'hello' from the townsfolk, who had come from all directions. This seemed to be the only word of English that was universally known. I was already aware of what a friendly and happy race of people the Thais were. My companions had begun to appreciate this too.

The road conditions had deteriorated from reasonable to a deep muddy potholed surface. We passed through Ratapoon towards Pattalung, where we had hoped to spend the night, but darkness closed in very quickly so we decided to stop as we entered a small village where there were just a few huts scattered around. (We were only seventeen kilometres from Pattalung.) As if by magic there seemed to be an instant gathering of the villagers. We were quite amazed by where they had all come from.

I indicated, by my hand movements, that we wanted a place to sleep. We were soon swamped with all kinds of offers. Eventually we were shown to a house that was balanced on stilts and taken upstairs to the veranda where an oil lamp had been lit for us. About a dozen of the villagers followed us up the stairs to watch the proceedings. They looked on while we lit the stove and made some tea. An old man came up the stairs and placed six eggs on the table before us. I offered to pay him for them, but he wouldn't take anything. A little boy of about six years old appeared on the veranda accompanied by his mother. He seemed to be fascinated by the fact that I was wearing shorts. Once he had found his confidence, he came over to me and tried to put his hands up my trouser legs. This was rather embarrassing, but everybody else found it amusing. I just tickled his tummy each time he tried. He giggled just like any other little boy would do.

After we had finished our meal most of the villagers melted away, but one young lad of about fourteen stayed for a while and tried to entertain us by playing his flute.

When we finally went to bed down for the night we found the mosquitoes were working overtime on us, so Louise and I went back down to the vehicle and tried to escape their attention for a while. However, when she returned upstairs again to lay out her sleeping bag she found space was so limited that she returned back down to the vehicle and slept in the back. I had already commandeered the front.

We left at 8.30 a.m. the following morning in the pouring rain. The villagers were there to see us off. We were soon driving through the mud again and bouncing in and out of the potholes. Before we reached Pattalung we had a river to ford. I waded across to test its depth, regardless of what might be lurking beneath its murky surface, before driving through. This was a practice we always carried out before fording took place.

We carried on through Trang and passed more large rubber plantations. The estates in Thailand didn't appear to be as well kept and tidy as those in Malaya. The rain hadn't stopped all that day; it had become more and more difficult trying to keep the windscreen clean. So much mud had been splashed up from the road that the wipers couldn't cope; this made progress very slow.

We pressed on until we reached the small village of Pagside, sixty miles north west of Huay Yod, where we decided to call it a day. We had heard that there was a monastery nearby just outside the village. We went along and asked the monks if there was somewhere dry we could sleep for the night. None of the monks spoke any English, which was surprising as in most of the religious organisations I had come into contact with throughout my travels you would always find someone who spoke English. But with the magic of hand movements they soon understood what we wanted.

They led us through a muddy bog and over a stile-like contraption where we arrived at a small wooden house. This was where we were to spend the night. We were unable to get the vehicle very near to the house, so we had to trek backwards and forwards through the mud in order to reach our gear. Nevertheless, we were very grateful for any kind of shelter that night.

There was a school for boys attached to the monastery and it wasn't long before half a dozen of the boys had joined us. Two of them who were learning English practised on us. They wrote us little notes asking questions.

"Why do you come to our village?"

"Where do you go?"

"Where from you come?"

We were kept quite busy writing down answers to all their questions. I was asked by one of the boys to write a song for them, and the one I chose seemed very appropriate at the time.

'Mud mud glorious mud.

There's nothing quite like it for cooling the blood.

Follow me follow.

Down to the hollow.

And there let us wallow in glorious mud.'

Before we left the village the following morning we asked some of the kids if they would pose for some photographs. We hadn't realised what we had let ourselves in for. Those laughing, shouting, happy kids ran from every corner of the village and virtually besieged the Land Rover. They climbed everywhere there was a space, on the roof, on the bonnet, on the bumpers and the mudguards. I doubted there had been any more youngsters left anywhere else in the village.

Pagside, Thailand. Children from the village besiege the Land Rover to have their picture taken.

During the next couple of days we had very little respite from the rain. Every time we left the vehicle we were soaked and covered in mud. After we had passed through the little townships of Krabi, Aowleuk, Tupput and Pangnga, the road narrowed to nothing more than a track. It became impossible to avoid any of the potholes, there were just too many. After we heard an unusual banging noise that came from the rear we stopped to investigate, and to our dismay found that one of the bloody trailer spring couplings had sheared off. The spring had gone through the bottom of the trailer and had finished up puncturing a tin of jam. I suppose with all the punishment the trailer had suffered over those few hours, something like that was inevitable. I wondered at the time if my decision to bring the trailer in the first place had been the right one. It had been the second major trailer problem since we left Sydney, Australia. We limped into Tungmaprouw pulling our wounded trailer, and hoped we might find a guy with welding equipment, but it seemed as though we had run out of luck; there wasn't any. The nearest welding gear was ten miles away in the little town of Taguapa. We didn't hang around; we had some lunch and moved straight out.

After a slow drive we eventually arrived in Taguapa at 6.30 in the evening. It was a dimly lit place with ramshackle shops and dwellings. I indicated to a young bystander, who was already looking at our lopsided trailer, that we needed a repair shop. He joined us in the vehicle and took us a mile and a half out of town (the same way we had just come in) to a dimly lit yard with pieces of junk metal lying all over the place.

A man who spoke little English came out and I tried to explain our problem. He immediately sent a runner to drag his welder back to work. When we unloaded the trailer we found the worst mess we had ever seen in our lives. Most of our supply of tinned foods had taken a real battering. We had everything from wet Nullarbor dust and sand, to wet and muddy tin labels at the bottom, all mixed up and flavoured with broken open tins of jam. None of the tins that had survived had any labels on. All of the meticulous packing of our supplies in Sydney, Australia had come to nothing. The only consolation we derived from that fiasco was that the trailer would be much lighter. It was just potluck after that as to what we would find inside when we opened the tins.

We unloaded the trailer and work was started on it straight away. In the meantime, we were invited by the repairman to stay at his humble abode for the night. They worked diligently on the trailer from 7 p.m. until midnight when the work was completed. It had been necessary to weld six angle brackets inside the trailer, giving it extra strength, with another three cross members welded on the bottom as cracks had been found along the seams. The exhaust system on the Land Rover had also undergone major surgery. I was very satisfied with what had been done and I wondered what the cost of all that dedicated work would be.

Next morning we had breakfast standing up around our newly refurbished trailer, scrutinized by the locals. After having discarded all the damaged tins and stores, we cleaned and re-packed the trailer. The contents of which had now been reduced by half. When I asked the repairman for the bill, I was amazed by his response. His words were:

"I work for you for nothing. I not want pay. You need help, I help!"

I smiled at him and thanked him for his very kind offer but insisted that I must pay him for all the work that he had done, but my words had fallen on deaf ears. He was adamant and would take nothing. Although this was a very typical example of the generosity, kindness and willingness to help of the Thai people, I felt very uneasy after having had all that work done and no payment made. It might be that their generosity was a step too far.

Before I left the repair compound I had what I thought was a bright idea. Whilst in Singapore I had been given a present by Les Champaign, who was attached to the intelligence bureau of the

Australian Embassy. I had intended to keep it for a special occasion when it might be most needed, but I offered my present, a bottle of Scotch whisky to the repairman.

The look on his face was pure joy. One would have thought that he had been offered eternal life. He rubbed the label that said 'Scotch Whisky' wondering if it was real or whether he was just dreaming. As the old saying goes, 'We all get our just rewards in heaven'. I believed he thought he had just had his down here on earth that day. I have often wondered if he ever drunk the whisky or just kept it as a status symbol.

With all the heavy rain we had experienced over those last few days. I knew what to expect on the next 120-mile stretch to Ranong. My team were about to find out. There was no road, only jungle tracks. There had been talk of some kind of road being constructed, but there was very little evidence of this on my outward trip.

When we arrived at the barrier, which had been the point of entry to the jungle stretch where a permit to enter was required, the guard at the barrier muttered, "Permit, permit."

We of course didn't have one. As he couldn't speak any English, I assumed he couldn't read any either, so I pulled my driving licence from my case, held my breath, and showed him the licence. I repeated the words, "Permit, London." He seemed happy.

I printed my name in his book and added my old air force number in the place for the permit number. The barrier was opened and we passed through.

I was a bit worried about Bruce at the time. Although he hadn't mentioned about not feeling up to scratch, he appeared to be very lethargic and not a bit like his old self. We weren't in one of the best places for anybody to get sick.

As expected we were soon driving down muddy tracks, then having to stop to paddle in mud in order to drag brush from the surrounding jungle to fill in some of the muddy waterlogged creeks. Although this was a frequent occurrence, we had at least managed to keep going at a very slow pace.

On one narrow track a large snake slid across in front of the vehicle and out of sight. To my great surprise, we had actually covered just over thirty miles in six hours. But as all good things come to an end, so did our hopes. We had come to an abrupt stop and were firmly bogged down up to our axles in mud. Even the four-wheel drive could do nothing to extricate us from our plight.

We worked for four hours, chopping branches, and dragging anything we could muster to sink into the mud to try and form a firm base under the wheels. All our efforts were in vain; it just would not budge. It was at times like these that there was only one thing to do, put the kettle on and have a cuppa.

After the effects of our inspirational beverage had had a chance to work, another attempt was made to free the vehicle. I removed all my clothes and wrapped a towel around my waist. This had meant immersing nearly half my body below the surface of the thick slimy mud to reach the bottom of the rear wheels, in order to try and push some stout pieces of branch underneath.

When I emerged from the mud a number of leaches had attached themselves to my body by burying their heads into my flesh. They were on my chest, back and legs. If you try to pull them off, it is possible that their heads will break off and remain in the flesh. The only effective way of removal is to pour salt over them. They will then normally just drop off. Another method is to run a lighted cigarette down their body. If you leave them on the flesh for any length of time, they will just fill up with your blood and then drop off when they'd finished their meal. As none of our party was a smoker, the girls very kindly gave them the salt treatment. The penetrations they made left blood trickling down my body like a bead of water on a windowpane. This would continue until the blood had congealed.

All my efforts and my mud bath had, again, been in vain. The Land Rover remained firmly stuck. After a painstaking four-hour slog of pushing and pulling, one of the villagers who was working nearby saw our predicament and said he would get an old truck they had in the village to try and pull us out. This old truck rolled up after about thirty minutes. It looked as though it had been borrowed from the hillbillies and was ready to expire at any moment, but we were certainly thankful it was there. We tied a towrope to the chassis of the rear of our vehicle and to the front of the rescue truck. The intention was to drag it back out of the bog the same way in which we had gone in. However, after two unsuccessful attempts, both of which ending with the towrope breaking, we had to think of something else. We then tried again using a tow wire. This time it was successful, and we were back on reasonably firm ground. My pride took a bit of a knock as I saw my faithful old Land Rover being towed out of trouble. But it certainly wasn't to be the last time.

Between Taguapa and Ranong. The remains of one of the many typical bridges we had to cross.

Although we were happy to be out of the bog, we had gained nothing. We were right back where we started. Fortunately more villagers had arrived with the rescue truck and they helped us lay a much firmer runway. We made it through on our second attempt. Every few hundred yards we had to stop to make a bridge through a bog, clear a path through thick patches of jungle with our machetes, or remove a fallen tree. Thank God I had anticipated some of the troubles we might face and invested in a good axe before we left Aussie. Some half-hearted attempts had been made in some places, near villages, to erect the odd wooden bridge over some of the larger creeks. These bridges were made with logs and pulled into position by elephants. The only snag was they never made any approaches to these bridges; consequently there was a gap of one or two feet, between the edge of the bridge and the beginning of the roadway. So we had to build a ramp of logs, or whatever we could find in the surrounding jungle. Then drag it to the bridge and make a ramp before we could drive on. We then dragged the logs across to the other side and made another ramp so that we could drive off again. But that wasn't the end of the problem. Sometimes a bridge would be so short that the Land Rover took up its entire length, which made it impossible to get the trailer on at the same time. We had to make two ramps so that we could place them at both ends of the bridge to enable us to drive on and straight off again in one go.

Eric and John building a bridge across one of the many creeks and swamps through the jungles of Thailand and Burma.

Stuck in a swamp when one of the homemade bridges fell apart.

Sometimes when we crossed these creeks, if we were lucky, we might find some logs that were long enough and of a manageable size which we could then drag to the creek and position them across to line up with the width of the wheels of the Land Rover. That would then enable me to balance the vehicle on the logs and drive slowly across without slipping off. I had my door partially open, and leaned halfway out of the vehicle so that I could see the offside wheels, and one of the logs, to make sure I was on course. This meant inch-perfect driving, and it was always a great relief when I reached the other side. If I had slipped off, it would have entailed hours of work to extricate us, and the tortuous effort of having to start all over again. I must blow my own trumpet a little and say I made many a successful crossing of these creeks at the first attempt. However, I must admit that on the odd occasions when I did slip off, we were well and truly not up the creek, but in it.

Most of our wallowing in the mud was done bare-footed and with the girls in bathing costumes. They had very little else to wear at times as their clothes were nearly always wet with the incessant rain. On those occasions I advised everybody to wash their feet with disinfectant in the water. This advice was rarely heeded. I made sure though that I practised what I preached. Later, some of the group were to regret not following my example.

Poor Bruce, who had been under the weather, had taken a turn for the worse. He had contracted some kind of fever, and had a bad leg which prevented him from being able to leave the vehicle unaided. We were without his help when we most needed all the help we could get. The girls had done everything to try to make him as comfortable as possible. We had no chance getting him to a doctor, or any idea of how long it would take us to get through this stretch of jungle to reach Ranong. That was in the lap of the gods.

The harsh conditions of the journey had begun to take their toll. By the end of the day, trying to keep the wheels of the Land Rover turning, come what may, left us drained and we still had to make camp and cook a meal before we could crash into our sleeping bags.

We had been fortunate enough to arrive at a small village just as another storm broke, and we were very thankful to be offered a small aluminium hut where we could spend the night. The hut had four shutter windows that opened outwards. We backed the Land Rover up to one of the windows and ran a lead from the vehicle, which gave us enough light to see and prepare our meal. This was a bit of luxury for us. Just to be able to get out of the rain and mud for a while and get ourselves dry. The villagers also presented us with a large bowl of cooked rice, which was very welcome and a good substitute for bread, which we hadn't been able to get for days.

The natural curiosity of the villagers had, as usual, got the better of them. The locals poked their heads through the open shuttered windows, which they occupied for the whole evening, while they watched and laughed at the way we prepared our food. They only melted away when we disconnected the lead from the vehicle and went to our beds.

After we left the village next morning, it wasn't long before we ran into trouble. We had to battle for every inch of road covered. We found problems round every corner, and at the bottom of every hill. One of the swamps that day proved to be a real bastard. It was one of the worst we had encountered. There was a deep stream which ran right through its middle, which made it practically impossible to judge its depth. Louise had a lucky escape there. While she was searching for wood in a deep ditch a snake had slithered over her foot. She made a hasty retreat from the ditch and understandably decided against going back in.

Bruce, who had been watching events from his sickbed in the

Land Rover, calmly informed me that I had nearly trodden on a snake during all the activity. That was the least of my worries; I had too much else to think about. I, once more, had reluctantly removed all my clothes for another dip into the muddy water to try to push a firm base under the wheels of the vehicle. As before, to protect my dignity I wrapped a towel around my waist and then immersed myself into the quagmire whilst John and the girls fed me anything and everything that could be dragged from the surrounding jungle DIY store. I was immersed far longer than I had wanted to be, but our efforts met with some success. I was under no illusion as to what to expect when I emerged from the mud bath; the leeches were there again on my body for the girls to remove with their salt treatments.

On the removal of my towel, in private, a chilling shudder ran up my spine. There it was, a big black bull leech fixed firmly to my undercarriage and which, by its size, had already enjoyed a good draught of my blood. My first thought had been to shout to one of the girls to bring the salt pot, but I cancelled that idea straight away. I had never had the experience of finding out what it was like to have salt poured on my dingle and I certainly had no intention of doing so! I was in a situation that I couldn't have even told my own mother about, so decided to let nature take its course and let the 'bloody' thing finish its lunch and drop off of its own accord. Telling my friends would have been an embarrassment too far. With their sense of humour, my life wouldn't have been worth living. It crossed my mind that if I had been a black guy, and the same thing had happened, I would certainly have had an identification problem.

After that whole freakish episode, it became necessary to rethink my strategy when I had to dive into swamps. After that I always made sure that my undercarriage was up and tucked firmly into a tight pair of underpants.

As previously mentioned our earlier attempt to pass through that swamp had been most encouraging. We had expected to get through unscathed but, unfortunately, I was unable to maintain momentum as the swamp had deepened. We were firmly bogged down. We worked for ten hours and tried everything we knew to free the vehicle. We were all very tired and very wet, and as night approached we had no option but to set up camp at the side of the bog and cook ourselves a well-earned meal. We all slept soundly that night, going to sleep to the sound of the vampire bats in their nearby homes and with the thought that the vehicle was still stuck in the swamp.

Another muggy day dawned as I peeped through the small crack in the front of the tent. It was raining and an early morning white mist rose from the sodden soil. I crept from the tent to have a peep at the Land Rover and secretly hoped that while we slept some kind fairy had waved her magic wand and rescued it from the bog. I hadn't been enamoured by the prospect of our continued fight against the swamp, but at least as the girls had cooked a good breakfast, we didn't have to start our fight on empty stomachs.

Cooking breakfast in Thailand

We tried to make a small contraption like a capstan by sinking a log in the soft ground, with about four feet of it remaining exposed above the surface. We tied a stout branch horizontally across it so it was fashioned like a cross, then tied one end of the rope to the vehicle and the other end to the sunken log, with two people on either side of the cross member; one side pulling and the other pushing. The object was for the rope to wind round the log and move the vehicle. Backed up by myself driving at the same time, the vehicle actually moved a little, but not enough to make much difference. The hole with the log in soon became elongated, as the ground was too soft. So that unlikely experiment was doomed to failure.

As so much of our time had been taken up and so much energy expended in futile attempts to dislodge ourselves, I took the decision that after one more effort, two of us would reconnoitre the surrounding jungle and look for a village that might be able to help.

We removed everything from the vehicle, and we were disconnecting the trailer when we were suddenly startled by the sound of knocking. We listened for a while as the sound became louder, then it changed to a crashing and tearing noise. When we saw what it was, we just couldn't believe our eyes. There was this huge elephant, complete with keeper sitting on his neck, heading straight for us.

'Jumbo' turns up to help in the Thailand swamps

He stopped a few yards away by the edge of the swamp. A big grin spread across his face. He shouted, "Chang, Chang," which I took to mean his elephant, and gestured with his hand that his elephant would pull us from the swamp. We were completely baffled as to how he could have known that we were there. We had seen nobody, and as far as we knew nobody had seen us. Maybe a kind fairy had waved her magic wand after all. Whatever the mystery that surrounded his arrival I wondered if someone up there was keeping an eye on us.

And finally the elephant gets us out of our spot of bother

The chains on the elephant were connected up to the chassis of the Land Rover. The keeper then coaxed 'Jumbo' forward a little, which took up the slack on the chains (just like you would if you were to tow a car), then he shouted a command which the great beast responded to. His backbone rose up from his back as he took the strain and the vehicle begun to move. It swept aside the mud in its path, then pulled three times with a few seconds rest in between, and we were back on firm ground again. Somebody joked that we should have taken the elephant with us and painted on his side 'RAC Thailand'. Then when we ran into trouble we could always make a trunk call to get help.

As a token of our appreciation, we would have liked the 'elephant man' to have accepted a reward for the help given, but it was no surprise when he refused the money offered. He did, however, enjoy some of our Ryvita biscuits spread with plum jam. So we gave him the rest of the packet, and the jam. Before he climbed back on his elephant he took great pains to make us understand that we had many problems ahead before we reached Ranong. Our enduring urge to keep going had taken a few knocks, but our determination was intact and still up and running. Our 'elephant man' scooped up some more jam on his biscuit, waved goodbye, then disappeared back into the thick jungle as mysteriously as he had arrived.

We packed up the tent, repacked the Land Rover and were back on track again. Bruce was still very poorly and we needed to move faster to get the medical help he so badly needed. Everything was against us and we hadn't yet covered half the distance to Ranong. Our nightmare drive continued.

It was never a matter of if we ran into trouble, just a matter of when. Some of the old bridges we came upon that did have ramps were so rotten with age that it was highly dangerous to even attempt to cross them, but nine times out of ten we had no choice. On those occasions everybody would leave the vehicle, with the exception of Bruce, to reduce the weight while the crossing was made. One such bridge stood about thirty feet high and spanned about twenty-five yards across. On examination, the whole thing was found to be rotten. I walked over and found the flat planks across had holes in them and were very spongy. The timbers creaked when walked on. Having summed up the possibility of driving over, my thoughts were that it was a bit of a dangerous thing to attempt. We looked for a way to bypass the bridge.

I had to check out this bridge thoroughly before attempting to cross it.

Fording the muddy waters below was never an option. To hack a path through the surrounding jungle would have taken days: that was time we didn't have. It was another of those occasions when it was prudent to put the kettle on and apply some clear thinking about what to do next. I walked backwards and forwards across the bridge a number of times, and each time I was more convinced that it would be stupid to try it. After a lot of wasted time flogging my brain to death wondering what to do, my thoughts jumping in all directions at once. I finally focused on the fact that I had been taking chances, in one way or another, since leaving England nearly twelve months earlier. After all, our current problem was just another risk that had to be taken, albeit a bigger one than most of the others. If things were to go wrong, I knew it would be the end of my dream.

We removed some of the heavier equipment from the Land Rover and trailer. Then with my heartbeat increasing its revs per minute, I engaged four-wheel drive and slowly mounted the rotten timbers of the bridge. Almost at once the front wheels sunk about an inch into the soft woods. By the time the back wheels of the vehicle had a hold the whole bridge trembled. I edged the vehicle slowly across bit by bit. Just over halfway across there was a resounding crash. The trailer wheels, which were narrower than the Land Rover wheels, had gone through the bridge up to its axles. I expected the whole thing to go crashing down into the muddy waters below. I dared not stop to take stock of the situation, so I carried on with the trailer tearing up the bridge behind me.

As my six wheels landed on firm ground I couldn't help but notice that my right hand had been a little unsteady. The rest of the group rejoined the vehicle after they had struggled across the depleted bridge carrying the luggage we had left behind.

We had only covered another four miles when Mother Nature,

again, showed her disapproval and anger and turned surly against us mere mortals who sought to ride roughshod over her. But my crew had thwarted her every inch of the way and matched our dogged determination against her capricious nature. She would not triumph over us. That latest attack on our progress was another of those rotten bridges. It was not quite as long as the last one but equally as obstructive.

Crossing an extremely dangerous bridge in the jungle

143

It became quite evident that those old bridges hadn't been used or maintained for many years; probably not since the Japanese occupation in the 1940s. I drove slowly across, without too many problems, but the trailer wasn't so lucky. One of the rickety bridge supports had slipped out of position as I crossed over with the vehicle, causing the trailer to drop down; it was now supported only by a few remaining tangled cross members. Fortunately, it hadn't disconnected itself from the tow bar. Being much lighter than it had been, I was able to accelerate and pull it back onto firm ground none the worse for its ordeal.

It crossed my mind at the time that if those naval guys in Singapore had managed to set off on their own expedition and successfully reached those last two bridges, they would not have been able to cross over without major repairs being carried out.

Darkness descended upon us once more as we stopped by an unfinished bridge with a bog on the other side. There was a small bamboo hut nearby beside the river. It was occupied by a man and wife with two little children. They offered us accommodation on the site of their humble home. Their bamboo hut stood on log stilts, and half of its underneath was taken up with a chicken enclosure. The rest of the space was offered to us, beside the chickens. We gratefully accepted, if there were another deluge, we would at least be in the dry.

When our hosts learned of our sick friend they invited him to sleep on their tiny upstairs veranda where, they thought, he would be more comfortable. John stayed upstairs with him. A fire was lit for us under the hut to cook our meal. I thought a fire there was a bit dangerous with his house just above the fire, but he didn't seem to have a problem with it.

The humble kitchen above the chicken house

We cooked some of our now much-depleted stock of dried beef curry and packet soups. Our soup was also enjoyed by our hosts and their children. We made ourselves as comfortable as possible in our very unusual bedroom and its equally unusual fragrances. We laid down our inflated airbeds and slid comfortably into our snug sleeping bags. I had slept in many strange places since the start of the expedition, but for me this was the first time I had slept two feet away from a big fat white cockerel with just a few bamboo canes between us. We had no problem waking up next morning. This bloody cockerel blasted my ear at first light, informing us and the world outside that it was

145

time to get up.

Whilst the girls prepared breakfast, John and I went down to the muddy stream to contemplate its crossing. We had a bath down there at the same time; that wasn't a good move. The water was very murky and a big black leech decided to make a breakfast of my leg. We returned back to the chicken house where Lyn covered it with salt before it dropped off, leaving quite a deep hole in my leg. It took longer for the bleeding to stop than normal.

Our well-practiced task of making runways through swamps swung into action once more, pulling the usual jungle waste of logs and branches into position. We had spent over an hour preparing, but sod's law hit us again, as one of our rear wheels slipped off a log whilst we attempted to cross. We were right back in the shit all over again. We uncoupled the trailer and started on the tedious task once more of freeing the thing all over again. We worked all that morning and around 12.30 p.m., with the help of a number of villagers who had been rounded up by our host, the vehicle was manhandled back onto firm ground again. We made a separate crossing with the trailer, which had to be pulled over by ropes. The only comfort derived from the many setbacks encountered on that 120-mile jungle marathon was that each mile covered brought us nearer to our goal of Ranong.

By late afternoon we had pressed on a few miles before our way was barred by a huge fallen tree. We saw at a glance that there wasn't a chance of us being able to move it. We tried towing it aside. That didn't work. To chop it apart, using our one axe would have been a mammoth task, so we went for the easier option of building a ramp over it. This took up a lot of our time. We had to search a wide area of the surrounding jungle for a number of much smaller logs. We tied them into bundles of varying sizes, like faggots. We then placed them both sides of the fallen tree. Stakes were then hammered in between each faggot to prevent any movement when we crossed over. On the other side space was very limited because of the way the tree had fallen. We were then forced to use the vehicle like a bulldozer, to bulldoze a way through the thick undergrowth to get back on the track.

As darkness closed in we came upon a building standing on its own in a clearing. We pulled over to investigate the possibility of kipping down there for the night. The place was all locked up but was obviously a school. A school meant there must be a village nearby. While the others waited Louise and I set off to look for it. We walked down a narrow track leading from the school. We had only walked about two hundred yards and were suddenly stopped in our tracks. A loud roar came from a clump of bushes a few yards ahead of us. We saw nothing but the sound was enough; a wild animal had probably been disturbed by our presence. I said to Lou that we had better get out of there and we doubled back more hurriedly than when we arrived. The others were quite amused at the reason for our quick return. We waited another half an hour before we returned back down that track again. I had my gun strapped on for added comfort. We walked for half a mile and arrived at a clearing with dead-end jungle. No sign of a village there.

We returned to the main track and had walked about a mile farther down when we heard strange singing coming from ahead. We closed in on the sound and arrived at a clearing with bamboo huts. I went to the nearest hut and called hello. An old man came to the door and murmured something, indicating for us to follow him. We were led to a hut where the singing came from. We climbed the bamboo stairs into a room and were met by a short thin man who by candlelight was teaching young children to sing. The scene was absolutely idyllic. About twenty or more young heads turned our way with their big eyes staring at us in wonderment. Who were we? Who had suddenly arrived at night in their tiny jungle village so isolated from everywhere? Where had we come from? Those unspoken expressions were written all over their smiling faces. The children's teacher spoke some English so we asked if we could stay in the schoolhouse. He just smiled and handed me the key.

We returned to the little schoolhouse, which was very neat and tidy with its rows of tiny wooden desks and seats made of bamboo. We rearranged some of the desks to accommodate our sleeping bags and cooked a meal. The energy we expended that day had taken its toll. We were all ready to zip ourselves up in our sleeping bags.

After breakfast the next morning we left the school as clean as we had found it and returned the key with our grateful thanks. We were ready once more to face another day with conditions that had become routinely predictable, ranging from bad, to worse, to almost impossible. It just rained and rained all that day as we meandered through dark sodden jungle track trying to keep moving any way possible. Even our food had to be prepared while we were all huddled together in the vehicle. A necessary pit stop that helped to fertilize our jungle toilet was carried out in what can only be described as a very uncomfortable operation.

As night descended upon us again, our thoughts and hopes focussed on the possibility that we might stumble on another village. We needed somewhere to dry ourselves out, but those hopes took a cruel knock. Mother Nature had again reared her ugly head and intervened to make life for us as difficult as possible. There was a wide creek right across our path, which was all we needed on what was already a miserable day. We had no option but to try and cross it, otherwise we were going nowhere. I tested the depth in the usual way and gave it a go. It turned out to be another of our many disasters. We were firmly stuck again.

We worked for over half an hour, pulling and pushing, trying to free the thing, but it was no good, and we were just too tired to move another inch. It was apparent we were stuck there for the night. We had to make the choice of staying in the Land Rover in the creek and sleeping the best way we could, or searching around for a clearing and putting the tent up in the pouring rain. Neither choice had any merit whatsoever, but we decided on the latter.

We struggled to make camp in the most appalling conditions imaginable. The only space locally available was two hundred yards away from the vehicle, and that was much smaller than was needed. The tent was pitched as the rain hammered down on us. It was difficult to erect as it became soaked as soon as it was unpacked. There was hardly enough room to stretch out the guy ropes; one of which had to be tied to a bush instead of staked into the ground. The groundsheet was laid onto the soft mud and our feet pushed it farther into the ground when walked on. To add to our discomfort, water leaked through the tent onto the ground sheet. We inflated our airbeds, covering the whole area of the tent. We were constantly reminded of the soft mud beneath our feet by the squelching noises below when we moved around.

Everything we needed from the vehicle had meant traipsing backwards and forwards through the creek, which wasn't very pleasant in the dark.

The cooking of our meal on moving airbeds was more like a comedy act. (The difficulties can only be appreciated by trying it for yourselves.) The burners with a billycan balanced on top had to be held in position by a pair of hands all the time cooking was in progress. Invariably, a shout of 'keep still' would go up from the holder when one of us rocked the boat when some involuntary movement took place. How we managed to finish up with a reasonable meal and a mug of coffee after all the trials and tribulations of the day was a miracle and only made possible by the sheer tenacity of the group. We spent a wet night in our sleeping bags trying to sleep and constantly moving the position of our heads to avoid the drips which came inside the tent and splashed onto our faces.

Lynette Baber, in a letter to her family in Sydney, mentioned about that night in the tent. Here is a quote from her letter:

'Another evening we got stuck in similar circumstances. That was the worst night I've spent so far. All night it poured with rain, both inside and outside the tent. We were almost eaten alive by flies and mosquitoes and nearly dying from the heat as well as trying to dodge the rainwater leaking into the tent. The creek had risen during the night and the Land Rover was firmly stuck in it; we could not budge it an inch.'

The morning brought no relief after our wet night's sleep. The rain continued to pound our tent. There was no way we could even have begun to think of trying to extricate the vehicle from the creek. The whole of that day was spent in the tent writing letters and making tea.

Around 3.00 p.m. that afternoon a villager walked by sheltered under a weird-looking umbrella made from bamboo slats with banana leaves for its canopy. He came over to our tent and invited us all back to his village, nearly two kilometres away. We would all loved to have taken advantage of his offer, but with Bruce so sick, and having to leave the vehicle so far away, it was a non-starter. However, it was decided that John and Angela should go to the village, while Bruce, Lyn, Louise and I remained behind to dodge the leaks for another night, and to keep the mosquitoes company.

When we awoke early next morning an eerie silence hung over us, broken only by the creature noises of the surrounding jungle. It wasn't apparent immediately, then we realized that the rain had stopped. Louise, Lyn and I made a quick exit from the tent and went back to the Land Rover. We found that the creek had gone down quite a bit. I made another attempt to drive the vehicle out, but it still would not budge. As we struggled with it, some villagers who were passing by gave us a hand. Just then John and Angela appeared from the opposite direction with another dozen villagers. With the sudden arrival of all that manpower we were soon out of the creek. It was marvellous how quickly things happened when the rain stopped.

It was good to be on the move again, but new problems were never very far away. The continued use of the four-wheel drive over those past few days had played hell with our petrol reserves, which had been used at the rate of only seven-plus miles to the gallon. The little drop we had left in the tank only looked good for a few more miles. We couldn't even afford to risk using any to refill our burners.

We were fortunate to arrive at a village and were amazed to find a tiny teashop. That was the first one we had seen at all on this jungle stretch. Also on sale were packets of Thai biscuits and surprisingly some tins of Nestlé milk. The teashop man was very pleased when we all sat down on the narrow forms in front of his counter and enjoyed glasses of his hot sweet tea. Our arrival had brought many of the villagers crowding round his stall. This was something we had long become accustomed to. Very often somebody amongst them would speak English, but sometimes nobody did and they would jabber away in their own language. Whenever this happened I would usually say, 'Yes, I had one but the wheels came off,' causing much laughter from them and us, even though they didn't have a clue what had been said.

We made known to the villagers our need to buy petrol. Although there was no supply in the village they told us of a small army unit holed up just outside. The army very kindly gave us two gallons, they couldn't spare any more. But when the chips are down one has to be grateful for small mercies, and we certainly were.

Our next challenge came by way of a muddy river with a very steep climb on the opposite bank. There was a large hole in the bank, half-filled with big rocks. At first sight it looked impossible to climb, but after a ten-minute survey I came to the conclusion it could be done. It must be done. The girls, John and I soon got cracking on filling in the rest of the hole with as many rocks that could be lifted. We made a track over the top of the rocks which took us over an hour. I drove across the river with little trouble, but the problem was getting up the bank. The vehicle slipped back each time we were a few feet from the top. There was no choice but to remove the trailer and pull that up separately. With that done and the others pushing the vehicle from behind, we managed to get over the bank first go. However, our self-congratulation of a job well done was short lived as we were confronted with another thorny problem.

We were driving along a narrow ledge with an escarpment about twenty feet deep on our near side. A part of the road ahead had subsided and left a bite out of its side about four feet long. This made the width of the road too narrow for the width of the wheels on the vehicle. A couple of us clambered down the escarpment in search of something to bridge that gap. We came upon some large fallen trees; one of them had long thick pieces of bark coming away from its sides. With some careful hacking away we succeeded in peeling off two unbroken lengths of about six feet long. They were placed on top of each other for extra strength and then laid across the gap, forming a shallow channel. To reduce the weight on the near side of the vehicle we transferred all the heavy luggage to the other side. That proved to be the bit of icing on the cake that was needed and we crossed over unscathed.

A break in the weather gave us the opportunity to dry out our wet clothes. So when a large clearing appeared in the middle of the road we grabbed the opportunity with both hands to put up the tent, build a fire and hang out our clothes. That was one of the few stops we made that hadn't been forced on us by the elements.

On moving off next morning, although we now had dry clothes to travel in, we also nearly had a dry petrol tank. The two gallons given to us by the army was almost all gone. I reckoned we had enough for about another ten miles. We kept going, waiting for that inevitable moment when there was no further response from the accelerator, but it didn't happen. The gods had smiled on us for a change.

We came upon a road gang erecting one of those wooden bridges where they forget to build the approaches. There was no petrol there, but one of the gang offered to walk to a settlement a few miles away and bring us some. An offer we were pleased to accept. We showed our appreciation to the rest of the gang while we waited for the petrol to arrive in true British tradition by making them some tea. The petrol arrived two hours later and we were on our way.

One of the Thai bridges where they 'forgot' to build the approaches

We had about twenty-five miles to go before we reached Ranong, but twenty-five miles in such a hostile environment was still one hell of a way to go.

155

We arrived at a small village that wasn't on the map. We learned its name was Bunghing, and it was close to a river that had to be crossed. We understood the river was tidal and would not reach its lowest ebb until 1.00 p.m. the next day. There was a P.W.D. (Public Works Dept) bungalow in the village, and we were invited to stay there until the water level was right for us to cross. These bungalows were often found in inaccessible areas and were used as a waterhole for government officials while they were on duty. Although this was the first one I had seen on that stretch.

During my travels to this part of the world I had frequently come into contact with people suffering from malaria and was sometimes able to help a little by giving them some of the pills we carried. Whenever the word 'malaria' is mentioned now, the little village of Bunghing always comes to mind. A villager came to us carrying a small child of about three years old in his arms, who was sick with malaria, and asked for our help. It was a pathetic sight to see the appealing look in his eyes, hoping we could help his little girl. One couldn't help but be moved by it. I had never felt so inadequate in all my life. If only I were a doctor or had some kind of medical training. I didn't have the heart to say that we couldn't help him. Although we knew the malaria dose taken by adults, we had no idea what the dose should be for a small child. Or, if indeed our Mepacrine tablets would be suitable at all. The only options we had was either to do nothing, or to take a calculated risk and give the child some of our tablets. I decided on the latter but reduced the dose by half. The tablets were then carefully cut in two for the father to administer them after we had left. It was very necessary to make sure that he completely understood the times that they should be given. That problem was solved by pointing to my watch, raising my arm, and turning it in a complete clockwise circle depicting a twelve-hour period. Then repeating the action again for a twenty-four-hour period. That way he understood the space he should allow in between giving the tablets. He nodded his head in approval. We gave the child half a tablet straight away. Whether the action I took was right or wrong I will never know, but faced with the dire situation I felt it was better than taking no action at all.

In the morning I made my way down to the river to wade across to test its depth for myself. I was joined by an uninvited chaperon, a lad of about eighteen who turned out to be a real nutcase. He practically dragged me up the river, splashing me as I went and stopping every few yards to indicate how deep the river was. He touched his chest then went up to his nose about a dozen times in five minutes. I only got the message when some of the locals looked on amused as we splashed around in the water. They touched their heads indicating that the lad was a few cards short of a full pack.

A start had been made on the building of a wooden bridge across the river, but the work wasn't far enough advanced to be of any use to us. There was a bulldozer at the scene, which for us was a sight for sore eyes. The level of the river had gone down but not by as much as we had hoped.

I extended the exhaust pipe and made ready to cross, when the bulldozer driver offered to cross the river in front of us in case we ran into trouble. We followed him down the winding, muddy track feeling much more relaxed than usual. The dozer crossed with no apparent effort. We crossed at a much slower pace and reached the middle, but that was as far as we got. We stopped right there in the middle, and I realized at once that I had forgotten to remove the fan belt and the water had whipped up into the engine. That inexcusable omission of mine I could only put down to my complacent attitude due to the presence of the bulldozer.

The bulldozer pulling us from the river

A chain was soon hitched up to the Land Rover. The driver appeared very happy that we had stopped so he could pull us out again. He dragged us up the opposite bank with great ease and continued to pull us for a further hundred yards through a deep swamp that we hadn't been aware of. He left us on firm ground to dry out the engine.

We gathered some pace over the next few hours and covered one of the best daily mileages since our start from Taguapa. We heard that there was a tin mine near Ranong and decided on a visit to see if a tour of the mine was possible. A visit to the manager's bungalow brought an immediate response with a cordial invitation to stay that night with a tour to be arranged next day. We had an excellent dinner served up by the manager's manservant. It was very relaxing to be able to slip into our sleeping bags that night with clear minds and not have to be concerned how we were going to extricate ourselves from some river or bog the next day.

The tour of the mine started after we had had a good breakfast. We were taken on board a large dredger engaged in excavating mineral deposits from below the mud in the river. The sludge dredged up was deposited on a large sloping sluice to be washed by powerful jets of water until only the residue remained. The mine manager mentioned that apart from the tin deposits they searched for, other minerals also occasionally came to the surface, including some precious stones. With our education on the extraction of tin from Mother Earth completed, and the killing of a snake outside our door by the manager's manservant, we left the mine and headed towards the little town of Ranong.

The dredger at the tin mine near Ranong

On Tuesday, 25th November 1958, we arrived in Ranong. It had been a truly incredible journey. The 120-mile trek from Taguapa had taken us nine and a half days to complete. Our daily mileages were 44-13-2-6-6-0-7-6-36. That same 120-mile stretch took me only two days on my journey out. I had nothing but praise and admiration for my team, who worked tenaciously throughout under very trying conditions, and it was only through all that dedication that it was made possible at all.

We made our way to the bank to change some traveller's cheques. A customer inside, whose curiosity got the better of him about our presence in Ranong, invited us to have some tea with him. He said he was a scrap metal dealer. I thought that sounded a bit ominous. I knew our vehicle had taken a lot of punishment but, surely, our Land Rover outside didn't look that ramshackle that he wanted to make an offer.

He took us to a nearby teashop, and with our tea he sent for six parcels of rice, all neatly wrapped up in banana leaves tied with green string. Inside, on top of the rice, was a brown leaf with which to pick up the rice. That seemed to be the perfect way of dishing up food. No arguments there on who was to do the washing up after. We couldn't stay too long with the scrap metal man as our priority was to leave there immediately and head for the capital, Bangkok.

It was imperative we got Bruce into hospital as his condition was deteriorating. The three girls had been having problems of their own. Their feet had begun to swell up, and a white fungus was growing between their toes. Louise and Lyn's feet appeared to be worse than Angela's. This might never have happened if they had taken the advice given to them some time ago to wash their feet in disinfected water. A similar situation might have been related to the fever that Bruce was suffering from. One particularly foul-smelling swamp we encountered was so obnoxious that, with the exception of Bruce, we all took precautions and gargled our throats. Some food for thought.

The 370-mile drive from Ranong to Bangkok didn't pass without incident. The roads were reasonably good, and we covered 139 miles before stopping at a small village for the night. We left early the next morning just after breakfast, and things went well for the next forty miles, until suddenly we heard a grinding sound coming from the offside rear wheel. On examination my worst fears were realized, the noise came from the wheel bearing and as I didn't have a spare there was no hope of getting the job done anywhere other than in Bangkok.

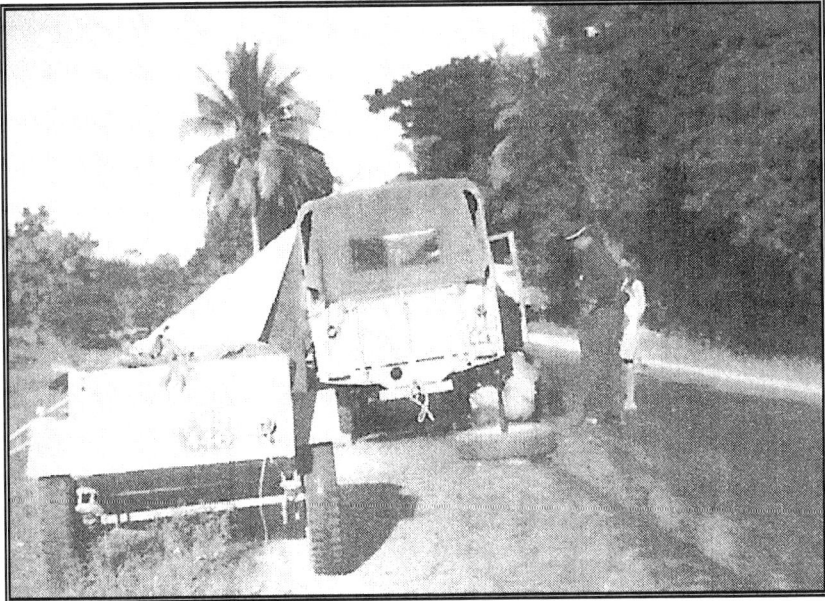

Wheel bearing problems in Thailand

There was little choice other than to carry on and hope for the best. Apart from the continuous reminder of our problem by the noise coming from the rear wheel, we made good progress. But that was tempered by a lingering unease in my mind.

We passed through the little town of Rajleurd and headed towards Nakorn Pathon when it happened. An urgent shout came from the back of the vehicle from Lynette, calling for me to stop. I braked but nothing happened. A rapid change down of gears enabled me to slow down quickly, but before coming to a stop there was a crash from the back. I looked out and saw the whole unit of the back wheel farther down the road. The bearing had completely disintegrated and apart from the jacking up of the vehicle there was nothing else that could be immediately done. Bangkok was fifty-five miles away, but we were in the fortunate position of being on a road with a sparse amount of traffic that headed towards Nakorn Pathon, with a direct route to Bangkok from there. Without further ado, I left the others and hitched a ride. Luckily, it took me all the way into the capital. I went directly to Edgar Brothers, the Land Rover agents, and the manager, who I knew from my previous visits, immediately organised a Land Rover and two mechanics, with the necessary parts, to drive me back to my vehicle. The whole journey, there and back, took just five hours and the two mechanics had our wheel back on in double quick time.

Our run into Bangkok was a pleasant drive, through flat country with palm trees, paddy fields and the odd few small villages. As soon as we arrived we took Bruce to the hospital, where he was admitted straight away. We were greatly relieved that our friend was now in safe hands at last. The girls received treatment while we were there for the fungus and swelling of their feet. They were all given injections before leaving the hospital.

We had a lot of running around to do whilst in Bangkok. It was the last capital city before Burma, so anything of importance had to be sorted out there. Our first priority was the health of the Land Rover, so we booked it in at Edgar Brothers for a complete overhaul and service. The Castrol agents, who were aware of our pending arrival, supplied all the oil needed and paid for the full service. The repair bill for all the other work carried out should have been equivalent to about thirty pounds but I was asked to pay just fifteen, which included their journey out to us when our wheel had fallen off. All this was kindness unlimited.

I went to the British Embassy for a prearranged meeting with Colonel Kim Lacey, the military attaché, where we discussed, among other things, details for what was to be my attempt to re-enter Burma. I passed over to him all my rolls of film for development. The colonel and his wife very kindly invited the rest of us in for a lovely lunch that was to spill over into teatime, where we finished up enjoying their extended hospitality. When we left the embassy we were presented with some tins of Ryvita biscuits, which were very acceptable. Our last tin had been given to the elephant man.

The same evening an invitation came from the Australian Embassy by way of Colonel Aitken, the Australian military attaché, for us to join him and his wife for dinner that night. John and the girls were quite chuffed to be invited for dinner in that little bit of Australia in a foreign field. I was quite pleased too.

It would appear word of our arrival in Bangkok had spread. A letter had been handed in to the British Embassy from the wife of Pol.Lt.Col. Cho-dti-Pad Bunnag, who was the deputy chief of the Mounted Police. That letter once again highlighted the kindness that the Thai people had bestowed on us throughout all our travels in their country. The letter received is copied overleaf in its entirety.

'Dear all of you the traveller

I am the wife of Pol. Lt. Col. Cho-dti-Pad Bunnag. My resident is here. I have heard from my husband that all of you come to stay at our club. I am very glad and I think that all of you should to have convenience in bathing and sleeping, if you don't mind please come to my resident and have your bathing. I'll prepare for you, please.

Excuse me my English is bad and I can say a little in English.

With my sincerely.

Mrs Cho-dti-pad Bunnag

29th November 1958.'

We were delighted to accept the invitation from such a gracious lady. The Polo Club was close to the king's palace and the stables, which housed the king's horses and the crown prince's pony. These were everything one would expect from a well run stable housing a string of beautiful horses. We felt really honoured to be invited to ride any horse of our choice. Only Louise and I took up the offer. For anyone who was a 'horsey' person to be able to stay at a place like that, was like a dream come true.

The Australian Information Service interviewed us at the Polo Club. They wanted a story for an Australian magazine. We didn't mind being interviewed, although we had some reservations as sometimes reporters tended to put their own interpretation on what was said, which wasn't always the storyline they were given.

John and the girls were taken on a sightseeing tour of Bangkok by the embassy staff. I didn't join them as I had been asked to meet the naval attaché at the embassy. He briefed me on the Singapore naval party and confirmed that they were to go ahead with the expedition, if their application for Burmese visas was successful. But he did admit to having problems. That hadn't surprised me. My own efforts had been stonewalled by the Burmese all the way along the line. Maybe I'd been using the wrong aftershave. Anyway, I intended to make a final bid before we left Bangkok. I left the embassy, wished him luck with the visas, but I was sceptical of his chances.

Bruce made good progress after his spell in hospital and had begun to look his old self again. It was a pity that he had missed out on being able to share our rather unusual digs at the Polo Club. Our enforced delay whilst we waited for him wasn't entirely taken up with socialising and sightseeing. It had given us a good opportunity to give the Land Rover a long overdue facelift, get some of the equipment cleaned, and all our clothes washed to rid them of the mud they had collected over the last couple of weeks.

But what had been of primary importance was being able to reply to all the mail that had accumulated at the embassy for us whilst awaiting our arrival. It always had a far better chance of reaching its destination when it was posted in a capital city. I was very fortunate that while we were in Southeast Asia my mail, when possible, was sent by the diplomatic bag as concession to me for all the information I passed on to them. My mail was then guaranteed a safe arrival in London.

While we waited to leave Bangkok, I couldn't help but feel a little concerned about the condition of the girls' feet. Although they had received medical attention at the hospital, the fungus between their toes and the swelling of their feet were still very much in evidence. They had been advised that the problem could take weeks to resolve. That was a bit of a blow. We could cope with things like getting stuck in bogs or swamps and the wheels dropping off, but the girls' feet were a different ball game. We still had thousands of miles to travel, with many of them out of the reach of proper medical help. All we could do was pray that their condition didn't deteriorate further.

The last day in Bangkok wasn't a happy one for us. Our final application to the Burmese Consulate for land-route visas had been turned down flat. They informed us, for the umpteenth time, that overland travel through their country was not possible. It was too dangerous and they were not prepared to be responsible for the safety of foreigners. Although their response was predictable, it hadn't lessened the impact it had on our morale. I finally knew

167

there was nowhere else left for us to go for approved entry into Burma. It was a big setback, but not the end of the world, at least not my world. My determination to continue was still very much alive and kicking. I wasn't yet quite ready to throw in the towel, or accept that my dream would end there, that day, and be gobbled up by the monster of failure all for the sake of a little bit of paper called a visa. When we started our journey from Sydney, Australia, my companions had joined me because they wanted to be a part of that great adventure and challenge of mine. They had faith that I would get them safely to England. I was determined to do everything that was possible so as not to disappoint them. It was only a matter of time before we were forced to open 'Pandora's Box'.

Leaving Bangkok

Our last undertaking before leaving the capital was to do some personal shopping. We wanted to purchase some of the famous silver jewellery, unique to Thailand, but which was sadly now becoming a dying art. The jewellery, handmade from silver and black shellac, when polished revealed the figures of Thai gods and goddesses emerging from the black shellac. It would be difficult to find examples of that kind of work today.

We headed out north for the start of the 750-mile drive towards the Thai/Burma border of Tachilek. As the delay in Bangkok had been unavoidable, it was important that we tried to make up some of the time that had been lost. We passed through the little town of Saraburt in the late afternoon and headed towards Nakorn Sawan. We had intended to spend the night there, but the need for sleep caught up with us before we reached our destination. As it was already very late and road conditions had deteriorated, we decided to call it a day. We had covered 200 miles and were happy with that. We pulled off the road and made camp in a small jungle clearing. Fortunately, it was a dry night.

We lost no time in moving out the next morning and entered Nakorn Sawan before the town was fully mobile. We stayed just long enough to fill up with petrol and have a mosey around the town. We then continued on towards Lampoon, nearly 200 miles away.

We hadn't travelled for long when we discovered, after hitting a huge pothole, that the tow bar section of the trailer had partly broken away from the chassis. One of the rear spring leaves on the Land Rover had also broken. That was all we needed. Whenever we tried to make up some of the lost time, something else happened to slow us down further. I then had two choices; either return to Nakorn Sawan for repairs, or carry on to the next town of Tak, about ninety miles away. As I always liked to look forward and not back, I decided to press on ahead.

We roped up the tow bar the best way we could and continued on at a much slower pace into Tak. The repair shop there found on examination, apart from the welding of the tow bar, four new thicker leaves were needed on the same bank of springs where the one leaf was found to be broken. In addition to that, both wheel bearings in the trailer needed to be changed. I was then fully convinced that bringing a trailer on this expedition had turned out to be a bad idea, and an expensive one. But having gone down that road I was determined to get the bloody thing to England after having towed it all that way already.

While we waited for the completion of the repairs we had some lunch. Over lunch somebody happened to mention about our Thailand visas, and when were they due to expire. Then the horrible truth dawned on us; they had already expired by nearly a week! That meant we had now compounded our problems at the border. With no valid Burmese visas to get in and expired Thailand visas to get out, there was no one else to blame for the cock up, only myself. I should have checked them in Bangkok before we left when it could have been sorted out with the Immigration Department, with some back up from our own embassy there if there had been any problems. I tried to glean a little comfort for my shortcomings because I had so much on my mind at the time.

We wasted most of that day waiting for the vehicle and trailer to be nursed back to health so as soon as the work was finished, we immediately hit the road again, just to get some mileage under our belts before we stopped for the night.

As we headed for Lampoon, the road narrowed and split into two narrower tracks. One of these tracks climbed up onto a ledge which ran adjacent to the other track. We chose to take the higher ground as there was less likelihood of driving through bogs. We continued our journey until the darkness made driving on a bit precarious and made camp on the ledge.

The jungle curtain climbed high above us, with a precipice falling below. There hadn't been a lot of room for manoeuvre. We had to be very careful each time it became necessary to leave the tent, and not forget we were perched on a narrow ledge. Especially during the night if we went outside for a pee while still half asleep.

Next morning, the first one to leave the tent had the shock of their life. Outside, impressed in the mud, were the footprints of a wild animal; it looked like a large cat. Everybody's thoughts immediately raced in different directions. Supposing this and supposing that, and what if one of us had gone out in the night and came face to face with the beast. Whatever it was I thought that something a little more than a pee might have resulted! It was possible that the smell of our cooking earlier had been enough to entice the creature into our camp. It also occurred to me that the ledge might have been a regular animal track.

We continued on for a while, and the two tracks gradually merged into one road again. We kept moving pretty well until tyre trouble interfered with our progress. We had to change the wheel, but at least this gave us an excuse for an unplanned brew up and something to eat.

We crossed a number of creeks and travelled through some small villages before we entered Lampoon. Our first port of call, and the most important one, was to fill the tank with petrol and have the tyre repaired. Whenever we arrived in a town there was always some repair or another that had to be carried out, either on the vehicle, or on the trailer, or on both.

We were soon back on the road again heading towards Chiang Mai. A town where more than a year earlier I had been in trouble with the police for trying to take photographs of the king, who just happened to be there at the time.

I can't deny that I suffered a few tummy flutters the closer we got to the Thai/Burma border, where all our expectations hung in the balance. Although I tended to put a brave face on events, I wondered if I had been too paranoid and obsessed. To bring about the realisation of my dream, was I ready to compromise the safety or well-being of my friends by risking everything to break into a country without their permission for a second time? After all, they had steadfastly refused us permission to enter. I pondered on this for a while, but decided to put my conscience back into cold storage for another day.

The place we chose to camp that night looked normal enough, just another jungle clearing, much the same as all the others we had used. We cooked ourselves a meal of dried curry and rice with a wedge of Kraft cheese from one of our twelve-ounce tins. The girls treated the fungus on their feet (which appeared not to have improved very much since the hospital treatment) before we all climbed into our sleeping bags. The girls, as usual, slept on one side of the tent, with the guys on the other side.

In the morning we noticed a few ants milling around on some of the underwear that had been laid on the ground sheet beside our beds. The horrible truth soon dawned on us; the ants had partly eaten the girls' knickers and some of John's pants. The knickers looked a bit like a dishcloth that had seen better days. Bruce and I were lucky as our pants had escaped unscathed. Maybe the ants were trying to tell us something, or the flavour wasn't quite up to their liking. It was quite evident that given the amount of fabric that was eaten, a swarm of the little buggers must have been involved. We found it hard to comprehend that with all those visitors during the night none of us felt anything crawling over us and we had slept completely unaware of their existence. The few we saw in the morning had probably come back for a second helping, or thought they had found the first jungle take-away.

After that rather unusual experience we all rummaged through our luggage for plastic bags, just in case. But one thing was quite certain, we didn't intend to spend another night there. After all, we wouldn't have wanted the girls to run out of knickers, or John his pants! We used to be more cautious with our clothes when we undressed at night, hanging them up on hooks that were attached to the poles inside the tent. But apart from the occasional creepy crawly in the tent, like a centipede in Lyn's sleeping bag, we had never attracted the attention of ants before, which had made us a bit blasé. We didn't bother to put the hooks on the poles; we just used the groundsheet for our clothes. Although the way we travelled made regular baths impossible, we did the best we could by using streams and rivers wherever possible. Washing our clothes while on the move was always a bit of a hit and miss affair. Therefore, it wasn't hard to understand why, with all our clothes so impregnated with the sweat and dirt of the day, the ants were interested in the underwear.

The road climbed steadily on for five muddy, slippery miles, round uncountable sharp bends and thick curtains of green jungle before we reached Thailand's northern capital, Chiang Mai, the second largest city. It was isolated by mountainous terrain and surrounded by enormous jungle-clad hills and boasted a character and charm all of its own. One couldn't help but be amazed by the sheer number of Buddhist temples and pagodas that covered the landscape. Chiang Mai bustled with the everyday life you would expect from a regional capital city. We wandered round the arts and crafts bazaar, where you could stand in awe while the silversmith skilfully turned a sheet of metal into a beautiful designed snuff box or other metal objects. The street markets stayed open well into the night, selling their vast array of coloured cloths and silks and many locally made carvings. Or you could buy a lungi, as worn by the locals. This is like a tablecloth that is wrapped around the waist and hangs like a skirt. An occasional circle of men could be witnessed gambling. By placing small pebbles in a ring on the ground, the pebbles were then manipulated around in the circle until one man finished with more pebbles than the rest. He was the one with the smile on his face at the end of the game.

We left Chiang Mai and continued north towards Tachilek, our ultimate goal and Thailand's most northern town at the Burmese border. We passed through the small town of Chiengdno and Muangngai, after which driving conditions deteriorated further due to heavy rain. Four-wheel drive and extreme caution was necessary as the Land Rover was prone to sliding in the mud when descending down some of the very steep inclines. We were all keen to keep moving as we were excited by the prospect that within the next few hours we would have reached the place that had occupied our thoughts and minds for so long.

We arrived at the small town of Fang, just a handful of miles from the border with Burma to the west. There the road turned and we headed directly to the east through thick jungle to the little town of Maesuey, then north again to Chiang Rai. The only similarity we found that existed between Chiang Rai and the charm of Chiang Mai was in name, and for a visitor to be able to say, 'I have been there'. There was little else to stimulate any interest, but as darkness had fallen and we didn't want to arrive at the border at night, we bedded down there. The following morning we drove the last forty-four miles to Mae-Sai where we arrived fresh and mentally prepared for the Edis expedition's invasion of Burma!

We booked in at the Customs and Immigration Department and handed over our passports. We secretly hoped that they wouldn't notice that our visas were out of date. However, that was a bit of wishful thinking on our part. As they rustled through the pages of our passports there was a lingering pause as they came to the Thai visa pages. The immigration officer, who spoke very good English, looked up, smiled and said that our visas had expired! I sheepishly tried to explain the difficulties that we had encountered travelling through his country. He told us not to worry; it wasn't a problem. But there would be a delay while he contacted the Immigration Department in Bangkok to get clearance to issue exit permits for us to leave Thailand. That could take up to three days. We didn't much like the bit about the three-day wait, but things weren't as bad as they might have been. Our situation

176

could certainly have been much worse.

We were invited to stay at the home of the customs officer and his wife while we waited for our exit permits to arrive. He suggested I send a message to our embassy in Bangkok to help expedite the permission. He relayed it for us by radio and I signed it from the six happy wanderers stuck at the Mae-Sai/Burma border.

Apart from giving us the chance to relax for a while, our enforced interlude gave me the opportunity to think long and hard about what my next move was to be when we left there. The river crossing of the Mae-Sai into Burma was less than two miles away. I walked down to the river more than once to look at the crossing point where I had forded on the outward journey. Apart from the river, which appeared to be flowing faster than I remembered, everything looked pretty much the same. The bridge, which had been bombed by the RAF during the war, was still down. The Burmese Customs and Immigration office was still in the same place at the top of the hill, where its flag fluttered from a pole nearby. I couldn't help but remember my sheer delight the first time I crossed that river into Thailand.

Our new friends, the customs officer, Chareon Coolshai and his second in command Sub L/T Chariun Swisubhaak, treated us like family friends that had come to stay for a while. They provided some excellent meals and there was always a glass of Thai whiskey on hand, to wile away our congenial wait. It wasn't quite like Scotch, but who was complaining?

We mentioned to Chareon about the possibility of the naval

expedition from Singapore passing though there if things worked out favourably for them. We asked him, should they arrive, if he would hand them a letter we had written. The letter read:

'Hello, lads. If you have reached here, you have done bloody well!

We enclose some pep pills for you for the next leg of the journey as you are sure going to need them. Good Luck. See you in England. Signed, Edis Expedition.'

I learned later from a naval attaché in India that their expedition never got off the ground. I also heard from Chareon some months later informing me that he still had the letter and the pills.

We wanted to show our gratitude to our hosts for the hospitality that had been showered on us but, unfortunately, we didn't have much to offer. We did, however, have two large tins of peaches left that we had brought with us from Australia. The tins had lost their labels; they had long shed their identity in one of the bogs or rivers they had been dragged through. We opened one of the tins to share between Chareon's wife and their two children. They were peach halves in syrup and as we offered them to the children, the older boy, who was six years old, took a nervous step back when we handed to him two of the peaches on a plate. The look of them seemed to frighten him. It was quite obvious that he had never seen anything like them before. He saw them not as something nice to eat but as something weird that he wanted nothing to do with. So much for all our good intentions.

By the second day of our wait, I had already formulated a bold plan of how I intended to press our entry into Burma. I took into consideration the fact that we had already had a type of Burmese visa issued in Australia. Those visas, of course, only covered us for a trip to Rangoon by air as tourists. They did not cover land-route travel, but it didn't say that on the visa. With those visas they issued another document, which asked us to give personal details, such as name, nationality, visa number, and address in Rangoon, which we gave as the YMCA. They had also told us many times that they could not be responsible for the safety of foreigners in their country. I thought that if I played my cards right, I could make all those ingredients work in our favour. If they wouldn't give us permission to enter their country, we would give ourselves permission. After all, if there were no recognised entry documents for overland travel, they might not recognise a homemade one if it was presented. We asked Chareon if we could use the typewriter in his office. We didn't tell him why we wanted it as we thought that he might not approve. I had some red carbon paper that I had brought with me from England (to cover such an eventuality) so I asked Angela, who kindly obliged, to type in red on the visa document the words:

'Valid for land route at holder's own responsibility. Motor vehicle FWG 446.'

The only snag was we noticed a typing error. There was no

way that we could take the risk of altering it. All we could hope for was that it wouldn't be noticed.

Later that afternoon, much sooner than expected, permission came through granting us our exit visas. We used the rest of that day to make preparations for the crossing the next day. We tidied up the Land Rover and stashed as much of our gear as possible in a position to keep it dry. Bruce and I prepared the vehicle for the fording. We removed the fan belt and extended the exhaust pipe with our rubber hose so that it was firmly fixed and long enough for the hose to curve upwards towards the back of the vehicle so that it could be held by somebody sitting in the back. If an extension weren't made, it would then be necessary for the driver to keep pressure on the gas pedal all the time throughout the crossing so that the pressure of the gasses coming from the exhaust pipe prevented the water entering into it. If the driver released the pressure on the accelerator, the water would shoot up the pipe in double quick time and the engine would stop. But all that would be academic if the river was too deep for a fording in the first place. I didn't think at the time that there would have been any more problems crossing on this occasion than I had had before. But how wrong I was. My plan had been not to seek permission first from the Burmese authorities to cross over, but to take the direct action approach and drive straight across. I thought that once we were on Burmese soil they wouldn't be able to send us back because at that point we would have no visas for re-entry into Thailand. I also wanted to try the psychological approach and instil in their minds our confidence that a problem didn't exist. That was why we hadn't needed to seek permission first. If only things worked out in reality as they do in one's imagination, life would be so much easier.

Customs officer on the Thai/Burma border

Our big day had dawned. We were ready to cross the Rubicon, but not without a few butterflies in the gut. We had a good breakfast. If we were going to get half-drowned, it might as well be on a full stomach. We said our goodbyes to Chareon and his family, and we all posed for some photographs. Chareon had seemed genuinely sorry to see us leave. He promised to write, and hoped that one day he might see us on a visit to England.

We drove down to the river. It was Wednesday 10th December 1958, and it had taken us nearly four weeks and over

1,700 adventure-packed miles to reach that spot, and at times I had wondered if we would ever make it. Angela and Louise remained in the back of the vehicle to take care of the exhaust pipe extension, and I opened both the doors to prevent the current pushing the vehicle downstream. John, Lyn and Bruce waded across so as to keep some of the weight out of the vehicle and to take photos of all the action. I ventured carefully down the steep embankment and rode along the bank for twenty yards, then turned surreptitiously into what I had thought was the shallowest point. Heading for the Burmese riverbank, water soon begun to pour into the vehicle. Angela and Louise started to bale out the water, but soon realised that they were fighting a losing battle; the water was coming in much too fast. The cab started to fill with water and the motor cut out right in the middle of the river. The water flowed through the open doors of the Land Rover and I was soon soaking wet as the water reached to my waist. Everything that could float did float. I had to grab items to prevent them floating out of the doors and away with the current.

On the Burmese bank a very irate immigration officer waved frantically for me to stop, whilst John, Lyn and Bruce tried to placate him. He need not have worried, as I couldn't do a bloody thing anyway. So much for my direct action approach, which had landed us right in the shit. There I was stuck between two countries, in what would normally be described as no-man's land, but in my case it was no-man's river. I could never in my wildest dreams have envisaged a situation like that ever happening; and I didn't' know how it would end.

The vehicle sunk lower into the mud and the water level had crept up to the map racks, just below the dashboard. Due to the fast-flowing current, I had great difficulty climbing from the cab and onto the bonnet, but eventually I managed to wade across to the Burmese bank to assist the others in trying to calm down the immigration guy, who thought we should have seen him first. We, of course, were very apologetic for our lack of etiquette and pointed out that we hadn't meant to undermine his authority in any way. Our apology helped a lot in removing the sting from his tail, but he remained adamant that he would not co-operate in any way until he had inspected the passports.

He stared, long and hard, at our 'do it yourself' document; it seemed like an eternity. He then pointed out that it was unusual to have permission to travel by land route due to the sensitive political situation. My thoughts ran wild with the uncertainty of our position, then suddenly without further ado he said, "You can come to Burma." When those gold-plated words flowed from his lips it took time to comprehend what he had just said. I found it hard to conceal the delight in my emotions. I felt like I had just scored the winning goal in the World Cup.

When I came back down to earth again, my thoughts drifted

back to the Land Rover still stuck, half-submerged in the mud, in the middle of the river with Louise and Angela still marooned in the back. We were told they had an old Bren-gun carrier that would pull it out for us.

Waiting for rescue in the Mae-Sai River

I waded back to the Land Rover and sat for half an hour while I waited for its arrival. That was the longest bath I had taken on the whole trip. I tied the towrope to the carrier, but the first attempt was futile. The rope snapped on take off as the driver had started much too fast. The second attempt was more successful. We appeared to jump from the water all of a sudden but the rope held, and the carrier towed us right to the top of the hill. Water poured out from the doors like miniature waterfalls splashing into the dust. I knew that we had a big job on our hands before our faithful old Land Rover would be on the road again.

The Thailand/Burma border at Tachilek. The sinking Land Rover, 'Tessa', being pulled from the Mae-Sai River by an army Bren-gun carrier.

Forbidden Entry Into Burma

After all the euphoria had died down, we were all invited to have a bottle of orange and a cup of tea with the immigration people. Our first priority, however, was to change into some dry clothes. That was if we could find any that the water hadn't got to first. We were given the use of the rear of their wooden building for our drying out.

We were interested to learn from the border officials that the Bren-gun Carrier that dragged us from the river was a vehicle that had been used by the British Army during the war against the Japanese in the 1940s. It was recovered from the jungle when the British Army left Burma. I found that very intriguing as I once saw a film about the war in Burma and all the indications had been that Errol Flynn had won the Battle of Burma all on his own; well, he was an American.

John and I soon got started on trying to get the Land Rover going again. I was very keen to leave there as soon as possible. I felt sure the immigration officers were still very suspicious of our presence. Unfortunately, things didn't work out how we would have liked. The damage to the vehicle was more extensive than we thought. Not surprisingly, the water had seeped in everywhere and all the oils had to be changed. When they were drained off they came out a milky colour, and it was evident that its viscosity had changed. All the electrics, even those above the waterline, had to be dried out. It soon became clear that we were not going to be able to leave that day. John and I continued to work on the vehicle for five hours before we were finally able to resuscitate it back to life. The rest of the crew had done a sterling job of drying out the inside and trying to salvage some of the gear that hadn't been rendered entirely useless.

Although our passports had already been stamped and returned to us earlier, we were very concerned when the chief immigration officer returned and asked to see them again. I was convinced that we had been rumbled and that he was ready to hang us out to dry. It was obvious he'd had second thoughts and seemed sceptical about our DIY documents. He told us that he was sending a message to Rangoon to confirm our visas and that we must go there and report to the Immigration Department immediately upon arrival. He wrote in our passports:

'Landed at Tachilek 10.12.58 - allowed to proceed to Rangoon with instructions to report to the Controller of Immigration at Rangoon on arrival without fail.'

I realised at once that there was now no way we dare go anywhere near Rangoon. That would have been akin to walking into the lion's den and giving ourselves up, and then we certainly would have had no chance of being able to continue on. I didn't mind taking risks, but that would have been a risk too far. Our main worry was whether they would receive a reply back from Rangoon before we left next day. We were invited to spend the night in the little café next to the Immigration Department run by a Pakistani. He kindly gave us sleeping space at the back of his shop. That gave us a little respite from cooking our own dinner.

We left at 7.30 a.m. the next morning, but travelled only the few hundred yards to the customs shed where we were delayed for an hour before we got clearance. But that wasn't the end of it; the bloody vehicle wouldn't start again. I couldn't deny feeling a little frustrated at yet another delay.

We worked on the vehicle for three hours, going back over some of the work we had done the day before, but she wouldn't start. I thought it was unwise to stay where we were any longer. It was important that we got the hell out of there as quickly as possible. As we were on top of a hill, I used that to my advantage, so with everybody on board I released the handbrake and we coasted down the hill. Halfway down, I engaged second gear, lifted my clutch pedal, and after a lot of spluttering the engine sprang back into life again. I felt very relieved that we were then well out of sight of the Immigration Department. Although those last thirty-six hours had been very traumatic for us, our entry into Burma had overcome the greatest challenge of my return journey. But that didn't mean we were home and dry. We had more than eleven hundred miles to travel through the jungles of Burma before we reached the relative safety of India. The irony was that although we had risked everything to get in, it was important that we made a sustained effort in order to get out again as quickly as possible. It was anyone's guess what would happen when we failed to report to the controller of immigration in Rangoon. That wasn't all we had to worry about, Burma was still a very dangerous place to be. The roads were unsafe for travellers, and large areas of the country were frequented by rebel and terrorist groups of varying political persuasions. There were communist insurgents who were busy trying to undermine the central government and armed bands of dacoits, who normally operated in smaller groups. Also, there were Chiang Kai-Shek's nationalist troops, the Kuomintang, who had fled across the border into Burma and sought sanctuary there when the communists defeated his army. Eventually an amnesty was offered to all those troops that agreed to return to Formosa voluntarily. Thousands took up the offer and returned. However, there were between 3,000 and 5,000 that elected to stay on in Burma. Chiang Kai-Shek then disassociated himself from all those who remained. They then became part of the terrorist problem.

All those factions with their different aspirations were responsible in one way or another for the lawlessness that gripped the country. Vehicles along the road were ambushed, bridges and trains blown up, and in some of the most dangerous areas a carriage chassis was placed in front of the engine to be pushed along ahead of the train. If an attempt were made to blow up the train, the chassis would take the brunt of the explosion and hopefully save the engine from damage. Thankfully, we were never that close to see whether it worked or not. We did, however, get close enough to photograph an armoured railway vehicle that travelled backwards and forwards along the line looking for saboteurs.

Armoured train looking for saboteurs

To travel between towns, vehicles would join in convoy with an army escort for protection. Even then some of the convoys came under attack. We were never able to enjoy the luxury of convoy protection as it was important that we avoided being asked awkward questions by the army. Our only protection was my Colt .45 revolver and .22 rifle, which were kept handy at all times. We just hoped they would never have to be used.

On the road towards Kengtung, progress was very slow. Hills thousands of feet high were commonplace and four-wheel drive had to be used most of the time. Our speed was only averaging ten miles an hour and what hadn't helped matters were the dubious noises that had started coming from the other rear wheel bearing on the Land Rover. It was particularly worrying considering what had happened to the one on the opposite side whilst in Thailand.

After covering fifty-three miles we arrived in the big village of Mongpayah late into the evening. There was no Dak bungalow, but there was a large wooden attap which the locals called the 'King's House'. Why it was so named nobody seemed to know. We contemplated an overnight stay there, but on reflection, as there was no garage or repair facilities in the village, we decided to carry on and drive through the night to Kengtung and hope the bearing would last out until we arrived. I must admit having erred a little about the night drive as it wasn't one of the wisest things to have done and went against all the advice that had been given to us at our embassy in Bangkok. My overriding priority, however, was to get through Burma as quickly as possible and with the thought that even insurgents and dacoits, or whatever else you would care to call them, have to sleep sometime!

From Mongpayah we followed the road through the valley of the Me-Len which ascended and descended constantly. The river, from fast flowing, gradually petered out to become nothing more than a gentle stream. Driving was difficult in the black of night, but we had good headlights and that was a blessing. Some of the bends were so sharp that we were unable to get round them in one movement and sometimes had to back up and take a second bite at the turn. With the trailer behind, the problem was made even worse. Bruce and I shared the driving and tried to take catnaps in between our stints, but sleep was never easy. In some places fallen boulders and precipices were a real hazard. We both came to the conclusion that two pairs of eyes were better than one, and safer.

We entered the town at 4.30 a.m. and intended stopping near to the hot springs until the town came back to life again, but the difficulty was finding them in the dark. We stopped at a few small bridges and scrambled down the banks to feel the temperature of the water as a guide to our location. Unfortunately, we weren't successful so we eventually gave up and drove on through the town for a couple of miles and stopped beside some paddy fields for a few hours shuteye.

We awoke covered in morning dew and found ourselves staring into the faces of some bewildered locals standing around the vehicle wondering who we were, and where we had come from. We returned to town to find a garage where we could change the wheel bearing.

Kengtung is a small, remote little town located in the corner of the Shan ranges where its borders merge with those of Indo China and Thailand. It maintained its own small airstrip, with two weekly flights, which operated between Rangoon and Kengtung using old Dakota aircraft. There was a Customs and Immigration outpost, and the army had commandeered the Dak bungalow.

We filled up with petrol at the B.O.C petrol pump. The garage man, who spoke a little English, very kindly guided us to what he claimed was the repair depot, but which turned out to be nothing more than a glorified junkyard.

We removed the wheel and, as expected, found we needed a new bearing and oil seal. The repairman invited me to join him on the back of his two stroke for a trip to the motor store to buy the parts. His driving scared the shit out of me. We hit every pothole he could find. The only trouble was he didn't bother to slow down when he saw them coming. I was up in the air more than I was on the seat.

We got the parts we needed for fifty-two kyats. (The kyat was worth one shilling and six pence each [7½ᵖ].) The removal of the old bearing nearly gave me a heart attack. He bashed the shaft repeatedly on an iron slab as he tried to get it off. The heavy hammer appeared to be the favourite tool of the day. The cost for the job was thirty-five kyats and my sore bottom.

Having wasted most of that day on repairs, we left Kengtung en route for Takaw, where we would cross the Salween River by ferry. As we were a little weary, our progress was slow, so we decided on another night drive to try and reach Takaw by morning. In some places, over the very high ridges, the road narrowed so much that it was impossible to see its edge from the side of the vehicle. All that was visible as we looked down was the long white winding river hundreds, and sometimes thousands, of feet below. It reflected in the moonlight, like an endless piece of white cotton on a black carpet of jungle. Fireflies, disturbed by our presence, darted around in the dark in front of us like mobile cat's eyes trying to reflect the way ahead.

As the light of morning broke through we came upon a bamboo shelter beside the track. As we were only a few miles from Takaw I thought it a good spot for us to freshen up, make some breakfast and to give the girls the opportunity to bathe their feet again, which were still giving cause for concern.

We crossed the Salween by the ferry, which was nothing more than a glorified wooden raft, and headed for Loilem. The map we had of Burma was only a little more than useless. It had been difficult to obtain a decent up-to-date one. Ours lacked detail and was nothing more than a sketch, but it was a case of make do with what we had and hope something better turned up along the way.

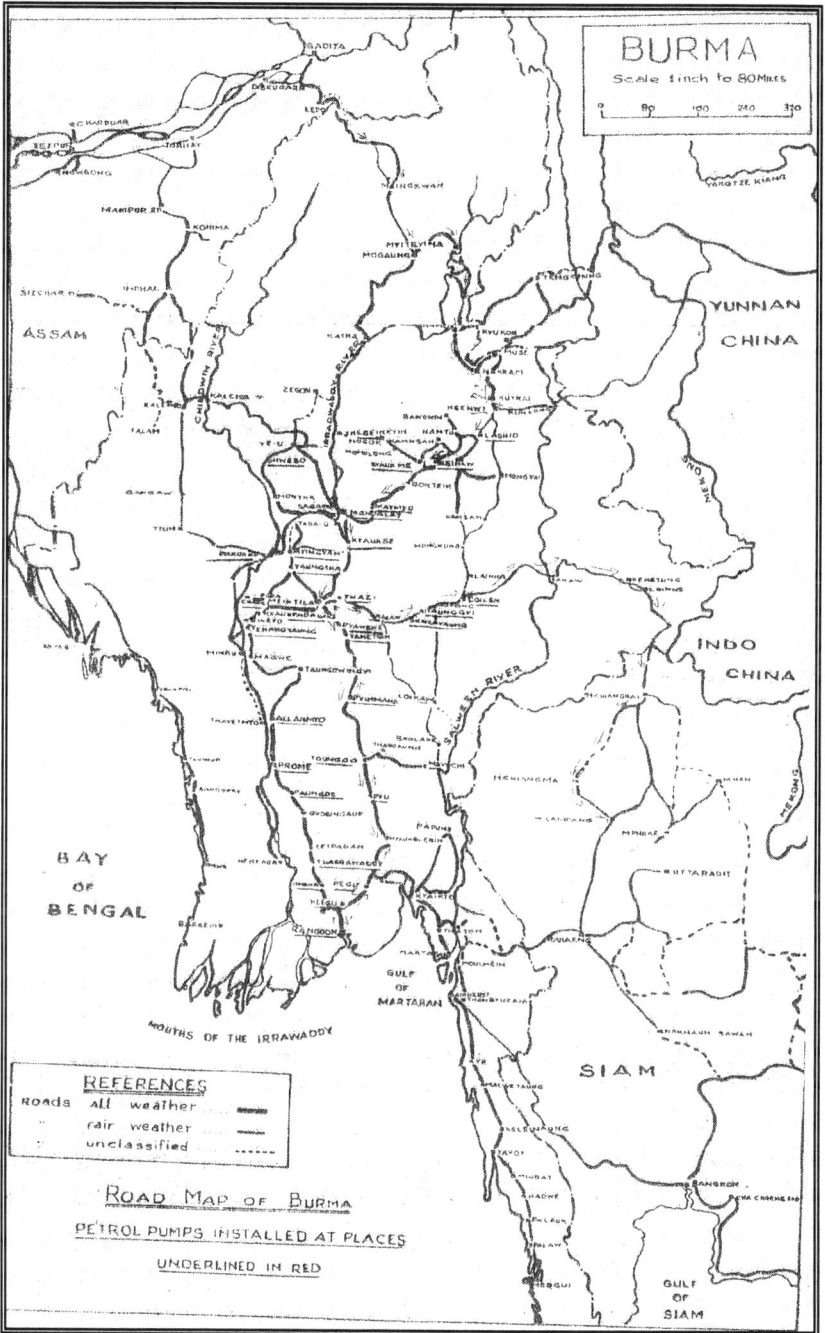

Our 'sketch' map of Burma

We had been warned again that we must take great care on that side of the river as ambushes and kidnappings were always a possibility. I tried to identify possible danger spots, particularly at places where we had to slow down for sharp bends. If we saw fallen trees or bushes ahead of us blocking the track we would assume they had been placed there in order to force us to stop. I kept my revolver strapped on most of the time. Although that had given us some feeling of security, it would have been little use against a determined ambush; vigilance was our virtue. The road ahead passed through large areas where the white poppies flourished, waiting to be harvested and its narcotic juice extracted to be dried and turned into opium.

Six miles from Loilem we made camp, pitching our tent beside the road. This was to be a stopover that will long be remembered by John.

After quite an uneventful night we settled down to an early breakfast. Before it was ready John did one of his usual disappearing acts by wandering off into the jungle with his camera hoping to find and photograph one of the exotic orchids found in nature's natural botanical garden. When he re-emerged to his cold breakfast, wearing a self-satisfied look, we knew 'eureka' he'd found it. Sadly, his jubilation was very short lived. Whilst folding his blanket in readiness to leave, he suddenly winced with pain as a big black scorpion dropped from his wrist.

Having heard many differing stories relating to the sting of the scorpion, we weren't really aware at the time of how serious it could be, but thought something should be done, and done quickly. I took a razor blade from the front of the Land Rover, and Lyn rubbed the wound with Dettol, while Angela and Louise applied a tourniquet at the bend of his arm. I cut with the blade at the point of the sting until it bled, then sucked the blood while the tourniquet was still applied. I then spat out two mouthfuls of blood and the pressure of the tourniquet was gradually loosened, then slowly removed altogether.

Nature's botanical garden: the Burmese jungle

We made him some sweet tea and he rested for a while. It had understandably been a great shock to him, but he recovered in a few hours. Whether our knee jerk reaction helped him in any way I didn't know. It might have been entirely wrong and not influenced the outcome, but in any crisis one can only act on what seems right at the time. At least I could be the founder member of the 'Overland Bloodsuckers Club'.

Our arrival in Loilem market place caused the usual crowd to gather round the vehicle, joined by the police soon after. They asked to see our passports and enquired if we had been to Rangoon as ordered. After convincing them we had, they politely allowed us to continue.

It was Sunday and Australia Day, and my Aussie friends celebrated with patriotic fervour in a local eating house and indulged themselves in gastronomic excesses. Bruce and I helped a little in their celebrations. But as all good things come to an end, so did ours when it was discovered the oil seal fitted with a new bearing in Kengtung was causing problems. The seal had a severe leak and needed changing again, but this was unobtainable in Loilem so we had little choice but to settle for an oversize one and file it down. It seemed that repairs to the Land Rover and trailer were becoming more and more numerous, too much so for comfort.

On the road out from Loilem we passed a large military training establishment as we headed west towards Taunggyi, Kalaw and Meiktila. We then turned north at the road junction en-route for Lashio, the capital of the Northern Shan States. Road conditions varied considerably from gravel to mud, with the usual river fordings and culverts. We passed through Laihka and were about to enter a small village when an army patrol stopped us. I was caught red-handed with my pistol strapped on in its holster.

Carrying a gun in Burma required a special permit, which I didn't have. When questioned by the captain of the patrol, who understood some English, I had to lie through my teeth to convince him that we had obtained permission during our visit to Rangoon to carry a firearm, but we didn't have it in writing, it was just verbal. I volunteered the bit about going to Rangoon as it was obvious he was going to ask to see our passports, which was exactly what happened. I think volunteering that information was what had swung the decision in our favour for him to let us go. He had no way of proving that we hadn't been to Rangoon. That was twice we had been challenged in a couple of days.

I'd had many unusual lunches during my travels but the one we had on the way to Lashio will be one of the most memorable. Included in the food supplies we carried were a variety of large sachets of soups which we thought had all been used. Then someone looking through a locker in the back of the Land Rover found a couple of packets that had somehow survived. Just the ticket for our lunch break that day! We prepared the soup in the usual way and sat around drinking it from our mugs. Bruce happened to remark that there were white bits floating in the soup. Closer scrutiny revealed hundreds of maggots. We all looked at each other with screwed up faces. John had already finished his, but the rest of us were, should I say, a little put off from finishing ours. When the packets were examined we found that they had somehow been punctured, and when we forded the dirty water of the Mae-Sai River the water had penetrated into the packets when

199

the vehicle was submerged. It was just as well they were our last two packets as soup was definitely off the menu for the foreseeable future.

A jungle lunch

We passed through Mongkung and Hsipaw before we arrived at Lashio, where we were at last able to sort out our oil seal problem by finding one of the correct size.

Lashio is nearly 3,000 feet above sea level and was the starting place of the old Burma Road which ran from Mandalay into China, and where supplies from India passed through in the Second World War en route for Chaing Kai-Shek's base in China at Kunming.

We still had six hundred uncertain miles to travel before leaving Burma. Up to that point, apart from the series of breakdowns suffered, we had been reasonably lucky. Our progress had been slow because of the problems, but I was pleased how we had been able to overcome them one by one, considering the limited resources available to us.

Although Lashio was a quiet little town, its peace and tranquillity was frequently disturbed by the sound of explosions each time the railway line from Mandalay was blown up by the insurgents. The little train would then have to return from whence it came until the line had been repaired. It must have been quite disconcerting for a would-be traveller to ask at the local booking office when the next train was due, only to be told it would leave on time if it wasn't blown up. If it had, you would have to wait until the line had been repaired, and that could take up to two weeks. I could hardly imagine a queue forming in order to take the train.

Apart from Pagodas, a Chinese monastery and other religious shrines, there was little else for us to be excited about in Lashio. It was always difficult for us to leave a place without the usual platitudes being churned out and Lashio was no exception, although this became boring at times we all seemed to have developed an extra sensory perception of what questions were coming next. We always tried to answer with a smile and to show appreciation of the interest they had shown in us. We left at noon that day and headed out towards Muse and Namkam. We were keen to reach Namkam so the girls could get some more treatment for their athlete's foot at the Mission Hospital there.

Thirty-two miles out of Lashio we passed through Hsenwi,

the capital of Hsenwi State and the seat of the Sawbwa. Located quite close to the town were some hot springs. During the Japanese occupation they took full advantage of all that unlimited supply of lovely hot water and built themselves a bathing pool in which their troops could relax. I wondered whether it was possible for anybody to relax in such a war-torn environment, with all the fighting taking place around them. Those hot springs later became known as the Nsenwi or Lashio Spa.

One mile through Nsenwi there was a Public Works Department bungalow perched on top of the hill. From that point heading east there was a gravelled branch road that ran through to Kunlong, fifty-two miles away, where it crossed the Salween and farther east eventually crossed the Mekong into the mountain province of Yunnan, China. That might be an interesting journey for another time.

Before we entered the little town of Kutkia we saw three very attractive Burmese girls coming towards us. They had baskets balanced on top of their heads and seemed to just glide along with such grace and balance. We stopped the vehicle and got out, curious to know what they had in their baskets. They lowered them to the ground for us and we found they contained green chillies, which I knew were very hot. I picked one out of the basket and pretended to bite into it. One girl became concerned and shouted something in Burmese and raised her hand. I took this to mean 'don't do it', so I went the whole hog and bit it in half, then acted out the antics of someone with a burnt mouth. The girls went into hysterics and a few minutes elapsed before they were able to regain their composure and get the baskets back onto their heads again. We often shared a bit of banter with the locals, especially the children. Laughter is always a good public relations exercise.

We filled up with petrol in Kutkia and bought bananas and fresh vegetables. We drove till midnight and made camp beside the Shweli River.

While having breakfast the next morning we were taken by surprise by an opportunistic raid on our camp. In the trees above us there was a troop of apes who showed their displeasure at our intrusion by thumping their chests. There were also a number of monkeys who jabbered away in sympathy with their larger neighbours. Then without further ado, one monkey swooped down from the trees, grabbed one of our mugs and was gone like Whippet Quick the cat burglar. He went back up the tree and proceeded to bang the mug against the trunk. That was something we could call 'real monkey business'. So with one mug light we drove into the town of Muse.

While driving alongside the river bordering China we stopped to buy some Chinese hats. Louise and I did a little rafting on the Shweli River. Although the river at that point was only about three hundred yards wide we chose not to land on the Chinese bank in case any problems were to occur.

On returning to the vehicle a Burmese policeman was waiting for us. He shook hands, looked at our passports and asked us to come to the police post about half a mile away. My mind immediately flashed back to our non-arrival in Rangoon and wondered if we had been found out. However, we were greeted at the post with the usual politeness we had now come to expect from the Burmese. After examining our passports and documents we were offered tea, and surprise, surprise they didn't even ask if we had been to Rangoon. My initial fears just melted away and we were allowed to continue.

Before leaving the police post I asked if there was a toilet I could use. A policeman beckoned me to follow him out the back of the post. He then pointed to what was their loo. I had seen and used many 'shit houses' on this trip, but without a doubt that one was the most precarious contraption I had come across. There was a long wet and greasy plank, around three feet wide and about seven feet long, protruding out over the edge of the riverbank at a height of seventy to eighty feet. It had perched on its end a box like construction made of bamboo and covered with brown leaves for the protection of one's privacy. Near the end of the plank was a small hole of about three inches wide, through which the fast flowing river could be seen below. The user would squat over the little hole and hope that their aim was true. During my air force days, I trained as an air gunner but those few minutes of privacy in that little house made me think that training as a bomb aimer would have on that occasion been far more useful. A gas mask would have helped a little too.

After a nineteen-mile drive, we arrived in the unusual,

remote, and colourful little village of Namkham. It was unusual because the little wooden houses were mostly quite different from those of other villages. They had a charm of their own, with their distinct flavour of Chinese architecture.

Namkham was the home of that excellent Mission Hospital run by Dr. Gordon Seagrave where, in that primitive place, he worked for twenty-five years with his family caring for the sick. When a larger hospital was needed the good doctor and his family, friends, Chinese coolies and even nurses, built one out of cobblestones with their own hands. Dr. Seagrave is also the author of *My Hospital In The Hills*, *Burma Surgeon* and *Burma Surgeon Returns*. We had the honour of meeting and shaking the hand of the great man himself when we attended his hospital for advice and treatment for the fungus that still plagued Lyn, Louise and Angela's feet. We stayed in the vicinity of the hospital until the treatment given was sufficient to allow us to continue on. The treatment included the scraping of the infected part of the feet, and irrespective of all the discomfort they suffered the girls had never let it get them down, they remained, as always, in good spirits. We were reminded while at the hospital of the importance of regularly taking our malaria tablets, I must admit I had become rather lax in that department and frequently forgot to take mine. I tended to think it would never happen to me, it was only others who caught malaria.

Before we left and headed for Bhamo we were advised that security along that stretch fluctuated from time to time and not to be surprised if we found ourselves held up by dacoits or insurgent bands at any point throughout the journey. We had started to become a little blasé about being ambushed or held up, but that last warning hammered home to us that the danger was still very real, and we became much more focused on that possibility.

Five miles out from Namkham, the Shweli River was crossed by a Bailey suspension bridge. The farther north we headed towards Bhamo, the more and more hilly the terrain became, and at certain points the road became very treacherous. Although we struggled in places it would have been almost impassable during heavy rains. Very often after a fording or crossing a creek, the brakes on the vehicle became so wet as to render them completely useless until they had dried out. It made driving rather dangerous when we had to negotiate sharp bends and steep hills. To overcome the drying out problem, and when prudent to do so, we would drive along with our brakes on. This created friction between the brake linings and the drums, and as friction causes heat, we found it a very effective way of drying them out, and saving time.

However, fate was never lurking too far away, and as we came down from the hills into flat country the offside trailer wheel dropped off and rolled into a paddy field, damaging the mudguard into the bargain. Although this was a further blow to our progress, things could have been far worse. If it had happened while we were high up in the hills and had dropped into the dense jungle below, it would have been lost forever. We had no new

206

replacement bearing to repair the trailer and had to rely on an old one that had been changed during servicing. I made a point of keeping some of the old parts that had been replaced just in case we were forced to use one of them again if no new part was available, which was the case when we arrived in Bhamo. Although there was always a bonanza of old wartime scrap laying around in towns and villages that could be picked over in a search for useful parts, it was rare to find just the bit you wanted, and if you did, it was the wrong size.

It wasn't unusual to find old war material, such as a motor vehicle, rusting away in the undergrowth with bamboo pushing its way through the rust. Only a few days before we had found an old Japanese tank that had been knocked out. Some enterprising individual had obviously found a good use for its engine as that had been removed. I wondered about that tank and thought of a story that might explain its being there. Did its occupants live or die? Did the soldiers who destroyed it ever make it back home to their families? My thoughts and imagination were tinged with a little sadness of not knowing the answer. There was a story within a story but there could be no ending.

While the trailer's mudguard was being repaired, we

wandered around the town and stopped in the little market place for bananas and tomatoes. Being the only Westerners in such a remote and unfrequented place we soon, as usual, became the subjects of curiosity. Whenever we stopped, people gathered around asking the usual questions.

Bhamo bustled with character. One old lady was sitting on the steps of her little wooden house on stilts smoking a peculiar-looking long pipe with a large bowl. After giving her a passing wave, she removed the pipe from her lips and smiled at us, revealing a set of teeth the same brown colour as the pipe she smoked. Hordes of children followed us around, wondering what we were about. I occasionally delighted them by trying to imitate a duck. That always went down well with the kids, who would then try to come back to me with their own ducky imitations.

Burmese priests with shaven heads wandered around in their orange coloured robes, with young novices trailing in their wake. They carried their wooden begging bowls in anticipation of receiving their daily donation of rice, with perhaps a little something extra to go with it; always freely given by generous benefactors.

Bhamo was also the terminus of the Irrawaddy Flotilla Company, the river steamer service from Katha and Mandalay. Motor vehicles could also be shipped from here to Thabeitkym, where there was a drivable road to Mogok. Just the job if you wished to buy or sell some rubies as Mogok is the ruby mining town where some of the world's finest rubies are found. If you are lucky enough to own a ruby ring or necklace, there is a good chance that they had their beginnings in Mogok.

With a healthy mudguard, a trailer bearing running on borrowed time and fingers crossed, we topped up with petrol and headed out of Bhamo towards Myitkyina. The road conditions varied considerably. This road was modified by the American Army during the war; for most part it was a shingle highway mechanically sealed and graded.

For the first nine miles up to Momouk the road had, at some time, been asphalted, but it was certainly ready for another topcoat. The remainder was in a fair condition. The use of the word 'fair' would normally indicate that we didn't actually get bogged down for too long at a time. If we could make fifteen to twenty miles an hour at any time, it was considered a good road.

We didn't manage the 116 miles to Myitkyina in one go. After fifty miles we arrived in the small township of Na Lone. There was a rather comfortable Dak Bungalow there so we called it a day. As we had missed out on lunch that day, for a change, we made chips for our evening meal from some of the excellent potatoes that were available in most parts of Burma. They went down well with fried tomatoes and boiled rice. Chips were a rare luxury for us because of our limited cooking utensils, and we always found it difficult to store the fat that was left over from the frying.

Three novice monks in Burma

One of the many visitors to the bungalow that night was a young Sikh. He spoke good English and mentioned he had a brother who kept a repair garage in Myitkyina and might be able to supply the bearing we so badly needed for the trailer. That was music to my ears.

Before we left the bungalow the next morning we all appended our signatures in the visitors' book, writing 'Edis 1957 Overland Expedition en route to London from Australia'. Not all the Dak bungalows had visitors' books, but those that did, only boasted a handful of names, some of which went back many years. They were mainly local government officers or Public Works Department (PWD) officials passing through. Frequently, army units occupied the Dak bungalows, and it was a case of hard luck if you had wanted to stay there at the same time.

Since their treatment for jungle foot at Dr. Seagrave's hospital at Namkham, Angela and Lyn's feet had begun to look a little healthier. Although Louise's feet had also improved regarding athlete's foot, another problem had reared its ugly head for her. One of her feet appeared to have signs of an ominous red shape forming under the skin. It was, at the time, hard to recognise what it could be. The foot was bandaged up and Louise travelled as much as possible with her foot raised, resting on whatever was convenient, but as always she never complained.

The last few miles to the ferry station at Kacchaw was a swampy marsh track. We boarded the pontoon ferry, operated by two outboard motors, for the crossing of the Irrawaddy. At that point of crossing, the river was about three hundred yards wide and took about ten minutes to cross. The ferry was quite small and could only accommodate about half a dozen vehicles at any one time. The town was three miles on from the other side of the river.

My return to Myitkyina was an important landmark for me on

my journey back to England; a place I had wondered in a brief moment of despondency if I would ever reach. Having arrived, a new mood of optimism passed over me. I felt like the cat that got the cream. Although it was important that we left the country as quickly as possible, in a strange sort of way I had grown very fond of Burma and the challenge that it had beset upon us. Mother Nature previously seemed to have thwarted our every move, but she had now come to terms with our presence.

Having found the garage workshop that the young Sikh guy had mentioned the previous day, we left the trailer with his brother, who assured us he could get the bearing we needed. He also broke the news that the axle was bent and needed to be straightened. I wasn't surprised; as I have mentioned before, the trailer had become a real pain, but I was determined to drag it back to England, come what may!

The market place was bustling with activity; there were all kinds of people, Chinese, Pakistanis, Shans, Kachins and others. They were mostly wearing lungis, the check tablecloth-like garment that is wrapped around the waist. It seemed hard to imagine that in such a tranquil place, with everybody going about their everyday business, that it could have been the scene in World War II of such savage and fanatical resistance by the Japanese garrison against the Allied armies coming in from India via the Ledo and Stilwell Road.

The Ledo Road met up with the old Burma Road, which ran from Mandalay into China. The British, with the help of fifteen thousand labourers recruited by the Indian Tea Association, started the building of the Ledo Road in early March 1942. It was expected that the first thirty-two miles would be in use by the end of May. However, the project was abandoned on the 11th of May as the labour was needed to help in the evacuation of refugees from Burma. The Americans took over the project in October 1942 and by March 1943 the road building was progressing at a rate of half a mile a day. It reached Shingbwiyang on the 27th of December 1943. They named the road after their General who built it. General Joseph Stilwell (vinegar Joe) who died in 1946. Eventually the road was four hundred and eighty-three miles long going to Wanting, and was first used for traffic to China in January 1945, but it wasn't finally competed until the 20th of May 1945.

As we tried to leave the market place and extricate ourselves from all those happy faces who still wished to ask questions of us, we were rescued by the executive engineer of the Equipment Division (Saw Rain Ban), who invited us to have lunch with him. An offer we couldn't refuse. After a pleasant couple of hours at his home while we waited for the trailer, he presented us with two baskets of lovely fruit as we left. He also warned us of the very difficult road ahead. Something I was already well acquainted with.

As it was late when we eventually became fully mobile again, we stayed the night in Myitkyina, by kind invitation, at the home of an American missionary, Mr Morrison, of the Mission of the

Assembly of God.

Thirty-eight miles out of Myitkyina we came upon a sugar mill near Namti. Outside the mill there was a queue of little ox carts, all loaded to capacity with the long stems of sugarcane waiting to be weighed, unloaded, and fed into the mill. We were all invited inside to see the various stages of production that the cane went through, from the molasses to the finely produced spoonful of pure white sugar you put in your cup of tea. It was interesting to learn that the mill was part of the reparations that the Japanese were forced to make to the Burmese after the war for invading their country and the damage caused to it. There was another mill near Pyinmana that was also provided by the Japanese under the reparation programme.

As we continued slowly northeast towards India, the terrain became more and more inhospitable. Although, I had travelled this road nearly a year before, I knew there was no guarantee that the conditions would be the same, and heaven knows it was bad enough then. Every monsoon takes its toll and alters the face of the place, with new landslides, subsidence, fallen boulders and trees down; it was no wonder that the Ledo Road had been dubbed 'the forgotten road'. Nobody had used it for twelve years, since the end of the war. It had been closed to the outside world and virtually abandoned. No maintenance had been carried out during that time. Most of the bridges were down and the few that had survived were in such a poor state that none but the brave, or the foolish, would attempt to use them. Only time would tell what nature's sometimes obstructive intrusion might have in store for us on the road ahead.

A rocky drive along the Ledo Road, Burma

As we wormed our way through muddy streams that crisscrossed each other and forded a number of rivers, I gave my daily thanks for my four-wheel drive gears, without which it would have been impossible to continue, a word I didn't tend to use lightly. We had driven on late into the night, albeit very slowly, but we did keep moving.

We were on a high ridge and as we descended we were startled by the faint movement of lights. They weren't like the twinkle of lights one would see from a distance, these lights were moving in all directions at the same time. As we came farther down the hill they became brighter. We could gradually make out the shape of the figures holding lanterns forcing us to stop.

Although a bit worrying at the time, I didn't believe that it had the hallmarks of an ambush as they would hardly have used lights to stop us. The mystery was soon cleared up; they were Katchin villagers who were waving their lanterns around to welcome us to their village. It was a bizarre situation. How on earth could they have known we were coming, or who we were?

Searching for a landing point in a Burmese river

We followed them through a jungle track into their village. In the middle was a large bamboo hut built on stilts, which we assumed was the village hall. We were invited to climb the bamboo steps to the room above, where there were villagers with their children seated cross-legged on the floor all around the room. In the middle there was a cosy log fire built on rocks. We were invited to sit down round the fire, where we were welcomed with handshakes by the village elders and laughter from curious, excited children. Two pretty dark-haired girls in their late teens then gracefully approached us carrying large banana leaves filled with rice, meat and vegetable dishes, which they placed before us. So as not turn their backs on us when they had delivered the food, they half-bowed then shuffled backwards away from us. I felt humbled by their politeness. We learned later that the headlights from our vehicle could be seen in the village from many miles away. They thought we must be strangers as it was very rare for a vehicle to pass that way, and it would never be in the dark of night.

During wartime the Katchins were always well known for their pro-British stance and this was certainly underlined by their camaraderie towards us during our stay in their village, and our journey all through the rest of their country. It would be hard for any outsider who had never visited a village like that to understand how these simple people could be so happy and contented without having any of the material things of life that we in the West take so much for granted. Perhaps one day, 'progress', as we know it, will reach this place. If that happens, I wonder if it will be the catalyst that will change their happy lives to something very different.

The very hospitable Katchin villagers

When we left, the whole village turned out to see us off. I felt like my family was waving goodbye to us as we left to go on holiday.

For two days of relentless driving we struggled through everything that the Stilwell Road could chuck at us, but we gradually closed the distance on our final run towards the Indian border. Apart from fording an uncountable number of rivers and creeks, we crossed three rivers in quick succession by ferry. One was at Tanai, where we stayed overnight at a mission run by the Reverend Rowland. Then we crossed the Tawan River by an outboard motor ferry, and then finally the wide Tarun River, operated by a cable-pulley pontoon ferry. I was very surprised to find that a number of simple log bridges had been replaced or repaired over some of the creeks. I was surprised because they weren't there when I passed through before. It made me wonder, after all the years of decay, if this could have been the start of the rebuilding of the Ledo Road.

Two Naga tribesmen in the Naga Hills of Burma

The road between Tanai and the Tawan River was nothing more than a narrow track surrounded by elephant grass about fifteen feet high. We were reminded, by the appearance of two Nagas walking towards us, that we were on the periphery of the Naga Hills. One was wearing something that looked like it had once been a white short-sleeved shirt; it was open at the front, exposing a fine bare chest. His head was covered in a brown cloth which was wrapped around like a hat. Over the top of the head, and resting across the shoulders, there was a wide string bow. A two-foot long knife in a wooden sheath was strapped around his waist and hung diagonally across the whole width of his body. For a Naga, whose tribe had a history of headhunting, his knife looked just the job for an executioner. His friend was decked out more or less the same, except that instead of a shirt, he wore a thick brown jacket buttoned up at the front.

The two tribesmen with the tools of their trade

We passed through the length of the Hukawng Valley fording many of the offshoots of the mighty Chindwin River, where we ran into a number of problems crossing over. It wasn't that the waters were deep, but rock falls were blocking our intended crossing points. It was very time-consuming lugging these rocks away in order to make a path wide enough for the vehicle to pass through. Some rocks were far too big to manhandle, so we used the Land Rover to drag them clear. A practice we were well versed in.

We arrived at the old abandoned airstrip, near the village of Shingbwiyang. Supplies were landed there by American transport Dakotas that flew in from India with vital equipment for the British and American troops in their desperate and unpredictable war against the Japanese. Pieces of wreckage from aircraft that hadn't made it back still littered the edge of the landing ground, which was now slowly being reclaimed by the jungle. The tarmac surface had bubbled up like a thousand miniature molehills; some of which had broken open at the top and jungle vegetation had pushed its way through to the light. We lingered on the landing strip for some lunch and a brew up and reflected on the happenings of those turbulent times of the 1940s.

As we travelled farther north the road became nothing better than a narrow jungle track. In places it was completely overgrown. We used machetes to chop away the undergrowth, when the track became obscured. We then used the vehicle like a bulldozer to push our way through until the track opened up again. That was repeated a number of times, and after a while it became a way of life. We'd only managed about forty miles that day. We forded two rivers, three miles apart and the second ford caused us a bit of a problem. We couldn't climb up the opposite bank; it was too steep, so we motored on upstream until we found a suitable spot to clamber out.

We stayed the night at a Baptist Mission School in a nearby

village. We hoped to get some petrol there but, unfortunately, there wasn't any to be had. The last of our reserves was in the tank and there was precious little of that. It wasn't that we had underestimated our needs but the constant extra thirst of the engine when using our four-wheel drive for long periods had again taken its toll on our miles per gallon. However, there was no point in crying in our beer, that is if we had had any to cry in. The only choice we had was to keep moving until the bloody thing ran out altogether. It wasn't as though this was the first time we had been in this position, and it wouldn't be the last.

The engine chose a most desolate part of the Stilwell Road to give its last gasp of life before it remained silent. True to the expedition's tradition, when in trouble we put the kettle on and took stock of our position. I decided after much thought that John and I had to walk to find petrol. I didn't reckon on one of the girls going with me because of the problems they were having with their feet. John, who had been a member of the Sydney Bush Walkers, fitted the situation perfectly.

We packed some food and started to walk. We had no idea how long we would be gone. It could have been days. Bruce and the girls had plenty of food to last them. Water in Burma was never too far away and was safe as long as it was boiled. They had the rifle for added comfort, but I wasn't happy to leave them in such an uncertain area of the Naga Hills to tough it out alone. Before we left we had agreed that in the unlikely event that a vehicle came along with some petrol, they would drive to meet us, keeping to the same track all the time.

John and I walked for hours, occasionally stopping for a short rest then pressing on again. That went on for nearly ten hours. As the light began to fade we were suddenly startled by a distant sound; we stopped to listen, then walked on a little, there was no mistaking it, the sound of an engine gradually became clearer. Then from round a bend in the track a jeep carrying a gang of men came towards us.

Only one of the men spoke a little English, they were a group of road workers who worked for the Public Works Department (PWD) repairing some of the small bridges across creeks. At the time this seemed to be further evidence of the possibility that attempts were indeed being made to repair parts of the Stilwell Road, albeit only a pinprick of what needed to be done.

John and I were invited to climb aboard the jeep, easier said than done, as there were already seven on board when we arrived. When we returned to the Land Rover, although having only been gone for half a day, it seemed like coming back home again. After pouring some of the nectar of life into our dry tank, which the road crew had so kindly given to us, the leader of the group, whom it transpired was also the chief engineer of the road asked us to join him. We followed them to a nearby village where they cooked dinner and entertained us in real Burmese style. Finally the chief engineer, and his road workers decided to travel on to their own village. At 1.30 a.m. they drove off into the mist singing 'Auld Lang Syne' which was quite amazing seeing that the chief engineer was the only one who could speak any English.

As Lyn quipped, "If running out of petrol always ended like this, we ought to do it more often." (She didn't have to walk for ten bloody hours.)

Bridge builders along the Burma Road

The early start planned for the morning went right out of the window. John and I were the culprits as we felt so knackered after our near ten-hour trek, and with the late night thrown in, we exited our sleeping bags rather late. By the time we'd finished breakfast and carried out the daily inspection on our bulldozer (Land Rover), it was nearly midday. We had hoped to reach the Indian border by evening, but that possibility became very remote.

We soon ran into thick muddy areas where it wasn't always possible for the vehicle to sustain momentum. Sometimes we came to a complete stop and would have to reverse back a distance and take another run at it. If that didn't work we dragged brush from the bush and laid it in front of the wheels.

Fallen tree on the road to the Burma/India border

We came upon a large tree that had fallen diagonally right across our track. There was no way that we could drive round it and it was a little too low to allow us to pass under. We solved that problem by using the axe and the spade to chop and scoop out enough of the jungle wall so as to allow the vehicle to pass under it.

To make up for our late start, we drove on into the darkness with headlights on. Even so, the blackness of the night made it very difficult to be able to see the edge of the road. Moveable searchlights, which unfortunately we didn't have, would have been a great advantage in those conditions. The road twisted, first to the right, then to the left, with rhythmic regularity for miles.

This photo was always thought to be part of the famous Burma Road located in Yunnan Province, and part of the Stilwell Road. Many years after the war, a Chinese World War II expert discovered that the multiple curves, known as '24 Zig', are actually in Qinglong, Guizhou Province. It was also discovered that they are not actually part of the route of the Stilwell Road but a nearby link road.

Progress was so slow that it made the night drive rather counterproductive. As the crow flies, the distance covered didn't warrant the continued risk of a mishap, especially when we were so close to the Indian frontier. At the first opportunity we turned off the road and looked for a clearing to make camp for the night.

We travelled on for some distance, still looking, when we entered a village with lots of little round huts. To my utter dismay it soon became apparent that we had entered a Naga village. The fact that we knew they had once been headhunters made us a little apprehensive about staying. Before I left England, I had seen press reports that the Indian Government had found it necessary to send troops to the area in order to subdue them, although I had seen no actual evidence of them on my first journey through.

The Naked Naga, as they were sometimes called, were demanding complete independence and the same freedom from interference with their tribal way of life as they had enjoyed when they were under British rule. The headhunting Nagas of the Assam-Burma border were a primitive people who lived and fought in the same way as their forefathers through the centuries. When India gained her independence from the British she tried to extend her rule over these primitive tribes but was met with violent resistance. Cases of headhunting were reported time and time again in the Indian press, forcing the government to act by sending troops into the Naga Hills. In their heyday, and when undisturbed by outsiders, the Nagas lived in an age full of crudeness and barbarism. They spent their lives in an atmosphere of perpetual war and danger, and only when well armed, and in groups, did the men venture into neighbouring villages. Pitched battles didn't appeal to the Nagas. They didn't wage war to destroy their neighbours, without whose existence much of life's zest would disappear, they just went in order just to obtain heads. For the Nagas, magical powers were inherent in the human skull and considered necessary to ensure the fertility and prosperity of both men and crops. The Nagas complained that since headhunting had been forbidden, their young men had lost their vigour and their crops no longer yielded abundant harvests as of old. Usually very little personal hatred existed between the individuals of two hostile Naga villages. War was just a sport they claimed, and no one was blamed if a head was brought home as a trophy.

The Nagas love to hold feast days and chiefs would call for a celebration on the very slightest pretext. On such occasions the men and women would adorn themselves in ceremonial costumes. A buffalo or two would be slain and carved for the celebrations, which would not begin until important rituals had first been observed. It would then be time for the chanting to start, which would ask for their crops to increase and that their food would last long. The end of the chant would be the signal for the real festivities to begin, where large quantities

Learning to use a crossbow the Naga way

of rice wine, served in cups made from banana leaves, were

drunk. A great day in the life of the Naga would be to hold a ceremonial dance to celebrate the capture of a head. Occasionally one would see the spoils of a raid dangling from the branches of trees with the shrivelled skins clinging to the skulls of conquered foes, with its features distorted into a gruesome grin. Life in the Naga Hills was primitive and precarious, yet seemed to yield a measure of happiness to their simple lives, and their needs were small.

Being mindful of stories, heard, read and seen in the press, and with no time for a referendum, my first instinct was to do a U-turn and get the hell out of there. But curiosity overtook common sense. If we left, would an opportunity ever occur again to tread the soil of such a place, where few westerners had walked before?

Suddenly, the vehicle was surrounded by curious villagers smiling at the strangers who had invaded their territory. There was no sign of hostility and we were soon invited to squat on carpets made of dried leaves, and given rice wine to drink from small round bowls made from banana leaves. It occurred to me that if headhunting was still in fashion, their gods had certainly made life easy for them to achieve six white heads without having to fight too hard to capture them.

Our arrival appeared to have activated an excuse for a celebration. A fire soon blazed in the centre of the village and the tribesmen sat in a large circle around it. We completed the circle. More wine flowed and the feast begun in earnest. It wasn't exactly clear what we were eating, but we suspected it might have contained buffalo meat as one had been seen tethered earlier; but whatever mysteries it held, we didn't look too closely. We were hungry and hungry men are never too particular what they eat, and as John mumbled, "You can't beat a bit of bush tucker."

As our hosts became more and more exhilarated (half-pissed) the celebrations went into full swing. Tribal music started to play. The instruments consisted of a large native skin drum, something that resembled a cymbal, and a large bamboo pipe. The tempo of the music seemed to be the queue for the chanting to begin. That was quickly followed by the dancing, but all we wanted to do was go to bed. As the celebrations were in our honour, we felt obliged, and indeed were expected, to join in. The dancing went on unabated. The tempo never changed and we all revolved in unison round the fire. It was a four-step movement, three steps forward and one big heavy step to the side that continued on with no sign of stopping. We were weary and stopped for a break to sit down, but that immediately triggered resentment. We didn't know why, but as we had no wish to alienate our hosts we started to dance again. That met with their approval.

A short time later and much to our relief, the chief raised his arms into the air and the dancing stopped. We realised then that it had been a mistake for us to stop before the chief had given the signal. At least a lesson had been learned. When in Naga Land, do as the Nagas do.

It was 2 a.m. in the morning when we were led to a hut in the corner of the village. The sleeping accommodation consisted of a platform, about three feet off the ground, with cross members made from bamboo covering the surface. It was a relief to unroll our sleeping bags on to it.

It wasn't easy to sleep as the band continued to churn out music for another two hours before silence finally reigned. We were in no hurry to get up next morning, but were very thankful after our rather sceptical entry into the village to have been able to take part in such a fantastic experience. Although very tiring, we all agreed that we wouldn't have wanted to miss one single moment of it.

The children of the village followed us around, just like other kids had done in the past, and chased one another around like all kids do. We never saw any of them trying to cut off the head of their native dolls!

With over two thousand miles of jungle, swamps, a thousand and one creeks and river crossings behind us, we finally arrived at the Pang-Sau Pass, the boundary outpost of the Burma Customs and Immigration Department.

Crossing Burmese rivers was never an easy feat.

It had been a gruelling experience for the expedition to reach

231

that point in our journey. We had overcome all the trials and tribulations relating to our illegal entry into the country and arrived comparatively unscathed. Whatever the Burmese immigration authorities could have done about our failure to report to Rangoon as ordered was now purely academic. I checked with them before we left, and they confirmed that overland travel was still not possible. No other Western vehicle had entered the country from India since my own entry ten months earlier on the 19th of February 1958.

For our last night in Burma, we stayed at the Dak bungalow in Pang-Sau village, leaving at 10.30 the next morning. A few miles farther down the track we arrived at the international boundary line which was not apparent at all but for the simple weatherworn tin sign at the side of the track. It read 'India-Burma'. That sign had great historic connections. When the building of the Stilwell Road was finished, it would have been seen by thousands of British and Allied troops coming in from Ledo, India. They would have trundled past along that road in their jungle-green camouflaged vehicles on their way to do battle with the Japanese. As the sign had such great significance we decided to recover it from its jungle home for posterity! The sign is now on display at the Imperial War Museum in London.

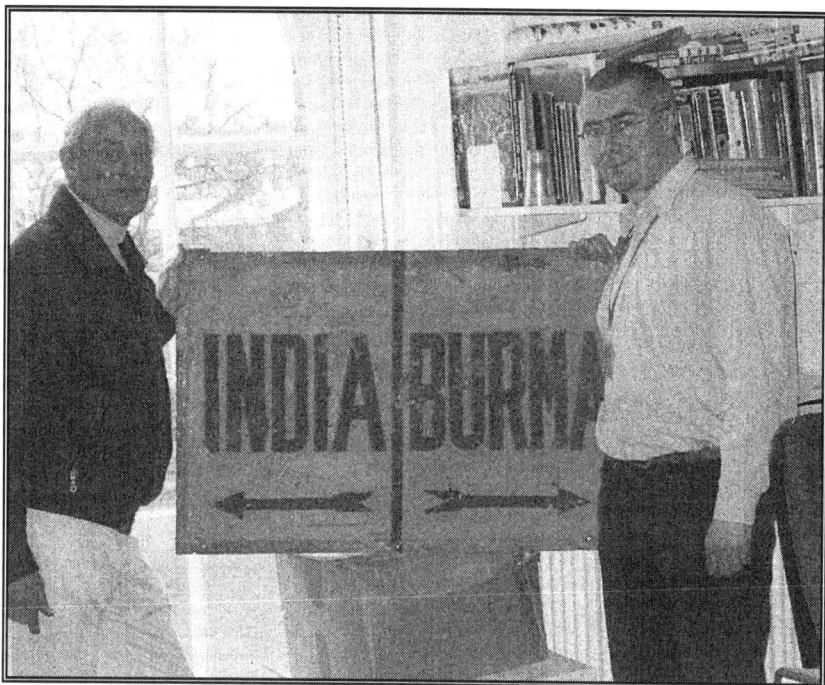

Eric Edis presenting the sign to the Imperial War Museum

India

Eleven miles along the track, we arrived at the Tirap Frontier Division Immigration and Customs Department at Nampong. After the surprise of our arrival had melted away, we were asked to unload everything from the vehicle and trailer. A request I was not happy to carry out. What the hell they thought we had to hide, apart from our mud-caked tents and equipment, we couldn't imagine. So as not to appear too obstreperous, we politely invited them to unload everything themselves, look at anything that took their fancy, and then put it all back again in the same place. In the meantime, while they deliberated, we procrastinated and set up one of the burners on their veranda. We made some tea and had some dry biscuit jam sandwiches. We offered some to the guys who wanted the vehicle unloaded. To our delight they accepted a mug of tea with a grateful nod and smile. I wasn't surprised when they decided that it wasn't really necessary to unload the vehicle after all. Such is the power of psychology.

With all the Customs and Immigration paraphernalia sorted out and Asia Minor ahead, we arrived in the village of Ledo in the tribal areas of Assam. The name had gained prominence in the 1940s by virtue of its important location to the war effort, but had slipped back into obscurity and would be difficult to find on any but the oldest of maps.

From Ledo we followed the Assam trunk road, which passed many of the large tea gardens of Assam, where a large percentage of the world's tea supplies are grown. We were very pleased to accept an invitation to stay for the night at the Bogapani Tea Estate at Digboi. My friends had heard me singing the praises of those fantastic tea garden 'waterholes', where on many occasions I had been invited to stay during the journey out. I had also promised to revisit them on the journey back.

A Waterhole/teagarden bungalow in Assam

I was pleased that my Australian friends were able to enjoy the same hospitality that I had enjoyed. It was also a good opportunity, in such a relaxed atmosphere, to catch up on some letter writing, update the diary and where possible enlist the services of a Dhobi Wallah. Most of the tea gardens we encountered were run by English or Scottish managers accompanied by their wives. The highlight of those visits was the chance of a hot bath. That wasn't always possible and depended very much on the hot-water supply available in the bungalow. That day I was the unlucky one and didn't come out smelling of roses, as when it was my turn to bath the hot water had run out. Hard luck for the others, who continued to suffer the effects of my overland fragrance a little longer.

From Digboi, we passed through Dibrugarh and followed the majestic course of the mighty Brahmaputra River, whose borders pass by the foothills of Nepal and Bhutan. The state of Assam is one of the most fertile areas in the whole of the country. This rich green land of rolling plains and dense forests, where tigers and other species roam free, has the ideal climate for what it does best, grow tea.

While driving along enjoying the day, we ran into an unfortunate incident. Perhaps, more apt to say, the incident ran into us. Out of the blue, from a bush-lined track a boy of about eleven or twelve years old on a bike suddenly emerged and ran into the offside of the Land Rover. There was absolutely nothing we could have done to prevent what happened. We stopped and picked up the lad. The girls then cleaned and dressed his grazed leg. Apart from that, he wasn't badly hurt.

The bike, which had no brakes, finished up with a buckled front wheel. In the meantime a small crowd had gathered. One guy, who spoke a little English, told us that we must pay for the damaged bike and pay many rupees in compensation. Although, we felt some sympathy for the boy, there was no way we were prepared to be intimidated into accepting responsibility for something we had no control over. It didn't seem to matter that we were completely blameless. We were Westerners, and Westerners are always rich. That label had been stuck on me many times before in India. As we got back into the vehicle a number of the onlookers stood in front to prevent it moving. We locked the doors and I moved the vehicle very slowly forward. Then gradually increased the speed until they broke off the encounter.

With the greatly improved road conditions we covered over three hundred and fifty miles in two days. That was the best progress we had made for many weeks. Louise thoughtfully enquired, "I wonder how many miles we've covered since we left Sydney, Australia?"

That was a good question! After we pondered and chucked a few guesses around, Bruce decided he would engage the mathematical side of his brain and have a count up. We always kept a record book in the front of the vehicle where mileages between principal towns and villages were recorded. After consulting the good book, he came up with a figure of 8,165 miles covered. That had taken us nearly five months and we still had more than halfway to go before we reached England. To look on the bright side, it was more cheering to look back and see how far we had come rather than look forward to see how far we still had to go.

As we continued our journey along the banks of the Brahmaputra valley near Jorhat, we called in at the Methoni Tea Estate to see Mr and Mrs Bill Mutch, who managed the garden. I had taken advantage of their hospitality when I stayed there some months earlier. It wasn't long before we were all holding a welcoming glass of wine in our hand and had an invitation to stay the night. We were taken on a tour of the garden. Men and women stood side by side, their nimble fingers plucking at a great pace from the endless rows of green bushes and tossing the leaves into conical cane baskets carried on their backs. In a large black shed we saw about a dozen women, some carrying babies on their backs, sitting in a big circle. There was a huge mound of tea in the middle. They had the tedious job of picking out by hand the tiny particles of light-coloured stalks that still remained in the tea.

After a good meal in the bungalow, followed by more wine, we were asked if we would like a bath. They were golden words indeed and I was determined not to miss out again. There was certainly no objection to my going first.

When it was time for our goodbyes to the Methoni Tea Garden, there was no adequate way of expressing our gratitude to Mr & Mrs Mutch. Not only for the hospitality showered on us but also for continuing our education on the history of tea, which had its beginnings on the Bogapani Estate. Apparently, there were a number of claims made about who first discovered the tea plant. A Robert Bruce was a leading contender. He claimed to have discovered the tea plant in 1823 while on a trading mission in the state of Rangpur. Subsequently, a G J Gordon was sent to China to purchase seeds and tea plants. The seeds from China were nurtured in nurseries and the small plants distributed. The first consignment of Assam tea was said to have been sent to England by sailing ship. The tea was auctioned in Mincing Lane, London in 1839 for an incredible 34/- shillings a pound. Amongst other contenders a Lt. Charlton, who served in Assam in 1841, claimed that it was he who had been first to send tea plants to the Horticultural Society ten years earlier. Being an insatiable tea drinker, I don't really mind who was first. I thank them all each time I put the kettle on. Whenever leaving a tea estate we always felt completely rejuvenated after that little taste of home comforts.

Riding an elephant in India

We continued to follow the course of the white water of the Brahmaputra through many small villages, miles of rice fields, banana plantations and coconut groves. We headed towards the ferry at Goalpara, 250 miles away, and hoped to make it before nightfall, but due to road conditions only managed a disappointing 141 miles, so we slept for the night in the circuit house at Gauhati. A circuit house is a luxurious version of the Dak bungalow, it is more like a small hotel, most have a few staff to tend to your needs and provide a meal, for which you pay a little extra. Permission has to be sought if you wish to stay there from a district magistrate, or government official; it was normally given.

Our original intention on arrival in Gauhati, before crossing the Brahmaputra at Goalpara, was to turn off the Assam truck road and drive through the jungle-clad Khasi Hills to Shillong (the capital of Assam). We carried a letter of introduction to Mr J S Hardman OBE, the Indian Tea Association adviser in Shillong. Unfortunately, those plans had to be abandoned because Louise's foot was still giving cause for concern, so we didn't want to delay our arrival in New Delhi, where it was thought a more effective treatment might be available for her, for too long. At the same time, others in the group wanted to go up into the Himalayas to see Darjeeling, so to strike a reasonable balance I decided to give the Shillong project a miss. It was a little disappointing but would have been even more disappointing for them to have bypassed Darjeeling when we were virtually sitting on the doorstep. Before we departed from Gauhati, I took a stroll up the hill to visit the poignant Commonwealth War Graves Cemetery for a moment of reflection and pay my respects.

After we passed through five villages and crossed over twenty-one bridges, we turned off the road for the three-mile detour to the ferry point at Goalpara. As there was a two-hour wait for the next crossing we took advantage of the interlude for some lunch and a brew.

This mighty river runs for 1,840 miles from its source in the

Himalayas to its delta in the Bay of Bengal. Although we had travelled hundreds of miles hugging the banks of the river, this was the first time we had seen any stretch of the river as calm as it was here. It is more than a mile wide at this point and it took fifteen minutes for the large motorised ferry to reach the little village of Jopigopaghat on the far bank.

From the ferry we headed out towards Cooch Behar. The roads across the wide plains were in a poor state. We had to keep our speed down so as not to punish our already fatigued vehicle more than necessary. We passed many more tea estates, miles of jungle and monkeys scurrying away from our approaching vehicle. There were banana trees, and small overloaded ox carts bumped their way along the potholed roads. After ninety-six miles we crossed the boundary of Assam near Dhubri into West Bengal. We followed the trunk road towards Siliguri, stopping overnight at the Dak bungalow in a small village not far from Cooch Behar. Next day we ran into better road conditions with long stretches of tarmac and occasional sandy riverbeds.

After filling the tank at Falataka, we headed to the Nedam Tea Estate, near Jalpaiguri, where I was able to fulfil another promise of a return journey visit to see Navsh Chaudra Dil, Inspector of Central Excise and Land Customs. An invitation to stay for lunch and freshen up was gratefully accepted. My group was, should I say, a little more than pleased that I had made so many friendly contacts to revisit.

We crossed the large locally famous Coronation Bridge into

Siliguri for the beginning of our ascent up to Darjeeling. At the time of the Raj, British troops and their wives spent their leave at this famous hill station nestling at over seven thousand feet high in the mountains of the Himalayas, where they relaxed in the cool of the hills, away from the heat of the plains.

Coronation Bridge

Although my first trip up to Darjeeling had been an exciting experience I still found it equally exhilarating driving up again. It is like going up into another world and probably as close to heaven as I shall ever get.

As darkness caught up with us we called in at the Planters Club to look up two Scottish Tea Garden engineers I met on the way out. We were all invited in for a drink. Foolishly everybody went into the club at the same time. It was a few minutes before we realised that the Land Rover parked outside had been left unattended. It had always been an expedition rule that one person at least always stayed with the vehicle. A quick exit from the club was, unfortunately, not quick enough. We paid dearly for our stupid omission; a biscuit tin containing new and exposed rolls of film had been lifted from the vehicle. We were not so much concerned about the new films in the tin but the irreplaceable exposed ones. Also removed was a tin of cheese, a hat and John's dirty pair of shorts. His comments were: "Good, now I don't have to wash them!"

Tibetan mother and child: beggars in Darjeeling, India

We left at 4 a.m. after a night's kip on the floor at the Planters' Club for the drive up to where we hoped to see the dawn break from Tiger Hill. I use the word 'hope' because there is no guarantee that cloud will not obscure this awe-inspiring sight that visitors come from far and wide to view. It has been said that to see the sun rise from Tiger Hill is one of the greatest sights in the world. We stood there on the strategically placed platform as dawn broke, but we were only rewarded with occasional glimpses of the tip of Everest between breaks in the clouds.

At the invitation of the two Scottish engineers we called in at the Gungaram Tea Estate at Bagdogra, which was managed by Mr & Mrs Miller, whom I had met before. An invitation to stay over for the night, with another hot bath, made it hard to refuse. The engineers wanted us to stay for an extra three days to attend the New Year's Party they were giving. It was a tempting offer but, unfortunately, we couldn't delay our need to reach New Delhi.

Crossing a river by pontoon bridge

From Bagdogra we passed through Jalpaiguri and headed onwards towards New Delhi, more than 1,200 miles away across the great divide of the Holy Ganges. We crossed over a narrow tributary by pontoon bridge before arriving at the ferry point at Manihari.

Although, described as a ferry, it was little more than a small, glorified rickety bamboo raft. After the vehicle had been positioned on board, the trailer, which had to be disconnected, was rolled on separately to allow enough space for a few passengers to board. It crossed my mind that if they were happy to cross their holy river on that thing, there was probably something in its favour that I had missed. The 'ferry', powered by a man with a long punting pole, was helped along by the current, which took us farther down river to disembark at Raj Mahal Ghat.

The road from there towards Dumka was just mile after mile of potholed surface. The trailer at the rear bounced around like a cork in rough water. We zigzagged all over the road trying to dodge the largest of the potholes. The Land Rover took such a shaking that one of the exhaust pipe brackets broke off leaving a hole in the pipe. After a bit of bodged surgery and the help of some binding wire, we managed to quieten the exhaust noise to a more acceptable level until we reached Dumka for a welding job.

I was always a bit apprehensive when having to stop for running repairs at one of those roadside repair places. They were of course always happy to earn a few rupees doing a repair, but it was essential that you stayed with your vehicle to supervise the work. Most of those little workshops seemed to have a bevy of young boys, from ten to about fourteen years of age, working in them. As soon as you made your problem known, these lads would hasten towards the vehicle, spanners and hammers in hand. Every nut and bolt in sight was fair game to be undone, whether related to the repair or not. When you protested they would look at you with surprise, raise their hand and tilt their head back in a way that told you not to worry. They knew what they were doing! That was the problem, so did we!

As Land Rover parts were unavailable in Dumka, our repair was a make do and mend affair. Bits of pipe from other exhausts were fashioned and welded together to a shape as near to ours as possible. After all that, we just kept our fingers crossed and hoped for the best.

We stayed the night, by the kind permission of the district magistrate, at a Dak bungalow some miles out from Dumka. He arranged for a Chokidar to prepare a meal for us. In the meantime he entertained and enlightened us on the history and tradition of the State of Bihar and the relics of its glorious past. He reminded us that the great Mahatma Gandhi, who was assassinated in January 1948 whilst on his way to prayers, had once called Bihar the garden of India. Also, Buddha had once sought enlightenment at the Great Temple of Bodhgaya. We found it all quite interesting, but after more than an hour of listening about Indian culture and traditions, our enthusiasm had taken a bit of a tumble and we were pleased to be liberated by the arrival of a meal of chicken curry.

Driving along Indian roads is not only an education but also an experience of survival. The Indian attitude to traffic is completely anarchic. Forget rules of the road, in India they don't exist. It is every man for himself. To drive with restraint or consideration is a complete waste of time. You have to develop a Kamikaze attitude of your own to survive.

There is a sensory overload of colour, sound, sight and a smell that is forever India. Brightly coloured lorries with all kinds of intricate designs painted in every available space rattle by belching black smoke, their cabs filled with passengers packed in together like sardines. Even the top of the vehicle is not spared. Passengers sit precariously perched on the roof rack complete with luggage. Some drivers carry a miniature temple in their cabs with a picture of their god, displaying their religious beliefs. It is quite common to see an overloaded, top-heavy, vehicle toppled on its side from taking a bend too fast. Travelling by bus can have its exciting moments. Apart from it being overloaded, don't be surprised to find yourself next to a couple of goats or a guy carrying live chickens with their wings tied up. It isn't unusual to see couples with as many as three children all riding around town on one motorbike. There are many modes of transport on Indian roads, but, perhaps, the most poignant is to see an undernourished wretched animal, whose ribcage can be clearly defined, struggling to pull an overloaded hooded buggy up a gradient. Little sympathy is shown from its driver, whose only response to its agony is a sharp crack at the whip.

In parts of India, the cow, sacred to the Hindu and worshipped as the Divine Mother, is found wandering at will on busy main roads. One has to be very alert not to collide with one of these animals. They are seen by the Hindus as a symbol of fertility and a source of life-sustaining milk.

Whether travelling by day or night between the larger townships, you are never too far away from one of the many roadside food stalls (Dhabas), where a quick, cheap and typically

Indian meal for the more adventurous eater is always available, albeit with a slightly limited choice. For the passing truck driver and hungry traveller, however, it is affordable, sustainable and convenient. Although the type of food may vary in the different regions, chicken and egg dishes are quite common throughout most of India. It is wiser wherever you eat to avoid salad dishes. They may look fresh and appealing, but you can never be sure if they have been washed in clean water. We always took care when eating fruit and made sure it was peeled first. Bananas, when available, became part of our daily diet. At lunchtimes we looked out for one of the many stalls making chapattis, but only purchased those that came straight out from the hot oven. We then wrapped them around a banana and hence, lunch was served. They go down well with a glass of hot milky tea. It is always well to remember that in most of these roadside places, the cleanliness and hygienic conditions can be highly suspect. You pay your money and make your choice!

Sixteen miles after passing through the town of Aurangabad, we boarded a rail train ferry for the crossing of the wide Son River to Derhi-Son. The crossing took a little over twenty minutes and cost twenty-two Rupees (about £1.75p approximately). After we had disembarked from the ferry at Dehri-Son, we were soon surrounded by curiosity seekers, who trotted out the usual questions in whatever words of English they could muster. Where were we from? Where were we going? Did we like their country? And so forth.

However, it was one elderly man in the crowd that caught my eye. He was dressed in a clean, long white shirt, sported a fine beard and had a white turban wrapped neatly around his head. Even with all the jabbering going on around, this man seemed to have a magnetic affect on me for reasons I cannot explain. My eyes repeatedly drifted back to where he stood. The look in his eyes didn't change; he just stared. After a few minutes I felt compelled to show my recognition of him with a long slow deep bow of my head towards him. He immediately responded in kind and moved through the crowd towards us. We shook hands and in perfect English he asked us to take tea with him.

We followed him to a nearby teashop in a little marketplace. He said his name was Dwarihapershad Panday and that he lived in Gorakhpur U.P. (Uttar Pradesh). We all talked for a while about Indian politics, and he told us that he had once been imprisoned by the British on the Andaman and Nicobar Islands for sixteen years for acts against the British Government, although we were not quite sure what these acts were. He admitted to joining a freedom movement that could undermine British rule. In other words he had committed the 'unforgivable crime' of wanting freedom for his country. Hundreds of others who had joined that movement were also transported to those islands and many were hanged. He showed no animosity towards Britain and admitted that many good things had come about under the Raj. He quoted the vast railway network that covered large parts of the country and the number of hospitals that were now available. On the downside, those who had worked for the British during the occupation no longer had jobs after they left. He went on to tell us that he had once been a member of the Legislative Assembly and that it hadn't been an easy transition into independence. India had made many mistakes, but they were their mistakes and they faced them as free men. It had been a pleasure for us to be in the company of the man in the crowd, who could still find it in his heart to be magnanimous toward us British.

As we headed farther on towards New Delhi, which, God willing, we hoped to reach in two or three days, our topics of conversation on the way stretched from Australia to London. We talked of the many good people with whom we had come into contact and would probably never have the pleasure of meeting again. Like the elephant man, who had arrived as if by magic and pulled us from the swamp. The man who had carried his sick child to us and asked for our help, and the man who had worked most of the night to repair our broken trailer and sought no reward. We laughed about our few days of luxury aboard the good ship *Charon*, where we stuffed ourselves silly with all that marvellous food for nearly six days. My friends discussed their hopes and aspirations for once they had reached England. Would they find work? Somewhere to live? Would Lyn find that long-lost relative she had never met? Of course, none of these applied to Angela or Bruce. Sadly, Angela would be leaving us when we reached Delhi to take up a nursery post, which had been prearranged before we left Australia. Bruce was leaving us in Teheran to take up a post teaching English.

On the outskirts of Benares we ran into an amusing little incident. We had just driven past a group of four pint-sized vendors, all holding little round baskets containing oranges. We stopped a bit farther down the road to check on the trailer. Seeing that we had stopped, the four kids, who could only have been between five and ten years old, charged towards the Land Rover thinking that we had stopped to buy their oranges. One little fellow, who looked the youngest of the bunch, fell over in the rush and spilled all his oranges in the road. He looked up at his friends now gathered round the Land Rover, and, having convinced himself that he had now lost any chance of a sale, began to cry. A couple of us walked back to where he was and helped to pick up his oranges. In the meantime, the other three were exalting with their sales pitch, all claiming to have the 'best' oranges. To keep the peace we used up all our spare annas and bought all the little fellow's oranges and some each from the other three. All four of them went away happy. We couldn't help but notice the smug look that had appeared on the little fellow's face.

We drove into Benares to explore. It is said to have been the religious capital of Hinduism since time began. Every year pilgrims flock in their millions to visit and bathe in the shadows of the derelict old palaces that line the left bank, overlooking the holy waters where they seek salvation. Throughout the whole length of the Ganges River, with its many Ghats, Benares is its holiest site. Every God-fearing Hindu wants to visit this place for the purification of body and soul, to cleanse themselves of sin and, where possible, to end their life there. It seemed ironical to us that a river so continuously polluted by the bodies of humans and animals could, in any way, be pure enough to cleanse the soul.

We visited the old city with its streets lined with colourful stalls, displaying everything from fruit and vegetables to Benares wares. We branched off into the maze of dark and dingy narrow alleyways filled with little shops. We were the constant target of beggars and children wanting to guide us down to the river to meet a holy man who for a few rupees would give us absolution. We had a bit of banter trying to decide which one of us needed it most.

Emaciated and unloved dogs wandered around, hopelessly looking for a morsel of food that may sustain life for a little longer. All they had to look forward to was the sharp end of a foot if they strayed into the path of a passer-by. If, as some might believe, there is a life hereafter, I would rather return as a holy cow than an Indian dog.

To see the sunrise over the Ganges was a more pleasant memory to cherish. It is quite breathtaking to watch this huge fireball slowly emerge to cast its intense beam of light across the waters and to rise gradually higher into the morning sky.

We left behind the noisy streets and smells of the old city as we listened to the clang of gongs and bells from the many temples and minarets fade away into the distance.

From Benares, we expected to take no more than a couple of

days for the drive to Agra, but poor road conditions decided otherwise. The road out started with a good tar surface, only to deteriorate after a few miles into a hard earth surface with the usual ration of potholes served up. This kept us awake as we bumped along. We passed through Allahabad, in the State of Uttar Pradesh, one of the most densely populated regions of India; then followed the course of the Ganges through Fateppur and Cawnpore. With so much change of scenery along the way there was enough to please and stimulate the sightseeing appetite of the most ardent traveller. It was a common sight to see people squatting by the roadside to relieve themselves. There were

Replenishing our water supply from a well in India

vultures circling overhead, awaiting that final moment to swoop down and tear apart the body of some luckless animal. Trucks, rickshaws, bullock carts and buses were all vying with each other for position in the already jam-packed narrow streets.

In the villages women gathered around communal wells, filling their pani (water) containers as they caught up with local gossip from neighbours. Washed clothes and colourful saris were spread out and graced the side of most riverbanks, where they bleached and dried in the hot morning sun.

If it was a haircut you wanted, no worries, as in most places there was always a guy with a chair and a pair of scissors on hand at the side of the road to chop away at your unwanted locks. If you were feeling really brave, for a few extra annas he would be pleased to trim your beard or give you a shave with his cutthroat razor. If you chose that option, it was always wise to have a bit of sticking plaster on hand, just in case.

The chance to find out what the future had in store for you was never far away. You could always find a fortune-teller along the road somewhere ready to tell you all the things you couldn't wait to hear.

Wherever you went in India, the word 'Bucksheesh' was never far from the ear. A bunch of kids, wearing as little as possible, were always on hand to utter that favourite word to any likely looking giver. Even when you had felt generous and parted with the odd rupee there was always another bunch up the road waiting to pounce.

We arrived at the small township of Manipuri at nightfall and decided to spend the night there. Unfortunately, the Dak bungalow, where we hoped to stay, was already taken, but we were grateful for the offer to camp in its grounds. Whilst we had a brew up and pondered on the offer, an onlooker offered to take us to a place a few miles away where we would have privacy and be undisturbed. That sounded too good to be true.

Our guide, who sat in the front seat of our Land Rover, directed us to stop at an old railway platform. You couldn't really call it a station, as there were no buildings. It was better described as a 'halt', where an engine would stop to fill its boiler with water. Our guide assured us we would be undisturbed as trains never stopped there anymore. We had slept in far worse places and the platform seemed ideal to prepare our meal and stretch out in our sleeping bags. We thanked our guide and gave him a few rupees before eventually settling down for the night on our platform.

About 6.30 the next morning, our slumber was suddenly disturbed by the unmistakable sound of the shrill whistle of a train. We couldn't believe our ears and we all shot up as one. As the train stopped at the platform, the doors flew open and a couple of hundred bodies clambered out with all their belongings; stepping over us and treading on all our bits and pieces. It was more like a bloody Wild West stampede. The driver of the train thought it was very funny to see us sleeping on a platform. I must admit that after the shock had worn off and we had our early morning cup of tea, we too all had a good laugh.

After passing through Shikohabad and Firozabad we arrived in Agra, home to one of the world's most famous buildings: The Taj Mahal. It was built on the banks of the Yamuna River by the Mughal Emperor, Shah Jahan, as a monument to his beloved wife Mumtez Mahal, which symbolised one of the great love stories of a bygone age. She was twenty-one when they fell in love and they married in 1612. His young queen bore him fourteen children, but sadly died in childbirth in 1630. Many stories surrounded her death. Legend claims that on her deathbed she begged her husband to build the most beautiful of monuments so that the world would never ever forget their great love. To honour his pledge, the creation of this exquisite white marble masterpiece began in 1632. With a workforce of more than 20,000 labourers and skilled foreign craftsmen, it took twenty-two years to complete and is known as the eighth wonder of the world. His plans to build an identical tomb nearby, in black marble, for himself came to nothing. He was overthrown by his son Aurangzel and imprisoned in the Agra Fort, where he remained until his death. From his prison, he was able to gaze across the Yamuna at his queen's final resting place.

An Indian lady at the Taj Mahal, India

Both Shah Jahan and Mumtez Mahal are buried side by side in the crypt below the tomb. The tomb of the queen is inscribed in Persian with texts from the Koran and the ninety-nine names of

God. The tomb of the king is inlaid with flowers only. During our visit to the Taj Mahal we were privileged to be invited to see the burial chamber (now closed to the public) for ourselves.

After we had descended the steps into the long dark tunnel, the guide striking matches made the only light through. On entry into the chamber, two coffin-shaped tombs stood side by side on high plinths, covered in smooth ivory-coloured marble. They were inlaid all over with intricate detailed flowers, with every petal and leaf perfectly crafted. An intricate marble latticework screen reminiscent of fine crocheted lace surrounded the tombs. I couldn't help but to be overcome by a feeling of tranquillity and wonderment for those few short moments in the presence of such historical splendour. When we left the chamber to walk back, we could literally see the light at the end of the tunnel.

One of the tombs in the Taj Mahal

With so many monuments scattered around there was much to see in Agra, once the centre of a great empire. It was a city that had changed hands many times from one invader to another until the British finally took over in the nineteenth century, when things became more stable.

Before leaving Agra, we only managed a fleeting visit to the Agra Fort, an imposing red sandstone structure built between 1565 and 1573 by the great Emperor Akbar on the banks of the Yamuna. It was a disappointment not to have been able to stay longer to learn more of its long history.

As we headed out for the G.T. road for the run to Delhi, we made a short detour to Sikandra for a visit to Akbar's tomb. The main gateway that led into the huge walled garden of the tomb was quite impressive. We were immediately struck by the great similarity of the tall, white marble minarets that stood in each corner of the magnificent red sandstone structure to those that stood at the four corners of the Taj Mahal. The sombre atmosphere normally associated with visits to tombs and monuments soon evaporated when we were treated to some light relief by the antics of troops of resident monkeys entertaining us.

We rejoined the G.T. road and within the hour passed through Mathura, a city with many Ghats along its riverside. A ceremony of the floating of small oil lamps on the river takes place from some of the Ghats each day after sunset.

We stayed that night at a P.W.D. bungalow in the small village of Palwal, about sixty miles from Mathura. We continued our journey to Delhi the next morning, and as soon as we arrived headed directly for the Birla Temple, just off Connaught Circus, where I hoped we would be able to stay again. The Birla Temple was built in 1936-40 by Seth Jugal Kishone Birla and is a fine example of the old Orissian style of Hindu temple. Fortunately, one of the temple elders remembered me from my last visit and was pleased to welcome us aboard. Most of the places we needed to visit around Delhi were in easy reach of the temple. It also felt safer to leave the Land Rover outside without the risk of it being interfered with.

After we had settled in, our first port of call was to the Australian Embassy, where we were pleased to leave Louise in the capable hands of their doctor, whom we hoped would be able to sort out her bad foot. In the meantime, the rest of us went off to collect our long-awaited mail from the British Embassy. At that point in time there was nothing more important to the group than the letters they clutched in their hands. So without further ado, we collected Louise with her now freshly bandaged foot and returned to the temple for everybody to absorb the contents of their precious mail from friends and family.

Our sleeping quarters in the temple were one large marble-tiled room. There were marble blocks about eighteen inches high placed strategically around, supporting long marble slabs, on which we unrolled our sleeping bags. The ablutions were housed separately, outside our room and along a narrow corridor. We set the burners up in the corner of the room just in case we did any cooking.

Next we set about applying for visas for the countries ahead of us, starting with a visit to the Persian Embassy. It came as a bit of a shock when they told us that no more visas were being issued at the present time for travel to their country. This was due to an epidemic of cholera in India and Pakistan. That was news to us. We had certainly heard nothing about any outbreak in either of those countries. I was a little concerned as something like that could last for weeks, time we didn't have. While we nursed that stumbling block, I decided to go ahead and apply for the visas for Afghanistan. After all, we had to have them eventually. However, all I got from the Afghans was another swift kick in the goolies. They kindly informed us that they could not issue a visa until we had the Persian entry visa. That was another bloody disaster, which needed a lot of thought.

I had an appointment at the British Embassy next day with the military attaché to be debriefed about my return journey through Burma. That gave me an opportunity to discuss with him the problem relating to the Persian and Afghan visas. After he made a couple of telephone calls on our behalf, he gave me some very interesting information. Apparently, it was still possible to obtain an Afghan visa, but only for a visit and providing you left the country the same way that you had entered it. They were, apparently, not too concerned about the cholera problem in India and Pakistan. Although that was good news, it wasn't the solution to our problem. It did, however, activate the devious grey matter in my head to formulate a plan that might possibly work. I thanked the attaché, but didn't share with him what I had in mind.

We returned to the Afghan Embassy and applied for visitors' visas, convincing them that we had now changed our plans. The visas were granted two days later, but that did not mean we were home and dry. The second part of the plan could not be carried out until we were actually in Afghanistan. Then, and only then, would we know if the plan could succeed.

Since the news of our arrival at the temple had become known, we had been inundated with visitors coming and going all the time. Even when we weren't there, they would wait for us to return. Some even arrived in the morning before we were up. Everybody wanted to invite us out for meals and to visit their homes. They all wanted to be so darned friendly and wouldn't take no for an answer. Students loved to practice their English on us and it became very tiring covering the same topics time and time again. Irrespective of all the kind attention and advice given to us about all the places we 'must' see before we left Delhi, if we had taken them all up, at least another two weeks would have been needed to see them all. However, we were quite flattered to have become mini celebrities during our short stay.

We did take some time out for sightseeing, and to visit places that were of particular interest to individual members of the group. We started with a visit to the Red Fort, another creation of the Emperor Shah Jahan. In 1857, after the Indian mutiny, it was stripped of all its lavish trappings and converted into a garrison.

The gigantic India Gate monument at the end of the mile-long Raj Path was built to commemorate British and Indian soldiers killed in World War I, and to those who fell in battle on the North-West Frontier. A visit to the Parliament House, where the constitution of India was drafted after independence, did not pass without some light-hearted comments and opinions from the locals. The building, said by some to be the largest circular building in the world, with a circumference of about half a mile, contains two houses of the parliament. These are the House of the People and the Council of States. The locals gleefully pointed out that they call their parliament building the monkey house. They explained that members of the house, in moments of passionate debate, when tempers are aroused and frustration overcomes their control, have been known to remove their shoes and throw them at their opponents. I could imagine that during some of the more contentious debates that took place in the house, the fun they must have had after sorting out all those shoes, especially if two opponents claimed the same pair.

One of our last tasks at the end of our five-day stay in Delhi was to have the repairs and servicing carried out on the Land Rover and trailer. We needed to replace a broken leaf on one of the rear springs, repair the exhaust again and weld a loose mudguard on the trailer. They were all things that had been repaired before and would again before we reached England.

Although Louise had seen the doctor a number of times during our time in Delhi, the condition of her foot still had a question mark hanging over it. All we could do was wait and see.

After we had packed up all of our gear and made ready to leave the temple, we cleaned our room and thanked all concerned for their hospitality. Then, after a final feed of samosas from the stall outside, we said our last goodbyes to Angela in the annex of the temple. It was sad to see her leave. She had been with us through the worst of our mishaps and adventures in Thailand and Burma. We wished her every success when she took up her new post as a kindergarten teacher, and we all gave her a parting kiss before she left us. Our team had now been reduced to five.

We left Delhi just before midday on Monday the 12th of January, and headed out in the direction of the Pakistani border. After passing through Karnal and having clocked up 164 miles, we pulled off the road five miles before Chandigarh, made camp and called it a day. After an early breakfast, I bathed and dressed Louise's foot before we left for the town.

Chandigarh was a new town, designed by the famous French architect Le Corbusier and was still under construction. Eventually it was expected to have a population of about thirty lakhs (1 lakh = 100,000) when the town was completed. We didn't stay long, we were keen to press on towards the border and if possible to cross over the next day. So it didn't help matters when we had a flat in one of the rear tyres. After changing the wheel, we killed two birds with one stone. As we hadn't eaten since breakfast, we handed in the punctured wheel at a nearby grotty repair place and had a meal of chapattis and bananas, washed down with a glass of tea, of course, at a place nearby.

Because of our enforced interlude we drove on for a bit into the darkness to make up for some of the lost time. It was never much fun at the best of times driving on India's roads, but at night there were added concerns. Some of the lorries were well lit up, so well in fact, that you could be forgiven for thinking that they were mobile Christmas trees going along the road. They were decorated with rows of fairy lights all around their bodywork. They were not the problem; it was the vehicles driven with no lights, indicators or brake lights that made life difficult. It wasn't hard to reason why so many crashed, battered and bruised lorries littered the verges of India's roads. Unlit ox carts could always be seen in our headlights, ponderously plodding along one behind the other, carrying their small loads. Sometimes as many as twenty or more travelled in convoy whilst their sleepy drivers nodded off as the oxen relentlessly followed each other in unbroken rhythm. When they came towards us in the darkness, the beast's eyes appeared to light up like cat's eyes on the road as our headlights reflected into them.

We passed through the town of Jalandhar on the road to Amritsar, the last big town before the Pakistani border. We stayed overnight at a Dak bungalow twenty miles outside, ready for an early run into the town the next morning.

Amritsar is the capital city of the Sikhs and the home of their holiest of shrines, the Golden Temple, where most Sikhs hope to make a pilgrimage once during their lifetime. Sikhism was founded and taught by Guru Nanak, born in 1469, in a village that is now in Pakistan. He preached the doctrine of one God and believed that God could be perceived through love and devotion to his fellow man. Sikh men can be easily identified by their wearing of a turban, a beard or the carrying of an ornamental dagger, although many of the modern Sikhs do not follow these religious traits or requirements.

As we entered the holy site, we removed our shoes and washed out feet. Although it was my second visit to this holy place, it took none of the shine off that golden clad marvel set in the middle of a large square of holy water. We were led across a narrow walkway leading from the bank and into the temple. To the sound of soft music we were shown into a large room surrounded by small arches. In the middle there was an enclosure with a large carpet in the centre. Patches of flower petals were strewn around the floor. Holy men chanted while their followers looked on, crowded round the enclosure. We were privileged to be taken to an inner sanctum where bearded priests sat under strong lights, peering into the pages of holy books, reading verses from their Holy Scriptures.

Sikhs have an historic hostility towards Hindus and Muslims and it has long been their desire to have a state of their own. When the British left the Indian subcontinent in 1947 and partition took place, the new boundary cut the Punjab, the natural home of the Sikhs, into two parts. Consequently, a two-way exodus started with hundreds of thousands of refugees fleeing from one country into the other. The Sikhs and Hindus fled from Pakistan into India and the Muslims from India into Pakistan. During the ensuing period of that religious catastrophe, many thousands died in the senseless slaughter they inflicted upon each other. Many of the Sikh shrines and temples in the Punjab were left in Pakistan after the exodus.

We took our leave of Amritsar and headed for the border, quite convinced that our education on shrines, temples, holy places and monuments in India had been more than enough to satisfy us for some time to come.

When we crossed the frontier into Pakistan at Wagah, there seemed to be an unusual amount of army activity taking place on both sides of the border area. I pondered on the reason for this and assumed that it was another of those moments of political unrest between the two countries. It happened with recurring regularity and usually resulted in more troops being sent to the area. After being cleared by Customs and Immigration, the army very politely advised us that as darkness had fallen, we should stay the night there and proceed to Lahore the next morning. We were allocated a very comfortable hut for the night.

West Pakistan

As Lahore is only a little over sixteen miles from the border, we soon arrived in the city centre. Small groups of soldiers could be seen stationed at strategic points around the city. Apart from our intense curiosity of their presence, everything seemed quite normal.

As an oil change had been arranged for us, our first port of call was to the business area, located along the broad avenue of the Mall. We had an appointment to see a Mr Hassan, the Wakefield Oil Company manager, whose office was quite near to the famous Kim's Gun, as portrayed in several of Rudyard Kipling's works. I mentioned to him about the presence of the troops on the streets. He commented that a political adjustment was taking place in Pakistan with a view to wiping out corruption. I thought that was straight to the point and as good a way as any of describing martial law.

As we drove around to do some shopping before leaving the city, we began to feel like VIPs. Each time we passed a group of soldiers, they came smartly to attention and saluted our vehicle. When we passed the police, they also shuffled to attention but without a salute. We had no idea of the reason for this, but assumed they were saluting the British and Australian flags that were flying on the front of the vehicle. Whatever the reason, we enjoyed the attention.

Heading out on the G.T. road towards Peshawar and the North-West Frontier, we passed through Gujranwala and Jhelum, where we noticed the first chills of a climate change. The weather was ready to become much colder and it was time to rake out our woollies.

After an overnight roadside stop, and whilst trying to light our petrol stoves to cook breakfast, a car drew up beside us. The driver was curious about all the names painted on the side of our Land Rover. He got out and introduced himself as the area representative of a tobacco company and said that he had seen our vehicle while he was in Lahore. He invited us all to his bungalow for breakfast. John was delighted, as it was his turn to do the washing up. The breakfast was more like a feast. Our tobacco man did us proud.

We were introduced to an American lady who was staying at the bungalow. She worked for the Pakistani Government as an economic adviser and travelled quite extensively in that capacity. She told us of the huge project taking place in the area of the Thal Desert, where the Thal Development Authority were cultivating and irrigating thousands of square miles of useless scrub desert to bring life and prosperity to the region. Great networks of concrete-lined canals had been built to channel the waters of the Indus and the other rivers that flowed into it. Large areas were grassed over beside tree-lined avenues. Thousands of dwellings were built to resettle the vast numbers of refugees that had fled from India. She went on to tell us that it was the largest and most important development in the country. There were many problems still to be overcome and that the whole project would take many years to complete.

We thanked our host for his hospitality and the American lady for giving us an insight into a most interesting project. We also reminded John that he hadn't gotten away with the washing up. He could do it the following day.

During our overland travels we were offered and enjoyed hospitality from many kind-hearted people in many places. Near Rawlpindi we were offered hospitality of a different kind and of a type least expected.

We stopped on the edge of a small village, and Lyn and Louise left us to go to the market to buy fresh fruit and vegetables. Bruce, John and myself were seated in the front of the Land Rover awaiting their return. A guy came over to us to see us, he couldn't speak any English, but by the gestures he made with his hands we assumed that he had something to sell. He raised his hands in a stance that indicated he was going away for a moment but would be back. We didn't have long to wait for him to reappear accompanied by two pretty young girls wearing white satin Punjabi dress. They looked about sixteen or seventeen years old. They smiled at us and said the man was their father. He, in the meantime, indicated that he wanted sixty rupees for favours from his daughters. They seemed quite happy to be used for the price of a few rupees. When it became apparent to him that there were no deals to be done, the price came tumbling down. It did something to the pit of my stomach to think how anybody could trade a daughter like some cheap object you would bargain for in the local market.

On our arrival in Rawlpindi we were informed by the police that a special permit would be required before we would be allowed to cross the strategically important Attock Bridge. Time would be saved if it were obtained there. They took us to the office of the district magistrate, which after a bit of friendly chat issued us the permit. It bore the seal of the deputy commissioner and allowed us to cross either by day or night.

With our flags fluttering from the bonnet of the Land Rover we approached the bridge. The guardroom could be seen from a distance. Once our vehicle had been spotted, a flurry of activity took place as they turned out the guard. Two rows of soldiers smartly formed up and presented arms as the officer in charge saluted our vehicle. I politely and with some amusement returned the salute, while slowly driving between the two ranks of soldiers.

We arrived in the North-West Frontier town of Peshawar en route to the Khyber Pass. Peshawar is one of the oldest cities in Pakistan and the terminus of the main railway line traversing the length of West Pakistan. Because of its central location, Peshawar has been the largest trading centre of central Asia and also serves as a base for the Khyber Pass and the regions beyond. It was a quiet town with the unpretentious dignity of an ancient city that has seen Persian and Greeks, Buddhists and Hindus, Mughals, Sikhs and the British come and go. It has the unusual romantic appeal and colourful atmosphere of the frontier and was built in two distinct parts, the Cantonment and the city.

The Cantonment was said to be one of the finest in Pakistan, with its pleasant tree-lined roads with bungalows and gardens on either side. In the city merchants from Afghanistan, central Asia, tribal territories, Swat and Chitral States, bring their merchandise for sale as they have done for hundreds of years. On display we saw rugs and carpets, sheepskins, Persian lamb skins, Russian crockery, gold thread and all kinds of dried fruit and silks. We paid a visit to the Kissa Khani Bazaar to buy some of the superbly crafted gold and silver embroidered zari shoes. It was the biggest bazaar in Peshawar. Kissa Khani bazaar means 'The Bazaar of Story Tellers', and it is where people would gather and hear charming tales of romance, travel or tribal feuds.

While we looked around the city for somewhere to change money, we met two lawyers who invited us to join them at a hotel for tea, and where our money could be changed. They told us the name of their village was Takal Bala and invited us to stay with them until we left for the Pass next day.

As the Khyber Pass closed at 4.00 p.m. each day, we would have been pushed to have made it in time, so we were grateful for the invitation.

Their house was a few miles out from the city through a long

271

muddy lane. We had dinner all seated cross-legged on a carpet round a large dish stacked high with all kinds of curried vegetables, with side dishes of salad. We all fed from the same dish, picking the food up with our fingers between large pieces of chapatti. When it became necessary to ask where the toilets were, the girls were shown to a small washroom with a hole in one corner. We, the boys, were taken outside into the yard and through a gate at the back. The lawyer opened his arms, which conveyed to us that we could choose our own spot. I looked out across the great expanse and thought, *The world is my toilet.*

We spent a comfortable night sharing a room in which there were four large beds. It felt very homely to wake up in the morning to the smell of fried eggs and freshly cooked chapattis, and with an excellent cup of tea from china cups. In Pakistan they had certainly learned the art of making a good cup of tea. A note in my diary reminded me that their cuppa was the best I had tasted anywhere.

We left the village at 10.30 a.m. The lawyers very kindly offered to guide us to the entrance of the Pass, where we thanked them for everything and said our goodbyes. We were a bit pissed off to learn that a permit to enter the Pass could not be issued on the spot, as I had been led to believe, but had to be applied for back in Peshawar. We had no option but to return there and apply to the Tribal Affairs Department, where we had to go through all the rigmarole of filling in application forms providing all our details. One of the questions on the form asked where were we going. That was a good question and ultimately depended on whether we managed to obtain that Persian entry visa refused to us in Delhi, but to answer the question we just put down 'England'.

The permits were issued to us and we arrived back at the Pass at 2.00 p.m. A big notice at the entrance warned that photography in the Pass was strictly forbidden. With our passports checked and our permits scrutinised, we entered the historic Khyber Pass with a warning that under no circumstances were we allowed to stop in the Pass for any reason. I didn't stick exactly to the rules on the way through. When you have travelled so far across the world to such a momentous and romantic place, the urge to take photographs becomes most compelling. Although we didn't stop, I managed to take a roll of 8mm cine-film through the windscreen of the Land Rover. It was a rugged drive for the thirty-one miles up to the Pakistan–Afghan border and took us about an hour and twenty minutes. A drive I would not have wanted to miss.

Afghanistan

We crossed the border at 4.30 p.m. with very little formality. No mention was made of our visitors' visas or that we had to leave Afghanistan through the same border we had entered. I hoped that was a good omen. Afghanistan wasn't a country that held a great deal of interest to many people and none but the most ardent travellers would choose to go there. Stories of Afghanistan had always intrigued me and I saw it as a country that offered the biggest challenge since we journeyed through the difficulties of Thailand and Burma. It was tribal, poor and unconquered. Many had tried, but all had failed. Probably only the most enlightened would even have had a clue where it was on the map.

The road out towards Kabul, the capital, was very rough and potholed. We knew that if it continued on like that for long the trailer was in for a very hard bouncy ride. We drove on until 7.30 p.m., when we came upon an abandoned mud hut partly sunken into the ground. As it had turned very cold and I was uncertain if another shelter would be found before it was completely dark, we moved in. The floor inside was covered with animal droppings, so we had some cleaning up to do before settling down. The burners were lit, hoping the heat coming from them would warm the place a little, whilst we cooked our meal of potatoes, rice and cauliflower.

An overnight 'DES-RES' in Afghanistan

It wasn't long after the meal was finished, the washing up done and the sleeping bags rolled out that things started to go wrong. Our peace of mind was suddenly shattered by the arrival of a mule caravan. There were about a dozen men and two women in the party. It was an awkward situation and something we hadn't reckoned with. It soon became clear that they were there to stay and there wasn't much we could do about it. The thought of us staying and spending the night with strangers who had arrived unannounced in the darkness didn't much appeal to us, so we packed up and moved out. After all, it was their country, and their need might have been greater than ours.

We bumped along for a while longer looking for a sheltered

place to bed down when we came to a small army camp and went in to enquire. The warm welcome we received was amazing. We were shown to a comfortable room with two single-sized army beds made up with white sheets, pillows and thick patterned blankets. Lyn and Louise had already decided who would be sleeping in those beds that night. The soldiers helped to carry our gear from the Land Rover and brought a portable charcoal fire to warm our room. One soldier was quite concerned at the sight of Louise's swollen foot when I removed the bandage to bathe it. He brought hot water to the room and insisted on bathing it for her.

Another soldier entered the room carrying five individual pots of tea, one for each of us, with white cups and saucers. Comparing our comfort at the army camp against that of the little mud hut a few miles back we were wallowing in five-star luxury. The soldiers clearly enjoyed fetching and carrying to make us as comfortable as possible. One guy, who called himself Aslam, spoke English with an American accent. He said he had learnt it from the Americans who, like the Russians, were working on repairing and building new roads. He pointed out that American road builders were good, but the Russians were very slow.

We thanked the soldiers of the Afghan army, who had made our first night in their country such a memorable one. They waved us off as we left the camp the next morning and headed for Jalalabad.

We followed the course of the Kabul River along part of the old Silk Road. Just as we entered the muddy town the vehicle ran out of petrol. We had no Afghan money at the time but still had some Pakistani and Indian rupees. These we were able to change at a local hotel. Rupees were far more acceptable in Afghanistan than their own currency; so we were able to carve ourselves out a good deal and fill up the tank.

A few miles out from the town towards Kabul, the road deteriorated to such an extent that it could only be described as absolutely atrocious. It was like running a gauntlet of loose gravel, rocks of all shapes and sizes with some having razor sharp edges. They were certainly no friend to our already well-worn tyres. It was a slow laborious drive through barren mountainous terrain until we came to a large hydroelectric power dam where construction work was taking place. It was quite interesting to watch all the activity going on while we ate a meal of goat's meat and potatoes from a nearby roadside stall. I was relieved when we arrived in Kabul, although a little surprised at how lucky we were to get away without a puncture given the state of the roads.

We booked in at the Kabul Hotel. The only room available had three large beds, which had to be shared. There was a stove in the room which could only be lit after we had purchased wood from the hotel. I wondered how it was possible for them to find any wood at all in such a barren place. We changed some more money at the hotel, at the excellent rate of 138 Afghanis to the English pound. A meal of meat and rice taken in our room cost only seven Afghanis each. That was equivalent to about five pennies (2½ new pence). I doubted if anybody would quibble about a ten-percent service charge with prices like that.

We met a Mr Court, an actor, who was also staying at the hotel. He told us that he had starred in the film *Titanic* as the first engineer, and that all the engine room scenes were taken at the Cricklewood Power Station in London.

The condition of Louise's foot had made it necessary once again for her to seek medical attention. We went along to the British Embassy to see the military attaché, Colonel Clifford, who arranged for her to see the embassy's British doctor. His diagnosis didn't surprise me. He told me that Louise needed urgent medical attention and advised a comprehensive course of streptomycin and penicillin injections for ten days. He also needed to do more tests, so in the meantime while we deliberated on the situation, the colonel gave us boys his spare room to stay in. The two girls stayed at the home of Mr & Mrs Niel, who were embassy workers, and we all met up again at the Niels' for the evening meal.

Bruce, who hadn't been without his problems already, was suffering from toothache. Arrangements were made for him to have the tooth extracted by a German woman dentist who looked after the dental health of embassy employees at a number of the embassies in Kabul.

As well as the setbacks we had suffered with Louise's foot and Bruce's tooth, we were also unable to replace a broken shock absorber for the Land Rover and there was a real possibility that some of the passes in Afghanistan could be blocked by snow, which had already begun to fall. There was still the problem of our entry visas into Persia to sort out, so there wasn't much time to piddle about.

I ignored the fact that we were committed to leaving Afghanistan the same way we came in and applied directly to the Persian Embassy for entry visas, hoping that they would not notice our Afghan visa commitments. Unfortunately, they did, and insisted on an Afghan police permit that would allow us to leave the country by a different exit point. With help from the British Embassy, and to my utter relief, the police granted my request for the permit. My devious actions taken in Delhi because of the cholera epidemic had paid off.

It wasn't possible for us all to remain in Kabul to the end of Louise's treatment, so it was arranged with the doctor that she would stay behind at the embassy until it was finished. They would then arrange for her to fly to Teheran and meet us there. However, not long after that, the arrangement was to change. The doctor confirmed what we already knew, Louise had guinea worm. He recommended that she should fly to England for treatment, which would mean a number of weeks in hospital there. It was a very difficult situation for her to come to terms with, but it didn't take long for her to decide that there was no way she was going to be left there to fly to England when the expedition moved out. She would take her chances and hope that her foot didn't worsen.

We heard that there was a Land Rover representative living

on the outskirts of Kabul. His name was Peter Baldwin, and he ran a small agency from his home. We went along to see him and thankfully he was able to replace our broken shock absorber, and also supplied a new speedometer cable. He kindly invited us all to stay for lunch. When he heard how poor Louise had suffered with her foot, he made a very generous offer to pay for her airfare back to Australia. She was very touched by this but refused the offer with grateful thanks. We returned to the Niels' for our last night in Kabul. They had prepared a lovely stew for our evening meal, which was just the job for a freezing night. That was the kind of weather we could expect from then on. We thanked Colonel Clifford and the doctor for all the help they had given us, packed the vehicle and departed with a gift of canned beer from the Niels. They had been goodness itself to us.

We left Kabul in the early evening and drove off into the snow, heading towards Ghazni. It soon became clear, weather wise, that we were not in for an easy ride. The weather was not to be our only problem. About an hour out from Kabul we ran into our first spot of bother. The dynamo had stopped charging, which meant we were going nowhere. I removed it in the bitter cold and found that the brushes were broken. We had no spares; they had already been used. We were in big trouble. There was no alternative but for me to start walking back to Kabul. We waited a while, hoping that something might come along to give me a lift, but that was wishful thinking. Only a fool and us would want to drive on a night like that. The clothes I wore were totally inadequate for walking in that kind of weather. My thoughts drifted back to my days in the meat freezer at Broome in Australia. I wore everything I could put on there, even my pyjamas. So that was what I had to do again. The only difference was that there was an icy wind to contend with also.

After a large mug of hot tea made with difficulty in the front of the Land Rover, I set off at a pace, following the wheel tracks left in the snow by our vehicle before the breakdown. My exuberant start, however, was not to last. Progress became slower and slower until the tracks were completely obliterated by the continuing snowfall.

As I began to stagger with tiredness, it had soon become apparent that I was in serious trouble. I was alarmed at my plight.

Unthinkable and negative thoughts penetrated my frozen scull as doubt began to tease my brain, I could no longer be sure I was heading in the right direction.

Each step had become a fresh agony. It was only sheer doggedness that drove one leg past another and another, leaving a furrow in my wake. The cold had long fought its way through the strips of newspaper wrapped around my body parts. The watch on my wrist had stopped and I lost all sense of time, or how far, I had walked. With the last of my human resources slowly ebbing away, my mind drifted back to the events of the last few hours. I worried how my friends were coping, and what would happen if I couldn't reach Kabul. Only John would be fit enough to attempt the journey. Bruce was still recovering from a fever and the two girls, from jungle foot. I tried to keep calm but was in a situation I had no control over. I was a slave and at the mercy of some capricious snow demon waiting to decide my fate.

The pain in my joints, made walking, a continuous nightmare. I was drugged with fatigue and wondering how much more my miserable body could take when I came to a signpost. It had fingers pointing in three directions. None of which could be read as they were completely covered by snow. I was totally frustrated and lingered there for a while to focus my mind. I tried to jump and swipe the snow off, but my feet hardly left the ground. With the support of the signpost at my back, I rested for a while. I knew that if I fell asleep, it would surely be my last.

As I stared into the distance, I thought I saw a light, then wondered if it was some cruel trick my eyes were playing on me, but it became brighter. It was the headlights of a car. As it came closer I could hear the noise of its engine as it struggled through the snow. It was an old beat-up Mercedes, but at that moment in time, it was the most beautiful car I had ever seen. Like a chariot from heaven. I stopped in front and raised my arm. The car stopped. Three men were inside with Afghan blankets wrapped around them, scarves covering their ears and wearing a shammagh on their heads. I repeated the word, Kabul, Kabul.

They opened the door to the seat in the back. There were guns on the seat beside the passenger, but he pushed them aside to make room for me to sit. The men didn't speak during the journey, which was probably no more than five or six miles. I uttered the words, "Mr Baldwin, Englishman," a couple of times. The driver just nodded.

As we reached the outskirts of Kabul, I recognised that I was close to the place where Peter Baldwin lived, the driver stopped the car, and with difficulty, I shook the hand of all three men, each of whom bowed his head in approval.

It was difficult to struggle the last few hundred yards to the house. My clothes were as stiff as boards. I walked like a man who was drunk. Mr Baldwin was surprised and shocked to see the state I was in. He immediately led me into a room with a blazing log fire. His manservant helped to remove my clothes and a heavy blanket was placed around my shoulders, I was then given a bowl of hot soup. It was a while before I began to feel my limbs again. After a hot shower, Peter gave me a pair of his socks to wear to help thaw out my feet while the rest of my clothes dried in front of the fire. After a meal of goats' meat stew, it was suggested that I remain there for the night and return to my vehicle the following morning in the company Land Rover when a new dynamo would be fitted. Although the offer to stay was very tempting, I couldn't help but be concerned about my friends. I needed to get back to them as soon as possible.

As soon as my clothes were dry, arrangements were made for me to be driven back to our vehicle. A new dynamo was made ready, for which Mr Baldwin refused to accept any payment. There were no words adequate enough to express my debt of gratitude to Peter for all he had done for me. I would never ever forget the sight of that blazing log fire when I came in from the cold. It was the early hours of the morning when I left the house with the manservant and mechanic for the journey back, still wearing Peters' socks.

When we arrived back to where the Land Rover and trailer stood, covered in deep snow, there was no sign of movement coming from the vehicle and no sign of movement around it. In the headlights, I lifted the canvas at the back and found them all cosily snuggled up in their sleeping bags. They had certainly not heard our arrival. I tried to wake them to tell them of the new dynamo, but they were completely uninterested.

Bruce tiredly asked, "Did you have any problems?"

I said, "No, no problems!" Then all went quiet.

The mechanic took about twenty minutes to fix the new dynamo, then gave our vehicle a jumpstart. Our own battery had been almost flat. As there was no further movement from the back, I retrieved my sleeping bag and made up my bed on the front seats. I left the engine running for a while to charge up the battery. The heater also warmed up the inside of the cab. It had been an eventful day and a thin red line between the Chariot from Heaven and the Angel of Death.

The following morning, whilst preparing porridge for breakfast, my friends remarked that they couldn't understand why I had bothered to come back that night as it was so late, and why I couldn't have waited till the morning.

The going became increasingly more difficult as the snow

continued to fall. We frequently had to stop to check which way the road was going. The last thing we needed was to plunge off into a snowdrift. Sometimes snowdrifts would build up right across the road according to the direction of the wind. We would then engage the four-wheel drive, and try to bulldoze our way through. In one way the snow sometimes helped a little, in as much as it filled in the grooves in the badly corrugated gravel road, which reduced vibration.

We stopped driving late at night beside another derelict mud house. This one had a dome roof with a large hole in the top but it was a shelter of a kind, away from the snow and wind. I had made the mistake of trying to edge too close to the house and the vehicle slid down a slope and finished up resting at an angle of 35/40 degrees, but it could have been much worse than it was. We cleared the snow from the slope that led down to the house the best way we could to make it easier for Louise with her bad foot. Our night's sleep, with the snow falling through the hole in the dome roof wasn't conducive to the feeling of being in a perfect Des/Res. We considered ourselves fortunate, however, that we had any kind of shelter at all.

I baled out from my sleeping bag next morning before the

others were awake. I wanted to get cracking digging out the Land Rover from its precarious angle. I had dug almost halfway round it before the others showed their faces.

Suddenly, we were surprised by the appearance of a bus carrying about twenty passengers. That was the first vehicle we had seen in a long time. Unfortunately, it hadn't travelled very far past us when it slid backwards off the road into a snowdrift. We eventually got the Land Rover righted and back on to firm ground again, when along came a Russian jeep. That too joined the party and slid sideways down the bank into the drift. I offered the Russian, who spoke very good English, and the Afghan driver our help to pull his jeep out, which he gratefully accepted. We unhooked the trailer, connected the tow wire and the jeep was on firm ground in no time at all.

The Russian told us that he was heading for Ghazni and was soon on his way. The bus, which had remained firmly stuck in the drift, had very little going on around it. The bus driver, who had seen me pull the jeep out with such ease, gestured for us to pull his bus out. I knew, by its position, that there was very little chance of us getting it out with the Land Rover, but felt very reluctant about leaving them in that predicament. I thought of all the kind people I had encountered on my journey who had helped me. I knew that at least I had to try to help them.

We fixed the tow wire to the bus and drove forward to take the strain. The bus just shuddered but hardly moved. I gestured to the driver to get all the people off and let the men push from the back. The passengers were very reluctant to leave the bus. I went on board, waved my arms around and told them to get off. I shouted, "If you want our help, get off your arses and help yourselves." I doubted if any of them understood a word I had said, but they all left the bus.

Problems with a Russian jeep

The women and the elderly men joined Louise and Lyn in the derelict house. The girls opened a large tin of biscuits and offered them some. Unfortunately, at some time, water had penetrated the tin, which had made them wet and inedible, so they threw them out in the snow. The passengers behaved as if Lyn and Louise were mad to throw them away and rushed out to pick them up and eat them. They took little notice of the girls' pleas that they were not fit to eat.

Only about half a dozen men were left to do the pushing. Bruce, John and I were already wet from trying to dig the snow from the wheel areas of the bus. We tried again and again, with the bus driver trying to drive it out as I pulled forward, but the

287

whole attempt was futile. After nearly two hours I called it a day, but agreed to take one of the bus passengers to Ghazni with us to arrange for heavy transport to go back and tow them out.

I was a bit low on petrol from having used the four-wheel drive so much, so I asked the bus driver if he would sell me a gallon, which would see us through to Ghazni. To my great surprise he was very reluctant to sell us any, although he had plenty. He eventually agreed to let us have a gallon provided we paid him two-and-a-half times the garage price. I thought at the time, *You ungrateful bastard; you won't get away with this.* I told him I would pay his price, but when the petrol was in our tank I only gave him the correct cost of the gallon.

The bus passenger who travelled with us stashed his bundle of luggage on top of our trailer alongside the axe and spade. As the snow had stopped, we followed the well-defined tyre tracks that had been left by the Russian jeep. After driving for more than twenty miles, the tracks suddenly disappeared but the Russian jeep hadn't.

There it was, well and truly stuck in another snowdrift with a very irate Russian shouting to us about what a bloody fool his driver was. He asked if we could pull him out again. That placed us in a bit of an awkward position. It was going to take longer this time as he was in deeper and we needed to get to Ghazni for arrangements to be made for the rescue of the bus passengers. On the other hand, we couldn't just drive off and leave him and his driver there. It would have helped if the jeep had carried a spade of its own.

288

More problems for the Russian jeep

All the digging had to be done with our one spade. We worked for over an hour before we were in a position to make the final pull to get him back on safe ground. The Russian was clearly delighted and ready to promise us everything.

He said, "When we get to Ghanzi, we will all drink Russian whisky and eat shish kebab together. Then we will play Russian snooker."

I asked what was different about Russian snooker.

"Our balls are bigger than yours," he replied.

I had to think about that one for a moment, but as it was too cold for a competition, I just took his word for it. We finally got underway again when it was practically dark and followed the jeep at a safe distance, just in case.

It was 9.30pm when we arrived at the Ghazni Hotel all absolutely knackered, cold and hungry. Unfortunately, it wasn't to be the end of our somewhat eventful day. We were soon to realize that fate hadn't taken a day off. The Afghan bus passenger found that his bundle of luggage was no longer on top of the trailer. It had dropped off along the way. Then to our utter dismay we found that the spade and the axe were also missing. That was a devastating blow. Those tools had been vital to us throughout the whole of our journey from Australia and were irreplaceable. There was no argument about it, we just had to go back and look for them. There was no point in us all going, so Lyn, Louise and John stayed at the hotel, while Bruce, the Afghan passenger, and myself set off on the search.

We had travelled about eight miles when a very excited Afghan raised his hands with joy as he spotted his bundle lying on top of the snow. We were very pleased for him, but there was no sign of our axe and spade. We carried on very slowly for another four miles and there it was, the axe! We found the spade another hundred yards farther on. It was time for Bruce and I to get excited. We lost no time in turning round, and as we hadn't taken the trailer with us, we were back at the hotel in double quick time.

We dropped the Afghan guy at a police post and hoped a rescue plan for the bus passengers would be quickly put into place. I felt that we had done all we could to help them, but I was sorry that it couldn't have been more.

Back at the hotel Bruce and I joined the others and were welcomed to a large room with five beds and a beautiful fire. We took no time at all stripping off to thaw ourselves out while clutching a mug of hot tea in our hands. It made a change that night for all five of us to each have a bed of our own.

Later the next morning the Russian, true to his word, invited us all to his room for that drink of Russian whisky and some skewered shish kebab. I thought the whisky was foul stuff. There were other Russians staying at the hotel. I pondered on their reasons for being there and asked our jeep guy. He just grimaced and said, "Insurance." (A word that has many connotations, and I suspected was politically motivated.) He was a likeable kind of chap with a smiling personality and we had an interesting conversation. I joked with him that he should come to England to sell his 'insurance'. He remarked that he would never be allowed a visa.

We left the hotel at 2.00 p.m. making sure that the axe and the spade were very securely tied. We then went through the ritual of filling up with petrol at Ghazni's only petrol point. In some places in Afghanistan, trying to fill up with petrol became a bit of a pantomime. You could see an isolated petrol pump sticking out of the ground someway off the side of the road with no apparent way of reaching it. Once you had managed to worm your way around any obstacles and eventually arrived by the pump, different sized copper jugs would be produced to be filled with petrol from an antiquated pump. This was operated by hand with the turning of a wheel. The petrol in the jugs would then be transferred into your petrol tank, which was all quite time-consuming.

Once again we bumped along the snow-covered corrugated road of this land of mountains and desert. Heading towards Kandahar, some 225 miles away, you could be forgiven for thinking that you were in the Antarctic. There was nothing but snow and more snow as far as the eye could see. We saw many wolves along the way as they searched for food. They could sometimes be seen in packs as they hunted together, and woe betides any luckless animal found stranded alone. Some dog owners, to protect their farm animals, had sharp pointed spikes fitted around the head or collar and feet of their dogs. That gave them the edge when fighting any wolves that tried to attack any of their master's animals. We, fortunately, never had to witness the aftermath of such a fight.

As night closed in, the moon was full and it became much colder. There was no wind and it had stopped snowing. The only shelter we could find, after a long search, was a small mud hut in the middle of a cemetery beside the pebble and stone-covered graves. We didn't relish the idea of having to put up a tent in the intense cold, especially with wolves on the prowl. To drive on to the next hotel was not an option. They were so few and far between, so we settled in the mud hut and hoped nobody would appear. We didn't want to be seen as strangers who showed no respect for their dead. Although the hut was very small there was just about enough room for us to spread out our sleeping bags. I slept with the gun stuck under the pillow, just in case we had to frighten away any four-legged intruders looking for a meal. The vehicle had frozen up during the night so we had to waste time in the morning heating water to help with the defrosting.

The afghan cemetery with its stone-covered graves

We left the shadows of the gravestones at 9.30 a.m. hoping that our presence hadn't disturbed the peace and tranquillity of the dead. Apart from frequently having to defrost the vehicle before we could move off in the mornings, there was always the added worry of whether it was going to start at all. Where possible during overnight stops we would try to pick a spot facing down a gradient. If starting then became a problem we would run the vehicle down the hill for a bump start. During the extreme cold it also became difficult to prevent our drinking water from freezing up in their plastic containers. It was most disconcerting when we needed to make a hot drink and had to break and melt the ice first. To try and alleviate this we transferred our large water container from its position at the front of the vehicle and placed it in the back with a blanket wrapped around it; this was reasonably effective.

The distance we were able to cover in any one day was governed solely by the state of the road. The treacherous conditions made it impossible to achieve what we considered to be a good day's drive. Driving on hilly terrain and iced-up roads was very hazardous and made us prone to slipping and sliding. Careful use of the brakes in those conditions was absolutely essential. On top of the trailer we carried some sandy gravel and if the vehicle slipped backwards on hills, or the wheels spun through lack of grip, those in the back would quickly jump out and throw some gravel under the wheels.

One night, when we could find nowhere better, we made camp in a culvert. Fortunately, apart from the snow, which we cleared out, it was quite dry. As we cooked our meal it wasn't long before we heard the howl of wolves, who had probably closed in on the smells of our cooking. Bruce, who had collected a toilet roll from the Land Rover, went over to some rocks some distance away to answer the call of nature. It wasn't long before an urgent yell came from him, shouting, "Eric, bring the gun!"

I immediately responded, gun in hand, to where he was, and was in time to see two wolves that were too close to him for comfort. One shot in their direction was all that was needed and they were gone. Bruce was literally caught with his trousers down. (I expect the appearance of the wolves helped him unload a little quicker than he normally would have.) That was another night's sleep we had with one eye open and gun under the pillow.

We eventually arrived in Kandahar and booked in at the hotel. We were all feeling a little travel weary and needed to rest up for a couple of days. We had been on the road for just over four months since leaving Sydney, Australia.

The word 'rest' might have been somewhat overstated, as there were lots of jobs that we needed to catch up on. Our clothes had to be washed, and most importantly we had to find a way of drying them. It would have been nice to have hot baths, but the very limited facilities at the hotel made that a non-starter. All we could hope for was the lesser luxury of standing up in a plastic bowl of hot water and washing ourselves down. Our cooking and eating utensils needed to be given a thorough wash and dried with clean tea towels, something we weren't easily able to do while on the move. Then there was our faithful steed, the Land Rover, which always needed constant love and attention.

We left the hotel and drove around to see the walled city of Kandahar, once the ancient capital of Afghanistan. We didn't stay too long and were soon on the road leading towards Farah. I wasn't feeling quite myself and seemed to have developed flu-like symptoms which came and went in cycles. For a few hours I would feel all right, then the symptoms would return and I would begin to shiver. I felt the need to drink more and more each time we stopped for a break. This went on for more than three days. All I looked forward to at the end of each day was to crawl into my sleeping bag.

On arrival at Farah we stocked up with some fruit and veg at the little market place, then carried on to ford the Farah Rud. As it was over two feet deep in places, we had to use our rubber hose extension to extend the exhaust pipe. The trailer was all but submerged during the crossing.

Our next target town was Herat, the last town we would pass through before reaching the Iranian border. The loose gravel road was very bad and bumpy. On some stretches the snow helped a little by welding together the loose gravel.

Forty miles out from Farah we stumbled on an American road builders' camp and enquired whether they had a doctor on site. Unfortunately they didn't, but they offered us the use of a caravan for twenty-four hours where I could rest up for a while. It couldn't be for longer as they were, as they put it, expecting a visit from the 'Big Boss Man'.

We rummaged through our depleted stock of medical supplies for something that might give some relief from whatever it was I was suffering from. I was given some tinned orange juice to drink, which helped my burning thirst and was indeed a change from the usual tea or coffee. The camp's Filipino cook brought hot food to the caravan for us. We were all very grateful for another night's shelter away from the cold and chill winds of the Afghan wastes. After a short stay at the camp, we enjoyed a good breakfast of sausages, fried eggs and homemade bread; we were then back on track towards Herat.

Passing through the small township of Shindand, we were surprised to see more Russian vehicles in the area, all driven by

Afghan drivers. They were the first heavier vehicles we had seen since our rescue of the Russian jeep. Having made better time than expected on the last stretch to Herat we arrived at the hotel at 5.30 p.m. It looked quite impressive from the outside, more so than others we had stayed at. Unfortunately, first impressions don't always stand up to the reality. The only room available to us in the hotel was an empty one with no beds, but we took it without hesitation.

There were a number of Russians staying at the hotel. We wondered what they were about and learned later that although they didn't wear military uniforms, their official function was to give firearms training to the Afghan Army. It was no surprise to find a couple of Americans, from the American Embassy, also staying at the hotel. Wherever the Russians were, the Americans were never too far away. They invited us to their room for a drink and by the amount of stuff they had there, they seemed to have brought everything with them bar the kitchen sink. There were wines, spirits and enough tinned foods to stand a siege. They told us, with grins on their faces, that they were there in Herat to have a look around, and they quizzed us about anything we might have seen on the way.

While exploring the hotel, Bruce discovered a door leading to a closed-off section and ambled through to investigate. He found an unoccupied room with two elaborately made-up beds. As curiosity got the better of him he asked a hotel worker who the room was for. From the inaudible reply, he gathered it was kept empty for any VIPs.

When it was time to turn in that night and all was quiet, Bruce and Lyn cheekily decided that they were the VIPs and went off to sleep in those elaborately made-up beds. For me, sleep didn't come easily. I was burning hot yet shivering, and my inner sleeping bag was wet with perspiration. In the morning I found it hard to stand without support from John, who helped me struggle to the toilet. I couldn't understand what was happening to me, but all the symptoms pointed to malaria. After all, I had been rather lax about taking my malaria tablets, but with such cold weather conditions I dismissed that idea out of hand.

Although facilities at the hotel left a lot to be desired, with toilets not working, water refusing to come out of the taps, and the extremely dim electric lights that kept going up and down all the time, we decided to stay on for another night. Bruce, John and Lyn went out to do some shopping and change some money, while Louise played nursemaid to me in our room. I spent most of that day in my sleeping bag.

We left the hotel the following morning having paid a mere fifty Afghani for two nights stay. Any food we had was paid for on delivery to our room. On inspection of the vehicle, I was a bit concerned to find that we had a slight leak in the radiator. I decided to chance it however, and hope for the best until we crossed the border into Iran, where the facilities were much better. The Russians and the two Americans came out to see us off and wished us all a safe journey as they waved us away.

Although still very cold, the snow on the road had thinned quite considerably, exposing more of the potholed and corrugated surface. We had been on the road for a little more than thirty minutes since leaving the hotel when we were to witness a nasty accident. A Russian fuel tanker had overtaken our vehicle a few minutes earlier and we followed about 200 yards behind. As we approached a very wide bend in the road, we were aware of another tanker approaching from the opposite direction. For no obvious reason the one we were following drifted across the road and straight into the path of the vehicle coming towards him! Neither sounded their horn to alert the other of their presence and no last-minute evasive action was taken to avoid a collision. They seemed quite oblivious of each other, and as they collided the front of both vehicles rose up like a pyramid before dropping back to the ground. I rushed from the Land Rover to see if I could help. The driver of the approaching tanker climbed down from his cab apparently unhurt. The other driver, whose tanker was then leaking fuel, stayed put in his cab.

It looked an unhealthy place for us to hang around and my first inclination was to get the hell out of it, but I knew I couldn't do that until I had checked on the driver. I shouted back to my friends to reverse the Land Rover and stay well back in case of an explosion, then I climbed up to open the cab door of the tanker. The driver was injured and couldn't move as his leg was broken.

It was a tense situation and we had to get him out as quickly as possible. There was no time to stand on ceremony, or apply all the medical techniques that should be afforded to an injured person. His cab being high off the ground made it even more difficult to extricate him, but I dragged him up from his seat and unceremoniously bundled him out into the arms of John, who had run up to assist, and with the help of the other driver we managed to get him down.

His leg was broken halfway down from the knee and was just hanging. I supported its weight with one hand to prevent the bone breaking through the skin and sticking out as we manhandled him over to where our vehicle stood. We then laid him lengthways across our trailer. He was in great pain, but that was only to be expected with all the rough handling he had received. Fortunately, we were able to give him some morphine tablets and I printed a large 'M' on his forehead. We turned the Land Rover round and left the tanker to carry on leaking.

We had passed a small building five miles back with a red cross displayed outside, so we took both the drivers there to be looked after. When we unloaded the injured man, the look in his eyes told us how grateful he was. He clasped his hands together as if in prayer and bowed his head. As I was feeling quite poorly at the time, it was hard to understand how I found the inner strength in my body that enabled me to pull the injured driver out from his cab. Whatever it was, I felt a little better when he was out.

After our unplanned interlude, we arrived at the Afghan customs point at Islam Gallee at 3.00 in the afternoon. We met an English guy there from Portsmouth who was hitchhiking his way to New Zealand. He had travelled from England by bus and any lifts he was able to pick up. We were able to give him a few useful pointers on his journey ahead.

While waiting at customs we went into a small post office at the side of their building to post some letters. Two men sitting in a dirty side room grunted at us and pointed at another room we should go to. In that room there was a small table and one chair. A guy walked in and we showed him the letters. After a quick glance he left the room and shortly returned with four other men. They deliberated for fifteen minutes to decide how much postage we had to pay. When the big decision had been reached, we were asked for 52 Afghanis and stamps for that amount were produced. We thought that was the end of our long drawn-out postal transaction, but not a bit of it. Another crisis had loomed. The ticket secretary, as he was so called, wasn't there and he was the one who stuck on the stamps and franked the envelopes. The 'four wise men' again went into a huddle and finally a second mind-bending decision was made. They would stick on the stamps themselves. For us to stick on our own stamps was never an option. We couldn't help but wonder if those letters would ever reach their destinations.

As we passed through no man's land towards the Persian border we stopped to gaze at a mass of hundreds of wild geese off the side of the road some distance away. Bruce decided that he would like to bag one and have it cooked later, after we had crossed the border. He took a couple of shots at them with the .22

rifle but after the first shot, they all rose up and landed again a hundred yards farther away. They were a bit smarter than he was. He had certainly cooked his goose all right. He didn't hit a bloody thing!

We arrived at the little border town of Yuosafabad at 5.45 p.m. and stayed the night at the customs post, where we tried to teach the custom officers some English.

After I had spent another bad night sweating, shivering and with little sleep, I knew that I had to seek medical help as soon as possible. The cycle of attacks was becoming more frequent. I was feeling so ill. To add further to my discomfort I also suffered bouts of diarrhoea. I didn't want my problems to cause too much inconvenience to my friends, so I tended to push my body to the limits of endurance just to keep going. We had come so far; I didn't intend to let sickness destroy the culmination of my dream. We thanked the custom officers for their hospitality and left the post at 8.45 a.m. I hoped the short English lesson given had had a measure of success.

Iran (Persia)

Although it would have been warmer to have travelled back across Iran by way of the South Persian Desert, the same way I journeyed out, I opted to take the very cold northern route to the Holy City of Meshed. I did this because I knew there was an American Mission Hospital there where Louise and I could get some medical advice and treatment.

The bridge that never was in Persia

After a four-hour drive over gravel and potholed roads, we stopped to talk to some gum-chewing American soldiers who were stationed nearby. They asked us where we had come from.

When told we had driven from Singapore, they at first thought we were joking. Then they eyed the vehicle and trailer up and down, and one guy said with an air of disbelief, "You mean in this?" he emphasized the word 'this' in a way that suggested that the Land Rover looked too knackered to even climb the next hill. Then a long drawn out 'wow' came from his lips.

We asked them if we could fill our water container at their camp. Most of our water had been used topping up the radiator, which had been leaking since we left the hotel in Herat. At the camp we were promptly invited to stay for lunch while our water container was filled and radiator topped up. They confirmed that, although there was a leak, it came from the water pump and not the radiator. They suggested that on our arrival in Meshed we should take the vehicle to their depot there, where the water pump could be fixed. That was certainly music to my ears.

After that unexpected lunch break, we left the camp and drove on till darkness had fallen, having to stop twice on the way to top up the radiator. It was a relief when the distant glow of the lights of Meshed came into view.

On arrival there we found a hotel near to the hospital so that Louise and I didn't have far to go. I was examined at the hospital by a Mr Scott, the doctor, who soon confirmed what I had already suspected, I had malaria. He told me that I needed to stay in the hospital for several days' treatment while further tests were carried out. I decided against his advice as we had lost so much time I thought it was important that we continued on with as little

304

delay as possible. He was quite concerned for my well-being and told me that I must, then, agree to rest for at least two days in order to allow the treatment he was giving me a chance to work.

He examined and dressed Louise's foot. Although there was partial improvement, there was still some way to go before she would be able to use it properly again. We were to return to the hospital at 1.00 p.m. the next day for treatment and to have lunch with Mr Scott.

I carried out doctor's orders the following day and remained in bed at the hotel. Louise stayed and provided me with hot water bottles and made orange drinks. When it was time to return to the hospital, I reluctantly dragged myself from the bed still feeling like death warmed up.

At the hospital, lunch was served to us in the nurses' home. In the meantime John, Bruce and Lyn had all been invited to the British Council, where they stayed for a meal.

On the second day I, again, rested up at the hotel while the other three took the Land Rover to the American Army depot for the water pump repairs. They also carried out a service and filled the radiator with antifreeze. That had certainly taken a weighty problem off my mind.

Louise and I returned to the hospital for our 1.00 p.m. appointment and found Mr Scott engaged in a heated argument in his office. The husband of a woman patient he had operated on was trying to beat the price of the bill down by half, and wanted to bargain just like he would have done in the bazaar. We felt very privileged to be invited to the nurses' quarters again for another lunch before we left the hospital.

Although the two days rest had been good, not just for myself but for my friends also, it was time once more for us to move on. I couldn't confess to feeling my old self again but the good doctor had done his best for me in the short time available. I was very grateful for that. He did, however, make clear to me that at sometime in the future it was very likely that I would need some prolonged hospital treatment. I just had to hope that it would be later rather than sooner.

We departed Meshed later that day for the 585-mile drive to Teheran. It was very cold. The vehicle and trailer had taken one hell of a beating over the potholed roads, and progress was slow.

We came to a small village and stopped by an old building that turned out to be a school. A young guy came out to talk with us. He called himself 'the Professor' and invited us to kip down for the night in the schoolroom. We shared our meal with him, and he kindly surrendered his bed to Louise and joined us to sleep on the floor. He told us that he was twenty years old and taught French to young children.

We were awakened the next morning by the sound of the Professor putting the kettle on. He hinted that the kids would be starting school at 8.00 a.m., so we tried to hurry making our porridge, but unfortunately we weren't quick enough. They started trooping in just before 8.00 a.m. and came in all shapes and sizes: tall, short, fat and thin and soon they were jockeying for

306

position around our cooking pots. That wasn't the only distraction to our breakfast. The local chickens and cockerels had filtered in from outside to join the party and pick up the odd morsel.

After breakfast the Professor gave each child one of our dirty dishes to wash in a pond in the school playground. We felt guilty having delayed lessons by nearly an hour, but at least the kids had learnt a little about making porridge, the staple food of overlanders.

It wasn't long after we had left the school when I noticed that the speedometer wasn't working again. It was only a little while back that a new cable had been fitted and we weren't able to replace it before we reached Teheran.

The changing scenery was very picturesque with its rolling brown hills half-covered in snow and the snow-covered mountains in the background. Nomadic groups of men and women struggled by the wayside, leaning forward to support the weight of the few possessions they carried on their backs. Some groups had the luxury of a mule or donkey to bear their load, or where a small child might be seated as they bumped their way along. Many of the small settlements had dwellings built of bricks made from a mixture of mud and animal dung. Dried dung was also used as fuel to heat their cooking pots and when fresh was sometimes stuck in pats to the walls of their houses to dry. Many houses boasted their own skinny dog that always barked at the vehicle as we passed by. Some would even chase after us until they had run out of steam. An occasional heavy truck would pass us by with its cargo of who knows what, leaving in its wake clouds of dust that we had to endure as it thundered ahead of us.

Mindful of the fact that villages and settlements were few and far between and hotels non-existent, we stopped at a gendarmerie post on the outskirts of a small village. It was manned by four officers, and we were given a small room in a dark corner of the building right next to a toilet. At first we thought that was great as we didn't have to go too far for a pee. That illusion was soon scuppered as we caught the first whiff coming from the gap under the toilet door. It stunk to high heaven, but as Lyn remarked, it was better than camping out in the bitter cold. Irrespective of the obnoxious smells, we still worked up a good meal on our burners and entertained the officers with a good brew of expedition tea. Nevertheless, we weren't too sorry to leave the post the following morning. We needed to take a good draught of fresh air.

A signpost we passed indicated that Teheran was 380 kilometres away. Our problems were much closer to home as the state of the road had produced another broken leaf in the trailer springs, so it was slow going until we arrived at the township of Shahrood. We found an old workshop there, but no luck in finding a leaf spring. Another garage offered to weld the broken leaf as a stopgap. The welder was so keen to do the job that he virtually pulled me into the workshop. Closer inspection revealed that things were worse than we thought. Three leaves were found to be broken. Welding them didn't appeal to me much as this was never a good option, but as we had little choice, I agreed a price of twenty-five tomans for the job.

Our clearly delighted welder set about the task like a kid with a new toy. We kept our eye on things whilst we made lunch in his workshop. The whole job took two hours. I did, however, have to point out to him a part of the job he had missed. When the money was handed to him he could hardly contain himself. He shouted, shrieked and ran from the yard waving the money above his head. We shrugged our shoulders and left nursing our own private thoughts.

I was very dubious about how successful that welding operation was going to be, but that wasn't the be all and end all of my concerns. Apart from the ongoing mechanical and medical problems, I was having trouble with the middle finger on my right hand. I had tended to ignore a small swelling at the bottom of that finger thinking it would heal by itself. Unfortunately, it didn't; it got worse. I bathed it in hot water and Dettol, but it became infected and more painful by the day. It began to affect my driving. I knew that as soon as we reached Teheran, a visit to the doctor was very much on the cards.

We drove on till 7.00 p.m. that night and ran into a heavy snowstorm. We pulled up alongside a light with a sign outside that indicated a place to sleep. The sign displayed two hands held together resting against a tilted head with the words 'Nis Pool' (No Money). That was the first time I had ever seen such a sign. The proprietor, of what turned out to be a teahouse, welcomed us and emphasized 'Nis Pool'. Two other men were seated at a table inside, both sporting a couple of weeks' growth of stubble on their faces. They were drinking from a bottle labelled 'Vodka'. From the moment we arrived their eyes never left the girls.

Once we had settled in at the back of the building, we were invited by the proprietor and his two cohorts to have drinks from their bottle. They were so insistent we became suspicious of their motives, but as far we were concerned, it was a non-starter. Lyn and Louise had already voiced their opinions of the men. One man asked Bruce if one of the girls would sleep with him. We kept watchful eyes on the men that night and slept with one eye open.

The next morning that 'Nis Pool' had changed with a request for ten tomans. We didn't argue the point and settled on five. Later that day, after taking another battering from the road surface, my earlier doubts about welded springs were well founded. They all broke off at the point of the weld. According to the map we still had about 140 miles to go to Teheran, so all we could do was repeat what we had done once before and put blocks underneath between the base of the trailer and the axle, supported by some thick bamboo canes we still had. This worked reasonably well for about ninety miles until the whole lot disintegrated. The bottom of the trailer was then resting on the axle. There was nothing further we could do but just drag it along as it was, which seemed to go on for ages.

It was very late when a cheer went up as we saw the coloured glow of the lights of Teheran in the distance. It was after midnight when we arrived and finding accommodation was difficult, but with help from the police we settled for a room in a boarding house. As it was too late for a meal we shared a battered tin of fruit and some biscuits between us.

Bruce and Lyn arose early next morning and went to shop at the local market for bread and eggs, which we cooked in our room for breakfast. There was a lot we had to do in Teheran, but the most important, as always, when we arrived in a capital city was first to collect our mail, then arrange for the necessary repairs to the Land Rover and trailer. We limped along Avenue Ferdowsi into the compound of the British Embassy at 11.00 a.m. that morning. The military attaché and Mr Cooper, the transport manager, arranged for the repairs to be carried out in the embassy workshop in the capable hands of the two Iranian motor mechanics. It was they who de-coked the engine on my first visit. I was to return the next day to discuss what repairs were necessary.

On returning to the boarding house I was approached by the proprietor, who spoke no English, but tried to convey to me that when we wiped our bottoms after using his toilets, we must not deposit the paper there. We must take it out with us and put it in a bucket at the end of the passage. I was a bit stunned by what he was trying to say and pretended not to understand what he was getting at. I accompanied him, as requested, down to the toilet. The blank look on my face prompted a masterly demonstration from him on how a Westerner wiped his arse, and then left the toilet paper to block the small drainage hole in the toilet floor. It was an embarrassing situation, but I did see his point. I made a discreet mention to the others and let them each sort out their own problems.

We returned to our room and planned how to make the best use of our limited time in Teheran. I decided to hang fire on a visit to the doctor about my infected hand until the repairs to the vehicle had been sorted out. We also needed to visit a hospital to check on Louise's foot and investigate the stomach pains she was suffering from. Bruce was to look into the possibility of taking up a teaching job in Teheran. He had often talked of his desire to teach English here. We celebrated our first full day in the city that evening by cooking a big meal in our room. We had missed out on food the night before so indulged ourselves in a little bit of gastronomic excess to make up for it.

I was back at the embassy at 9.00 the next morning, while the others explored the city and did other things. The two mechanics had lost no time removing what was left of the trailer springs. They found its bearings were also on their last legs. The rear springs of the Land Rover had been removed and needed to be reset. Two engine mountings had completely broken down with the engine resting on the cross-member of the chassis. The exhaust system needed welding repairs and that was just for starters. I was given use of the embassy Land Rover, driven by one of the mechanics, to transport me with our springs and exhaust pipe to the market.

I agreed a price of 110 tomans for the remedial work on the springs and ten tomans for welding the exhaust pipe. We found new engine mountings, and a new cable for the speedometer, but we could find no suitable size bearings for the trailer. That problem was eventually overcome by using two similar sized bearings, given to us by the embassy. We then made an alteration to the bearing housings to make a solid fit. As there was no embassy doctor we were able to see, they gave me the names and addresses of two in Teheran that they could recommend.

At 8.00 the next morning, before returning to the embassy, I accompanied Louise to see one of those doctors. He examined her and recommended she be checked out at the hospital. The doctor looked at my hand at the same time. An arrangement was made for me to return there and see him before we left Teheran.

At the hospital, as Louise was feeling so poorly, they decided to keep her in overnight. John returned with me to the embassy and we went with the mechanic to pick up the springs and exhaust pipe from the market. Then we both worked putting the trailer back together while the mechanics tackled work on the Land Rover. I was feeling quite upbeat on how the work was progressing. I wondered at the time if that would be the last major repair needed before we reached England.

Bruce's aspirations to teach English in Teheran took a massive boost when he met a Mr and Mrs Channel in the city. They invited us all for a meal so as to enlighten him on what life there was like for a teacher. They told us they had hitchhiked out from the UK some months earlier to check out job prospects. They were taken on by the British Council as English teachers and were happy to be earning £300 a month between them. Bruce didn't take long to make up his mind. He decided to go for it and would apply to the British Council the following day.

Before we turned in that night, we all trooped up to the hospital to see Louise. Although, she was deemed by the hospital to have improved, she looked far from being her old self. They insisted, however, that we take her out the next day.

Bruce was up early next morning and soon rummaging through his limited wardrobe to find something suitable to wear for his job application at the British Council. Lyn went along with him to give moral support, and we all wished him well. For me, it hadn't been a good night. I had had little sleep. My malaria and the pain from my hand had reminded me I had an appointment with the doctor.

John and I returned to the embassy to work some more on the vehicle, albeit with my own one-handed contribution being rather limiting. We worked up until 12.30 then returned to pick up Louise from the hospital. As we wandered through the city on our way back to our boarding house it wasn't hard to feel that, with its population of over two million, Teheran was firmly rooted in the present and had few links with Iran's mighty past. Even its best-known symbol of identity, volcanic snow-capped Mount Damavand (18,600ft) and rich in myth and legend is some fifty miles away.

Although Teheran had a unique and fascinating character, it was hard to explain exactly what it was. Part of the city's charm evokes in its quieter parts an atmosphere of an earlier and more peaceful age, contrasting pleasantly with the hustle and bustle of the city centre with its tall buildings and energetic traffic. It had all the facilities of modern life that one would expect from the largest city in a radius of nearly a thousand miles. The city lies at an altitude of 3,750 feet. It is situated on a rapidly rising slope with a difference of several hundred feet between its northern and southern limits.

As befits a capital city, Teheran had a vast array of goods in the supermarkets, department stores and bazaars. We saw natural sheepskin coats and lamb's skin hats at very reasonable prices. Shops in the Upper Ferdowsi Avenue and the bazaar had the best selection of Esfahan hand-printed fabrics, silverware, painted jewellery, turquoise, Shiraz inlay work and carpets from Kashan. Even with so much choice our own purchases were very limited. Some of the more spectacular attractions in and around the city included the world's most exotic display of diamonds, rubies, emeralds, sapphires, pearls and gold. Exhibited in a vault of the Bank Markazi (Central Bank), prime pieces include The Peacock Throne, gold and massive gems, the Dar-E-Noor, which is one of the world's greatest diamonds, a jewel-studded globe and the Imperial State Crown, which is used for coronations. Of the many mosques and tombs around the city, perhaps one of the most important is that at Rey, some eight kilometres south of the city.

Built in modern times on the site of Rhages, one of the mightiest cities of the ancient world, which was destroyed by the Mongols in 1220. The Mosque Shrine of Shah Adbul Azim is a major Shi'a place of pilgrimage, visited by over one million pilgrims a year. Non-Muslims, particularly women, should not enter it. Also at Rey is the Tomb of Reza Shah, a mid-twentieth-century shrine in honour of the founder of modern Iran, who was the father of the Shah.

On arrival back at the boarding house, Bruce and Lyn were relaxing with a mug of tea. By the satisfied look on Bruce's face I knew that he had come up trumps with his job application. I also knew he would be greatly missed.

Dinner in our room that night was a bit special. It was one of the last that Bruce would share with us. After the meal, he, John and Lyn went into town to see a film. Louise retired into her sleeping bag while I bathed and dressed my hand. I couldn't help but wonder that if my infected hand deteriorated more, how would I cope driving farther across that snow and ice-coated land?

We left for the embassy early the next morning to collect the Land Rover and trailer. That was to be our last visit there. The vehicle stood in the yard facing us and with its reset springs it stood higher off the ground. It seemed to convey to me that although, again, it had been bruised and battered, it remained proud and unbeaten and ready to pull its trailer into the next round of whatever lay ahead. I paid the small charge made to cover cost and time spent on the vehicle by the two mechanics. Adding my own appreciation of them. We thanked the embassy for all the invaluable assistance they had given and Bruce drove from the compound for one of his last stints behind the wheel.

After lunch the time had come to get my infected hand sorted out. Bruce, again, behind the wheel drove me with the others for that appointment with the Persian doctor. My hand was so swollen and painful it felt ready to explode. During the examination the doctor asked if I could bear pain as he needed to lance and drain the infection. I told him I could. I was no stranger to pain. Even so, I expected him to freeze the hand with an injection of some kind, but that wasn't the case. He just poured a liquid over it, which I believed to be some kind of surgical spirit. Then cut into my flesh with his lancing knife. I nearly ran up the wall; the pain was excruciating. Beads of sweat poured from my forehead as I gulped for intakes of breath. The doctor, obviously used to such reactions, carried on nonchalantly to bandage and rest my hand in a sling.

We spent our last night at the boarding house with Bruce reminiscing about all the adventures we had shared during our four and a half months together. We knew that when we left the next morning it would probably be the last time we would see him. Although trying to keep a brave face on things, it was always hard parting from a good friend.

On the morning of February 18th 1959, with all cylinders firing, it was chocks away for our rejuvenated vehicle as the four of us left the city. With my right arm still in a sling, I had little choice but to drive using my one sound hand. With the mountainous snow-covered route to Tabriz that lay ahead of us, I wasn't prepared to pass the responsibility on to Louise (whose foot was still bandaged) or Lyn, both of whom had had no experience of driving in such weather conditions. The few lorries we saw on the road were all equipped with snow chains, something we didn't have and couldn't get, so I knew what we were up against.

We drove on till well after dark that night, during which time I was able to develop the technique of a very fast gear change, enabling me on the rough surface to let go of the steering wheel, then to quickly grab it back again after the change without too much deviation of the vehicle. Of course that was only possible on a straightish road. When we negotiated the sharp bends one of the girls sitting next to me would make the gear change for me, according to my instructions, when I depressed the clutch pedal. This worked quite well most of the time and only caused an occasional hiccup when four-wheel drive was used in combination with other gears. The farther we headed out towards Tabriz the colder and more treacherous conditions became. Some of the passes were thousands of feet high, covered in fresh snow and black ice. We prayed that it wouldn't be necessary for us to stop for any reason or to lose momentum for fear of sliding back. We approached one nightmare bend about 3,000 to 4,000 feet up. Although the steering was on full lock, we just couldn't get round it. I brought the vehicle slowly to a halt about two feet from the

318

edge of the drop. Things looked pretty grim. I asked Lyn to put the handbrake on for me. I didn't want to let go of the steering wheel with my one hand. At that stage we found we were still moving slowing forward, slipping on the ice. Louise and Lyn just stared at me. They said nothing. I asked them to get out before I attempted to reverse, but they opted to stay.

There was so little time. John, who was in the back, had already seen what was happening and jumped out. I couldn't lose valuable seconds for Lyn to engage reverse four-wheel drive. I removed my hand from the steering wheel and did it myself. I told them to keep perfectly still. I straightened up the front wheels and let the clutch in very slowly, praying that the wheels wouldn't spin and cause further slide. It was a terrifying moment, but the Land Rover gradually began to move slowly backwards. I couldn't bother to worry what was happening to the trailer. At that point I just didn't care. I just wanted to be as far away from that drop as possible.

While that was going on, John had grabbed the spade from the trailer and had rammed it into the icy surface, behind one of the rear wheels. This helped prevent the vehicle from sliding again. The trailer did sustain a little damage, but nothing too serious. We were very lucky that night not to have all been killed. We had been inches from disaster.

Sadly, sometimes reality is never too far away and has a much crueller face, for as we slowly continued our curving descent our headlights picked up a diesel truck with its eight wheels up in the air, smashed to pieces. It had fallen from a ledge 200 to 300 feet above, and was resting on another with a sheer drop of heaven knows how far.

As there were still many wintry miles to travel, I was determined not to be caught in the same predicament again when driving over high ground. At the first opportunity we dug and filled one of our washing bowls with sandy gravel and tied it to the top of the trailer. This was to be used to throw under the wheels of the vehicle at the first sign of a slippery slope. We rehearsed that procedure before it was necessary to use it for real. From then on it became an integral part of our equipment whenever we travelled in adverse conditions.

It took three uncertain days to reach Tabriz. During which time I found the painful lancing operation carried out in Teheran had all been to no avail. My hand had again taken a turn for the worse, with the pain becoming more intense. To make life even more difficult a lump had appeared under my right arm. It became very tiresome having to spend time visiting hospitals and doctors whenever we arrived in the big towns, but there was little choice. We heard there was an American Mission Hospital in Tabriz, so when we arrived late at night, nearly out of petrol and all very cold we went straight there.

The house doctor was away. Only a young American woman doctor was there at the time. On seeing my hand she immediately gave me a penicillin injection and stressed that one should have been given to me in Teheran. The three middle fingers of the hand had all become infected, and there was the possibility of losing them if the infection spread to the tendons. The doctor decided she would anaesthetize me and operate the next day. She was going to open up the hand and scrape away the pus from the affected area. Although very grateful for the prompt attention, I didn't much care to have it done so soon. I asked her to wait a couple of days to see first what effect the penicillin and other injections given would have. She agreed to this providing, in the meantime, the hand was bathed as much as possible.

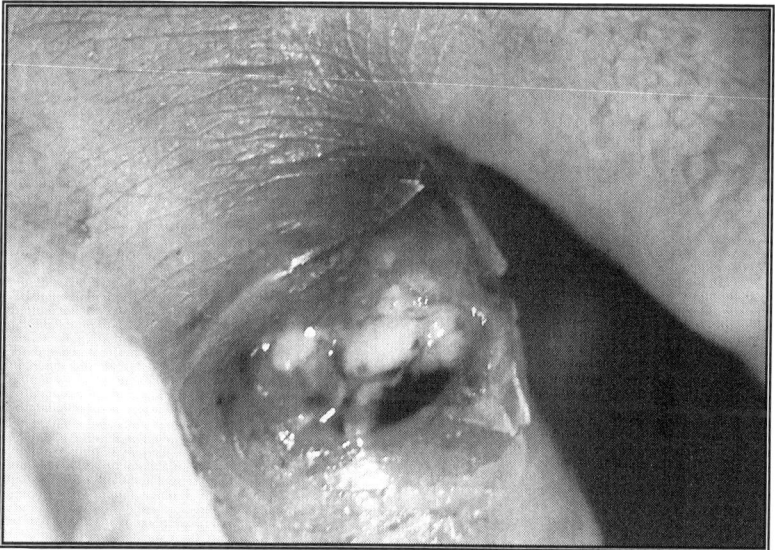

The gruesome infection that I had to pick at to get rid of the puss

The hospital was a small friendly place, akin to a cottage hospital. During our stay there we were given use of the house doctor's accommodation while he was away. We had full use of everything. We were able to have hot baths, wash our clothes and cook. On that first night we burnt the midnight oil. With the easy supply of hot water, I was able to keep up the bathing of my hand using the hottest water I could bear. I used the tweezers from our medical kit to pick away at the epicentre of the infection. It was like a thick plug of gristly pus. I pushed the tweezers into it as far as the pain would allow, removing little bits at a time. This went on until 3a.m. Lyn and Louise then redressed the hand and we went to bed. I slept more comfortably that night but next morning my stomach couldn't quite come to terms with eating the soft-boiled eggs that the doctor had kindly sent in for our breakfast.

The doctor saw me later that morning. On further examination she was quite amazed at the way the swelling had receded overnight, and by the amount of pus that had flowed from it. I explained my actions with the tweezers before going to bed. She remarked something about it being a brave thing to have done. I saw it quite differently, as nothing more than an act of desperation. Whatever it was, the pain had subsided and so had the possibility of having to have my hand spliced open. However, I wasn't entirely out of the woods as the doctor insisted I rest up for a couple of days, continue with the drugs given and pop in a sleeping pill when I went to bed. The news was also encouraging for Louise as there had been some improvement to her foot.

We took advantage of our short stay, living with home comforts and cooked one of the best roast dinners of the whole trip. When the time came to leave the hospital, I paid for all the drugs used on my behalf and expressed my sincere gratitude to the doctor for all the kindness and consideration shown to us. I can't help but admire all the good work of the missionaries in their mission hospitals around the world who, without question, will help people like ourselves who knock on their door.

As we headed on towards the Turkish border, it was still necessary to continue driving one-handed while my arm remained rested in a sling a while longer. This didn't help our nerves over the last few miles as the road narrowed and became more hilly on the run up to the frontier. We arrived at the Persian/Turkish customs post at 5.30 in the evening and had no problems with clearance from Customs and Immigration on the Persian side of the border. It was a different story when we crossed the few yards to the Turkish side.

Turkey

On examination of our Carnet, we were told by customs that it was not in order and that we could go no farther. I was totally stunned by what had been said and thought that some small misunderstanding had occurred which could soon be sorted. After all, every other country whose border we had crossed had found no problems with our travel documents. So what the hell were they talking about? They explained that the Carnet had originally been issued by the AA in London, but now bore the seal of the National Road Motoring Association (NRMA) of Sydney Australia, which as far as they were concerned made it unacceptable. I explained that as my journey had been unusually long, I had as a consequence, used up all the detachable pages in the book, so it had become necessary to have the Carnet extended to cover my return journey. The extension of that document was carried out in Sydney, Australia by the NRMA quite legitimately at the request of the AA in London. This cut no ice with the bloody-minded Turks. They just dug their heels in and insisted that it had to go back to London to be stamped. I even pointed out the printing on the cover of the Carnet, which clearly stated that an extension was permissible and could be carried out within the country you were in at the time. That was what had been done. It made no difference to them. They were determined we were going nowhere and were quite rude to us into the bargain. They knew we had already been cleared by the Iranian Customs and Immigration but still insisted we return there.

As it was getting late, I asked if we might stay at the post for the night, and get things sorted next morning. They laughed and mocked us. They then locked their door and left us in an icy corridor.

I couldn't understand the reasons for such a hostile attitude toward us. We had always been accepted with friendliness and respect whenever we arrived in a new country. Maybe they had still not forgiven us for Gallipoli! In the end, there was no alternative but to return over to the Iranian side. Their building was attached to the Turkish one but was a much friendlier place. We were welcomed back and given an empty room with a beautiful oil fire in which to contemplate our next move. We knew, even if we were allowed back, returning to Iran was out of the question and slept nursing that thought.

Next morning, with feathers still ruffled and in a militaristic mood, we returned to the Turkish customs determined that we would not continue to be denied entry for no valid reason. At first they showed the same contempt for us as the night before. I then opened my account and impressed upon them that we were in Turkey and that was where we intended to stay. To remove us they must first contact the British and Australian Embassies in

Ankara some 900 miles away, and state a good reason why we were, in effect, being held.

We sat in their office for four hours, trying to look unconcerned. An army captain came into the office, and he spoke better English. I started speaking to him about the disgusting way we had been treated by a country that was supposed to be our friend, and of my intention to report their conduct to our embassies when we reached Ankara.

They then started to show some interest by making an offer, which I immediately rejected out of hand. They told me I could go to Ankara alone by train, pay all my own expenses both ways and have my Carnet endorsed by their own AA.

I again impressed upon them that I had no intention of going anywhere without my vehicle or my friends. After another stand off they came up with another offer. We could continue on to Erzurum over 300 miles away, providing we took a customs officer along with us and paid all his expenses. Although I accepted that offer, I had no intention of being coerced into making promises about their man's expenses that I knew I wouldn't keep. He would eat and sleep in the same way we did.

When it was time to leave, not one, but two customs officers settled into the front seat. I wondered what the hell was going on. The extra guy, without having the courtesy to ask, had decided he was having a lift to somewhere or the other. I soon put the block on that. He was going nowhere and soon reluctantly removed himself from the vehicle.

When we eventually got moving, our man from customs made it clear that he wasn't happy to be driven by a guy with his arm in a sling and a girl changing gears. We weren't too happy either, but that was the way it had to be. I must admit I derived some small pleasure at his discomfort. We felt it was retribution for the way we had been treated.

We soon arrived at the rugged frontier town of Dogubayazit, ideally situated for a visit to Turkey's highest mountain, the volcanic Mount Ararat (Agri Dagi) which at 16,850 feet is perpetually covered in snow and dominates the arid plateau. Many myths and legends have evolved around Noah's Ark, Mount Ararat and the great flood. But did the Ark really exist? Many fragments of ancient timbers embedded in the ice have been discovered by Ark-hunting expeditions, but carbon-dating tests carried out have proved inconclusive. Whether the Ark existed or not, its history and location have been good for the local economy as it keeps the story alive.

Dogubayazit had a large Kurdish population, equally matched by a large military presence. Three kilometres up hill from the edge of the city was the Ishah Pasa Palace. Completed in the late 1800s it is decorated with beautiful stonework. The interior of the building is amazingly ornate. A fantastic blend of Georgian, Ottoman and Persian styles. A large area of the interior was set aside for the Pasa harem. Apart from the palace and an interesting circuit of walls, the city didn't hold much appeal.

After driving through the snow for more than an hour, our

customs man decided that he wanted to stop for the night in a village we were passing. I managed to get through to him that we had no intention of stopping there and would be going on for sometime. He was hopping mad and obviously under the impression that it was he who was calling the tune. I put him right on that score straight away. The longer we went on the more agitated he became, and who could blame him. Heavy snow was falling and we were prone to spasmodic skidding, plus the one-handed driving technique was all a bit more than his nerves could stand.

A few miles from the little town of Agri, we really struggled to maintain momentum. That was when he lost it, waving his arms around shouting, "Yok, Yok!" (Turkish for no.)

I shouted for him to shut up. We were not stopping until Agri. Not that he knew what I meant. He was like a frightened child. Eventually, when we arrived on the outskirts of the town, he was clearly delighted and kept repeating its name. The poor man must have thought that he had survived a trip through hell and he had aged ten years.

We stopped for the night and stayed in a cheap hotel. I offered to pay for the guy's meal, but he refused. He also turned down the offer of the bed we had arranged for him. I came to the firm conclusion that he didn't like us very much and that he had something up his sleeve. My suspicions were well founded. Next morning, when we were ready to leave, he came to tell us that the road was blocked and impassable and there was no way that we could continue. I didn't accept that at all and informed him that we would press on at all costs. I pointed to the spade and indicated that if we got stuck, he would dig too. I gave him the option to remain there if he wished, although I didn't think his boss would be too happy if he did.

The snow was deep. There was no doubt about that, but I had faith that our four-wheel drive would see us right. We kept moving, albeit very slowly, but we were moving and that was all that mattered. We were able to just bulldoze our way through some snowdrifts, but for others we had to back up and take a second run at them. On occasions it was necessary to leave the vehicle and use the spade. John, Louise and Lyn did sterling work. Although I wasn't able to dig, I sometimes took the spade from them and handed it to the customs guy to take his turn. He never volunteered to help. Ever since we had been forced to carry him from the border, he had made himself cosy by the heater in the front of the vehicle while the others took turns sitting in the back, where with no heating it was very cold. I formed the opinion that he should also have a spell in the back, sharing some of its discomforts.

We pulled in for a break at a small village teashop to buy glasses of hot sweet tea. On leaving, Lyn and Louise installed themselves on the front seats before the customs guy got in. He was most unhappy to be told that he had to join John for a stint in the back, which he stubbornly refused to do. So I gave him the option to get in, or I would leave him there! He probably thought I was bluffing, I wasn't. We drove off and left him in the snow outside the teashop. Looking back, we could see our irate 'friend' dancing wildly in the snow, waving his arms in the direction of the departing Land Rover. We hung our heads in shame.

After travelling another fifty miles, we found ourselves following a snowplough pushing its way ahead at five miles an hour through high snowdrifts. I thought at the time it was prudent to remain behind him but had second thoughts about it. We had stopped for a while to let the snow plough get well ahead when we saw a jeep coming up from behind, and who should be in it but none other than our customs guy. He was very annoyed, but oh so relieved to have caught us up and made a big show of his willingness to ride in the back.

After another night spent in a crummy hotel we arrived in the town of Erzurum and were taken directly to the office of the chief customs officer by our reluctant travelling companion, who was delighted to see the back of us.

In his office we were confronted with the same belligerent attitude we had experienced at the border, without so much as the courtesy of allowing us to explain our position. This chief customs guy informed us that we would not be allowed to journey on with our vehicle any farther, and told us that it must be transported to Ankara by train, for which we would have to pay the freight charges.

I objected strongly as I tried to get through to him that we had done nothing wrong to justify that. The ignorant man was not interested in anything I had to say. He went on to tell us that the vehicle would be impounded and we would not be allowed to leave Erzurum. On hearing this I became angry and told him to go to hell. He could impound the vehicle, that was his choice, but he could not impound us.

He then lowered his tone a little and became more conciliatory. I felt a pattern was emerging in his attitude and sensed we were being set up for something. All would soon be revealed. When he thought we were right for plucking, and that he had done enough to dent our morale, we would then be prepared and ready to accept anything in order to continue on with our journey. He then kicked in the real reason for all the hostility and played his master card. He was after a bribe. He told us that it was possible he could help us to continue on with our vehicle to Ankara if we paid him 300 lire (£12.00).

I immediately made it clear I was not prepared to be ripped off in such a way and would report his conduct to the town governor. He refused to give me the address of the governor's office and said the governor was far too busy to see me. Nevertheless I left his office to seek out the governor for myself.

I stopped the passers-by for directions, but it wasn't easy to make myself understood as very little English was spoken. After a while I was lucky enough to encounter a guy who spoke perfect English and who had once worked for an American Consulate as an interpreter. After I explained my problem, he agreed to take me to the governor's office and interpret for me.

The governor agreed to see us straightaway, and through my interpreter I poured out my whole story of everything that had happened since we entered his country. He listened intently without interruption to every word that was spoken; he then picked up the telephone, uttered a few words and replaced the receiver. Then he turned to me and said he was so sorry for the way we had been treated. We would be allowed to carry on with our journey to Ankara without further interference from customs. He promised an enquiry into the way we had been treated at the border and also why we had been asked to pay 300 lire to customs. Everything was then passed on to the chief of police to arrange our departure. I thanked my interpreter friend and the governor for his time and understanding of our problem.

The police chief did everything possible to help us. He asked me to bring my friends to join him in his office. Tea was laid on and he sent out for a large box of Turkish delight. While John, Lyn and Louise remained at the office a police jeep drove me back to customs, where I signed a paper relating to the Land Rover. When I came face to face again with the customs officer, it was a treat to see the expression on his face. If looks could kill, I would have been a dead man. His only comment to me was to say:

"Mister, this thing is very bad."

I just smiled and replied, "Mister, this thing is very good."

He then took the Carnet and wrote on its back cover and returned it to me. That was the last time I saw him.

In the meantime, back at his office the police chief had been busy kindly booking us into an all-expenses-paid hotel. He remarked that it would not be safe for us to leave Erzurum that day. What was meant by 'not safe' we never found out, but at least it gave us the opportunity to explore the town.

Erzurum was a modest city set in the middle of the barren eastern Anatolian plateau at an elevation of over 6,500ft. It was a crucial waterhole along the old Silk Road trade routes and was completely covered in deep snow during the harsh winter months. A number of cannon could be seen around the city, left by the Russians, who occupied Erzurum three times from 1828 but were finally ousted after being defeated by the Ottomans in 1918. More than a year later a congress was held in Erzurum where a national pact was drafted defining Turkey's republican borders.

The next morning, when we were ready to leave the hotel, a police jeep was sent to escort us to the outskirts of town, where they wished us good luck. Although we had tried to take all the bureaucracy and uncertainty caused by our tormentors in our stride and not be browbeaten by them, it nevertheless had been a bit mentally traumatic for us. However, by exposing their attempts to extract a bribe from us, it might have helped to prevent the same thing happening to others.

The miles unrolled under the wheels as we headed west towards Ankara. Except for a few diesel trucks equipped with snow chains on their wheels, there was little else on the road. We made good progress on some sections where snowploughs had earlier passed through, but these were few and far between. After Erzincan, on the way to Sivas, the road deteriorated and we were lucky if we made twenty miles an hour. We passed through many small hamlets, where villagers struggled through the snow with heavy bundles of firewood on their backs to warm their humble homes. Fuel piled high in neat bundles was stacked at the side of many of the small houses. It was normal practice to stockpile wood as they could never be certain when, or for how long, a village might become snowbound in such an environment.

In some of the more isolated areas of Turkey basket weaving and other cottage industries flourished. They were a mainstay of the village economy and its way of life. The practice of bartering for goods and services was commonplace among the local people.

The moon was high and scudding across the sky amongst a few thin clouds. With the reflection of the moonlight on the snow, it was almost as bright as day. We took advantage of this and kept going for a while longer. Apart from the sight of some wolves leaping through the snow to make headway, everywhere was quiet.

It was 11 p.m. when we called it a day and booked into a small hotel on the outskirts of Amasya. We were feeling upbeat on the way our moonlight drive had gone as it was unusual to have a day without some problem or another. Before we left the hotel the next morning, I felt the time was right to remove the sling from my arm. It would be a treat to be able to hold the steering wheel with my right hand again, get the fingers working properly and do all my own gear changing.

We didn't stay long in the town, just time enough to look around, learn a little of its history and do some shopping. Amasya was an appealing little place, sitting in a narrow valley along the cool Gesilirmah River with old Ottoman houses along its bank. An old fortress dominated the high ground above the town, which was immersed in history and said to have been founded by the Amazon Queen Amasis to become the first capital of the Kingdom of Pontus. This lasted for more than 280 years, after which it changed hands many times and was once chosen as a Roman provincial capital before fading into obscurity during the Byzantine era. Amasya progressed under Ottoman occupation and the area was frequently used as a staging post to launch campaigns into the eastern territories. In later Ottoman history three destructive earthquakes hit the city over a period of three centuries.

As we travelled towards Corum we passed the turn off heading north for the Black Sea coastal town of Samsun, eighty-two miles away from where the coast road linked the main towns of Sinop, Ordu, Giresun, Trabzon, and Rize. It looked interesting on our map, but it wasn't our chosen route for that day.

A few miles out from Corum, the going became easier and the snow on the ground thinner. Brown patches had started to appear through the snow on the hills. We were cheered by the thought that the worst of our struggles through snow and ice were now behind us.

Traffic on the road gradually increased, which made night driving an unnerving experience. Drivers of oncoming vehicles frequently didn't use their lights until the last minute, then would suddenly switch them on and dazzle you completely. Agriculture vehicles and horse-drawn carts drove with no lights at all. Donkeys with loads strapped to their sides with a passenger perched on top and camels loaded to capacity all made their way along the darkened roads. Small groups of men seeking a lift would sometimes signal to us to stop, but we never responded to these requests.

On our arrival in Ankara, our first job was to visit the office of the Customs and Immigration Department and take along the Carnet and the other document given to me in Erzurum. I was, understandably, very reluctant to go there at all. It was against my better judgement to go anywhere near a customs office until I reached the border. However, as I had given my word to report there when we arrived in the capital, I felt the need to honour that commitment.

Unfortunately, that was a big mistake. Honour didn't always bring the reward that might be deserved. It soon became clear that customs had prior knowledge of our pending arrival, probably from their man in Erzurum. I handed the document to a weasel-faced man who had hostility written all over it. After he had read what his colleague in Erzurum had written on the cover of the Carnet his reaction was spontaneous. He said he was going to take the car away and impound it until the Carnet had been stamped by the AA in London. However, this time I had pre-empted that possibility and parked the Land Rover well away from their offices. My reply to his threat was to tell him that it would be difficult for him to impound the car as I had parked it in the British embassy compound, and that was where it would stay. I picked up the Carnet still lying on his desk and he immediately demanded that I hand it back to him. When I refused he tried to snatch it from my hand, but he wasn't quite quick enough. I put it in my jeep coat pocket.

He exploded with anger, thumping the table with his fist shouting 'give me, give me,' like a kid who'd been deprived of his sweets. I shouted back that I would not give until I had been allowed to phone my embassy. As I made to leave the office he pressed a button on his desk which soon alerted the customs police, who entered the room to prevent my leaving. During all the kafuffle, and with the thought that things could get rough, I managed to slip the Carnet to Louise, who had accompanied me to the office.

Despite all his shouting and raving I was determined not to let his antics intimidate me. If I had given him the Carnet, God only knows what would have happened to it. It would certainly have been a problem for me without it.

After things had quietened down a little, the police left the office and stood guard outside the door. There was a silent stand off for a while, so I thought I would try a little psychology. Hanging on the wall behind his desk was a picture of Turkey's national hero, Kemal Ataturk. I pointed to the picture and wearing an enquiring look on my face, I then pointed to him, indicating whether the picture was one of himself, although it looked nothing like him. Then, with a flattered look and half a smile on his face, he shook his head in denial. As my charade appeared to have lowered the tension, I pointed to the phone on his desk and uttered the word 'embassy'. After a short pause of contemplation and much to my surprise, he agreed to my making a call to our embassy.

I spoke to the Consul, who was very helpful, he told us to sit tight, be patient and he would come back to us as soon as possible. True to his word, the phone rang an hour later, but it wasn't quite what we had expected. When the customs officer answered the call, he immediately sprang from his chair and virtually stood to attention, his head nodding in agreement with whatever was being said. It was obvious that he was speaking with someone of importance. We were soon to learn that the call came from the Director General of Turkish Customs, who had summoned him to bring us to his office, which was in another part of the Turkish capital.

The Consul was waiting for us there with the director general. After once more going through all our tales of woe, a letter from the director general was attached to the Carnet with the added assurance that whilst in Turkey we would have no further trouble with customs. He also promised to look into why his officials hadn't followed the guidelines clearly laid down with the issue of a Carnet, and apologized on their behalf.

With the customs yoke at last removed from our neck, Louise and I were able to catch up with John and Lyn at the small hotel they had found in the centre of town near Ulus Square. It was a good base from which to explore the city, pick up the necessary visas and other essentials needed. It had been an eventful day so we relaxed and went out for an evening meal to unwind.

We left the hotel early next morning as we were anxious to pick up our mail from the British and Australian Embassies, and then went on to suss out the area for some sightseeing.

Ankara was once nothing but a dusty small town in the middle of the Anatolian plateau but on the 13th of October 1923, it was chosen as the capital of the Turkish Republic. Modern Turkey was largely the creation of one man, Mustaff Kemal, who became its first president. He was later to change his name to Ataturk (Father of the Turks). To achieve his reforms Ataturk formed the Republican People's Party. His aim was for its members to establish a local leadership in every town and village throughout the land. He was determined to westernise Turkey and started by reviving the Turkish language, banning the veil and the fez.

Modern Ankara with its asphalt tree-lined roads, modern buildings, well-maintained parks, many cultural institutions and its well-developed social life is the symbol of today's forward-looking Turkey.

Ataturk died unexpectedly in 1938 at the age of fifty-seven. One of his many great sayings that we saw displayed on banners and in buildings throughout Turkey was 'How happy is he who can say he is a Turk'.

Driving around the capital there were constant reminders of him everywhere, from statues to streets that bore his name. The Mausoleum of Ataturk was built on the highest hill of the town Rasattepe, now called Anittepe, which means 'Memorial Hill'. It was the most imposing structure in Ankara and could be seen from all corners of the town. Construction was started in 1944 and completed ten years later. The ashes of Kemal were taken to the mausoleum in a solemn ceremony on November 10th 1953, the day of the fifteenth anniversary of his death. No visitor to Ankara could fail to remember the name of Mustafa Kemal Ataturk.

The two main shopping and business districts of Ankara were at Ulus Square and Kiziloy, the latter being mainly a fashionable district with its hotels, restaurants, movie theatres and sidewalk cafés. A favourite pastime for many of its people was to stroll along the Ataturk Boulevard after the working day or just sit in a pavement café and watch the world go by.

Ankara wasn't as enchanting or as bustling a city as Istanbul (Turkey's former capital). We were told that its inhabitants eagerly awaited the arrival of summer when they would take off to spend their vacation in Istanbul.

A visit to the Archaeological Museum on the south-western slope of the hill by the citadel was not only interesting for its rich and largest collection in the world of Hittite works, but also the buildings themselves. One of them used to be an old caravanserai and the other a bedesten (Turkish market place), both were built half a millennium ago by a Turkish Sultan. Numerous research and excavations undertaken up to that time had proved beyond dispute that the region of Ankara had been inhabited since prehistoric times. Nevertheless, it was only possible to trace the history of Ankara with clarity from the beginning of the Hittite period.

A few minutes walk from Ulus Square stands the Temple of Augustus built by the Galatian Princes in honour of the Roman Emperor Augustus. It was particularly interesting for its inscription in Latin known as the 'Testament of Augustus', which was in reality a kind of biography of the emperor. There were several mosques of historical interest in the city, namely the Alaeddin (1178), Aslanhane (1290-91), Ahi Serafeddin (first half of the fourteenth century) and Haci Bayram (sixteenth century).

Two important monuments erected in Ankara during the earlier days of the republic were the Victory Monument in Ulus Square, and in the park near Kiziloy the Confidence Monument with its inscription 'Ogun, Calis, Guven', meaning 'Be Proud, Be Industrious, Be Confident'. Also close by were the Roman baths which dated back from the first half of the third century.

Much has been said about the virtues of having a real Turkish bath, so before we left the city John and I decided to take the plunge and experience one for ourselves to find out if it was all that it was cracked up to be. After we paid our few lire all our clothes were removed and replaced by a large towel wrapped around our waist. We were then led into a large tiled room so dense with steam that other bodies in there looked like shadows in a mist. The heat was such that almost at once our bodies were exuding sweat. Then some tall, muscle-bound, black-moustached Turk with a long towel wrapped around him was let loose on us, manipulating our limbs into positions they had probably never been in before. After pounding our bodies with the sides of his large hands, which seemed to go on forever, a rough cord cloth was produced with which he robustly scoured our bodies to remove from the pores all the dirt that you didn't realize was there. A bucketful of cold water was then chucked over us as we lay on our marble slabs. This was followed by a hot shower. When we began to feel that we would never get out alive, we were wrapped in another large bath towel and sat down on the warm tiled floor propped up by a tiled wall. We were given a glass of hot Turkish tea to sip while we relaxed for at least thirty minutes. When we left the baths, John and I felt as though we were floating on air and had never felt so clean. I remarked to John that all the filth that had been removed from our pores probably had its beginnings in the swamps of Burma and Thailand.

Having seen as much of the capital as time would allow, we bought fresh fruit and vegetables from the market, filled the tank with petrol and left the hustle and bustle of the city for the near 300-mile drive to Istanbul.

We chatted on the way about Istanbul being the last city

before we crossed into Europe and that our Asian adventures were nearly over. It was more than five months since we had left Sydney, Australia and nearly seventeen months since I had left London. It seemed hard to come to terms with the realization that I could be home, back in London, within a couple of weeks, unless of course some nasty gremlin spiked our cannons.

Road conditions were a bit of a mishmash and varied from good asphalt and gravel to long stints of dusty potholed surfaces. Thirty miles beyond the town of Bolu, we were driving through a small village when the police, who wanted to know where we were going, stopped us. As soon as they saw that we were foreigners they suggested that, as it was getting dark, we stay at their police post. It was a cold night so we were happy to accept.

The post was a dingy place with hard mud floors and was lit by an oil lamp. We were shown to a large room with a round stove in the middle. A long pole was strapped to it with binding wire. Fixed halfway up the pole was a tin containing fuel oil. A narrow pipe with a fuel cock attached led from the tin down to a small aperture in the top of the stove from where the oil dripped into the fire at five-second intervals. Although it was a bit of a Heath Robinson affair, it kept the room warm rather efficiently.

After we had cooked a meal of vegetables on our burners in the corner of the room, we asked the four officers if they would like some of the coffee we were making. At that time coffee in Turkey was almost unobtainable for some reason. We had a job convincing them that what we had was real. I tipped some into one of their hands and they all had a sniff. It was obvious they hadn't tasted coffee for some time. Before we left the post the next morning we made their day by giving them a whole tin to share between them.

After a three-hour drive over a twisting undulating surface, the road ran through a military zone passing one of the largest barracks I had ever seen. There was absolutely no stopping or lingering for any reason in any of these military areas. We passed through Uskudar on the coast road down towards the Bosphorus, one of the world's busiest shipping lanes. It links the Mediterranean to the Black Sea via the Sea of Marmara. With our flags fluttering in a gentle breeze from the bonnet of the Land Rover, we made our descent down to the ferry point for the sea crossing of the Bosphorus. It seemed incredible that in just eight minutes we had left the Asian continent and arrived on the continent of Europe.

Our first port of call was to establish our base at a campsite along the Yalove Road, a few kilometres from the city centre. Istanbul is the largest city in Turkey, rich in historic and artistic diversity and the only city in the world that sits astride two continents, with Asia to the east and Europe to the west and almost encircled on all sides by sea. Of all the cities of the world that it has been my privilege to see, Istanbul must be ranked one of the most amazing and cosmopolitan places of them all. There was so much to see and do that we were in a quandary about where to begin. We settled that small problem by each feasting off a delicious freshly caught fish just landed from one of the small fishing boats and cooked at the side of the harbour by the vendor while we waited.

The Galata and Ataturk bridges over the Golden Horn linked the two main districts of the city, old Istanbul and Beyoglu, both of which are situated on the European side. On the Asiatic side are Kadikoy, Haydarpasa and Uskudar. Then there is the Bosphorus with its Anatolian and Asiatic shores. The easiest way to cross from Galata to Beyoglu was through the tunnel, built in 1873 and said to be the oldest subway in the world.

The Galata Tower was an important landmark around the city, said to have been built by Emperor Zeno in the fifth century, later captured by the Genoese who called it the Jesus Tower and used it as a lookout post, as did the Turks after the conquest. We decided to climb the 140 steps to the top of the 224-foot-high tower, and although we were knackered when we reached the top, we were rewarded with a sweeping view of the city below.

Shopping in Istanbul was a veritable shopper's paradise. As we explored the world's largest bazaar there was so much choice that it would have left Aladdin's cave sadly found wanting. The Grand Bazaar was a labyrinth of seemingly endless vaulted arcades and passageways of markets within markets. Although part of the Grand Bazaar had recently been destroyed by fire, most of its souvenir shops remained intact. Gifts made from silver and gold, copper tabletops, narghiles, antiques, jewellery, embroidery, ceramics, cloths and much more were always available. Anything could be bought as long as you knew where to look. Prices weren't fixed and bargaining was customary. My bargaining pitch was to haggle from around half the asking price and work from there. It normally paid off. I bought myself a Hookah, sometimes called a 'hubble-bubble' and secured it for exactly half the asking price.

Strewth! John splashed out on a new pair of shorts to replace the dirty ones somebody had nicked way back in Darjeeling. We had kept on telling him it was time he changed the ones he was wearing.

We didn't have to search long to find the old spice bazaar. It found us; we just followed that unmistakable aroma of rich spices from around the world until our eyes feasted on an array of colour by way of rows of dishes heaped with an intoxicating mix of ginger, curry powder, paprika, sage, tamarind and nuts of all descriptions. There were trays of all kinds of colourful mixed dried fruits, yellow, red, brown, blue, green and black. Not to mention large pyramids of Turkish delight filled with hazelnuts and tins of halvah, which suited the palate of most Turks. If you were a spend-a-holic you would certainly be broke when you left the treasure house that is the Grand Bazaar.

Taxim Square was the Piccadilly of Istanbul and the commercial hub of the city. In the centre of the square was the Memorial of the War of Independence, which was erected in 1928. One side of its circular pedestal represented Kemal Ataturk and his colleagues at the proclamation of the republic. The other side represented him as commander-in-chief giving the attack order to his troops.

Many ferry services operated around the Bosphorus and the Golden Horn, and it was just as convenient to hop on a ferry as it was a bus. We took the ferry that ran a service from the Galata Bridge to Kadikoy. A few minutes before our arrival, it was interesting to see the medical school where Florence Nightingale set up a hospital during the Crimean War.

Another ferry ride took us to Canakkal and the World War I battlegrounds to see the immaculately kept ANZAC Memorial Cemetery. In 1934 Kemal Ataturk wrote:

'These heroes that shed their blood -
And lost their lives -
You are now lying in soil of a friendly country -
Therefore rest in peace
There is no difference between Johnnies and the Mehmets to
us as they lie side by side -
Here in this country of ours.
You the Mothers who sent your sons from far away countries.
Wipe away your tears.
Your sons are now lying in our bosom and are in peace.
After losing their lives on this land they have become our
sons as well'.

It was thought that Istanbul stemmed from a small settlement named Lygos, which existed on what was then called Saray Burnu or Seraglio Point. On the 11th of May 330 AD Istanbul became the capital of the Roman Empire, renamed Constantinople after the emperor, and when the empire was split in two it became the capital of the East Roman (Byzantine) Empire.

Following the proclamation of the Turkish Republic in 1923, Ankara superseded Istanbul as the capital of Turkey and the name Constantinople was dropped. The city then became universally known as Istanbul. The region will long be remembered in British history, when in 1915 during World War I, British and French warships attempted to fight their way through the narrow straits of the Dardanelles (Hellespont), which separate Europe from Asia, to reach Canakkal in support of the disastrous Gallipoli campaign. Some of the fiercest fighting took place around the area known as ANZAC Cove, where Australia and New Zealand forces suffered very heavy casualties. The allies eventually admitted defeat and were forced to withdraw with a bloody nose at the hands of Lieutenant Colonel Mustafa Kemal, who later changed his name to Ataturk.

Many of the signposts in the city relating to Troy took me back to my school days where I believed, and was fascinated by all the tales about Trojan Wars, Helen of Troy and the great wooden horse that the teacher had tried to instil in me. But did the Trojan Wars really take place? Did Helen exist? And was there ever a wooden horse? Was it possible that a handful of Greek warriors were hidden inside the horse to slip out in the dead of night to open the city gates? The truth is we will never know for sure.

In 1870-71 a German named Heinrich Scheliemann tried to prove that the tales were true and carried out extensive excavations on a hill overlooking the Dardanelles that he believed to be ancient Troy. Diggings soon revealed treasures, including a fabulous headdress comprising of thousands of pieces of gold. After more extensive excavations in the 1890s and again in the 1930s evidence of Bronze Age occupation was discovered, but no firm evidence of Trojan Wars or the existence of a wooden horse. Before we left Istanbul in 1959 we heard that excavations were continuing.

As might be expected in such an historical place, Istanbul's architecture and innumerable historic monuments must make it unique in the world. Also its museums house priceless collections of exhibits from some of the world's oldest civilizations. The city was still evocative of its legendary past. At every step we met history and the old stands side by side with the new in delightful and harmonious contrast.

The three days we spent in the city wasn't enough to explore all that we would have liked, but to have visited every place of interest, plus 101 mosques, would have taken three weeks, not three days. We couldn't, however, leave without a visit to the famous Mosque of Sultan Ahmet (The Blue Mosque), said to be the only one in the world with six minarets, constructed in 1609-1616 and a masterpiece of Turkish architecture. The adjective 'blue' came from the priceless coloured tile work that adorned its interior and gave it an atmosphere of peace and tranquillity.

After a last swim in the campsite pool we broke camp and headed out of the city for the 150-mile drive to the Turkish/Bulgarian border at Edirne, where we spent our last night on Turkish soil. Early the next morning, armed with our letter from the Director General of Customs in Ankara, we presented ourselves at the Turkish customs and immigration post. The customs officer took a long hard look at the letter and showed it to his two colleagues, after which we suddenly became VIPs, albeit only for a few minutes.

Bulgaria

The Iron Curtain was raised enough to allow us entry into the Balkan police state of Communist Bulgaria. There were border guards swarming all over the place. The Customs and Immigration officers politely, but thoroughly, checked our passports and travel documents, then carefully scrutinized the inside of the Land Rover and trailer before allowing us through. We had been informed that on reaching Sofia, the capital, we must, if staying there, book into a tourist hotel. I had already heard of these tourist hotels in communist block countries from our own military attachés.

After a six-hour drive over reasonably good roads, we arrived in Sofia and made our way straight to the British Consulate. We had been advised to let them know of our presence in the capital. We were kindly invited by the security officer there to have some tea. He told us how suspicious the police were of strangers and how they thought of them as potential spies. He also mentioned that during one of his many security checks of rooms in the consulate he noticed some very fine white powder on a carpet in one of the rooms. On closer inspection he discovered a pinhole in the ceiling where a bug had been placed from the roof. I suggested to him that I couldn't believe that it was only the communist block that was engaged in those kinds of devious tactics. He just grinned and made no comment.

We left the consulate and were on our way to the hotel when we decided to stop to look at some shops. Our Land Rover immediately attracted a group of onlookers. A couple of men asked us if we had any jeans we could sell them. We apologized and told them that we only had ones that were in use. At that time jeans in the Eastern block were very hard to come by. A few minutes later we had a rather strange request. A guy wearing a smart pair of jeans approached us and in a lowered voice, and in perfect English with a strong American accent, he asked me if I would smuggle him across the border. He added how difficult life was in his country and that they were not allowed to leave or be granted visas for any reason. I was stunned by his request and could give no ready answer. I told him that I would think about it and meet him the following day.

We booked into the hotel and were shown to an apartment with two large rooms and four beds. In one of the rooms there was a large mirror attached to the wall. In the other there was a freestanding mirror on a chest of drawers. I had heard about the two-way mirrors that were fitted in some of the rooms so I was already genned up with that prospect in mind. It was the large mirror that immediately came to my notice and I promptly hung a towel over it to cover it up. Not long after there was a tap on the door and a maid entered. She looked over to where the towel covered the mirror and said, "No, no," and pulled the towel down. She then smiled and asked Lyn and Lou if they had some nylon stockings she could have. That was another small luxury in short supply in Bulgaria. The girls dug out a pair of fine tights for her that I suspected had been put aside for use in the UK. That certainly made her day. As soon as she left the room I hung the towel back over the mirror, and that was where it remained. We ignored another knock on the door.

I gave a lot of thought to the guy's request to smuggle him over the border and we all discussed it in hushed tones for some time. I felt that there was something not quite right about the whole thing, and yet I couldn't really put my finger on what it was, but my suspicions were aroused by the smart jeans he was wearing. I just wasn't happy. Then common sense kicked in, why on earth, when I was on the home stretch, should I have even contemplated such a thing and risk all that we had achieved together, and with the added possibility of starting a diplomatic incident, or worse? We all agreed that we should pass on this one.

There wasn't a lot in the city to hold our interest so we left in the late afternoon of the second day and headed for the border. It was dark when we arrived, but that was about to change. Floodlights suddenly saturated the vehicle and it wasn't long before the Bulgarian immigration officers were crawling all over the Land Rover and trailer. They searched everywhere, on the roof, underneath and then everything was removed from inside. When one lot had finished, others took over for another look. It was obvious they had been expecting to find something or somebody stashed away in the vehicle. We couldn't help but wonder what connection the guy who wanted to be smuggled across the border might have had to the whole episode.

After crossing into Yugoslavia, we deliberated on what life would have been like in a communist prison if we had gone along with that guy's smuggling request. From the border to Belgrade we had no problems, but as soon as we hit the Auto-put, a lot of niggling hold-ups kicked in. First we had a puncture, quickly followed by a broken exhaust pipe, which we repaired with an old jam tin. About thirty miles from Zagreb the bloody dynamo packed in, but we were lucky to fall on our feet. Coming from the opposite direction was a Rolls Royce. Seeing our union jack fluttering, it stopped and offered help. It was a car from our embassy in Belgrade, complete with the ambassador sitting in the back. They very kindly gave me a lift, some forty miles, back to the embassy, where a repair, 'while-you-wait', was carried out. I was then returned to where our vehicle had broken down, travelling in a lot less comfortable van, but still very grateful for all the help given.

We crossed the border into Austria at Maribor, travelling via Graz to the beautiful area around the city of Salzburg, where we camped the night and did some sightseeing. The rest of the route through Germany, France, via Munich and Strasbourg toward the cross Channel Ferry Port at Calais, was pretty much plain sailing. When we boarded the Dover ferry, it didn't seem real that after a journey that had taken us more than one and a half times the circumference of the earth (nearly 40,000 miles) through monsoon rains and snows, mountains, deserts and jungles for nearly eighteen months, I was actually sailing to England and would soon see my family.

It was Saturday the 21st of March 1959 when we rolled off the Dover ferry, my first reaction was to drive onto the wrong side of the road and curse an oncoming driver, until I suddenly realised that I was back in England. I felt then that my dream had been fulfilled. I had accomplished everything I had set out to do, and even more than I had intended.

Pat and Roger, on the outward journey, had also succeeded in their endeavours. Roger to join his mother in Singapore and Pat to realise her dream and reach Australia. Of my three remaining Aussie friends, John, Lyn and Louise, who joined me in Sydney Australia, they too had triumphed over adversity and survived the tough conditions of their overland adventures to reach England.

Those who had joined the expedition in London at the start, and had undertaken to return with me but fell by the wayside, created a situation that left me destined to be the only one to complete the entire round trip.

As we drove along the Dover road to towards London, the state of the vehicle was very much an issue. Apart from its mud-caked body, the trailer was listing to one side, with thick bamboo cans making the effort to prop it up. There was noise and smoke coming from the jam-tin repair of the exhaust pipe and we were being flashed by other drivers who assumed that we had no idea of what was going on at our tail end. We had no tax disc and no insurance. We kept our fingers crossed and were fortunate not to have been stopped by the police before we reached Trafalgar Square. We drove once round the Square and headed for home. It had been a long drive to Australia and back and I thanked my faithful travel-worn Land Rover FWG 446 for bringing us, and that 'bloody trailer' safely back to my home in Woodford Green, where it was time to put the kettle on.

Four weeks after arriving back home. The trailer was stolen from outside my home. I uttered a few unprintable profanities and sincerely hoped that the thief would have as much trouble with it as I had.

Mr. Scott, the good doctor who treated me for Malaria, was spot on when he warned that when I returned home I may need, at sometime, prolonged hospital treatment. Three weeks later, in a state of delirium, I was taken to the London hospital for tropical diseases, where I remained for nearly three weeks. It was also discovered there that I had hookworms eating away at my intestines. I am pleased to say that I fully recovered after excellent treatment.

At the time of my return home, our local cinema were showing a film called *The Journey*, and as an advertising ploy, they borrowed the Land Rover and placed it in their foyer for the duration of the showing. Later on, reluctantly, and with a heavy heart, I sold the vehicle to the local Land Rover agents hoping that it would go to a good home.

Pat, who was the only one that stayed with me throughout the whole of the journey to Australia, eventually travelled on to New Zealand, where she ran into Ken again, one of the two hitchhikers. They returned to Australia where they married and had two children. Ken, with an accomplice, became involved in an armed robbery and was sentenced to ten to fifteen years. He finished up doing eleven of them.

Many years later, in England, I met up with Pat again after she had traced me through the Charlie Chester radio programme. I went to see her and found her confined to a wheelchair, living alone, and suffering from multiple sclerosis. She poured out the story of the path that her life had taken since she had left me in Australia. She said how thankful she was to be able to take part in what was to be the highlight of her life. I was so sorry to hear a few weeks later that Pat had passed away, but I was pleased I had been able to see her once more and thank her for being such a loyal member of my group.

Roger, our seventeen-year-old, the baby of the group, stayed with the expedition all the way to Singapore, his final destination. He stayed on there for eighteen months, living in Changi. On his eventual return to the UK, he worked for a while in his father's wholesale business in Newquay, then went on to work in a local hotel for a few seasons. He eventually found his vocation as a flight steward with BOAC for eighteen years. It turned out to be the perfect job for him, just flying around the world staying in luxury hotels. All that was to end when he met Maria at a party in a bedsit in Chiswick. They married and were soon to be blessed with two sons. Going away for long periods then became less appealing, so it was goodbye to what was then British Airways. They moved to St. Ives in Cornwall and went into buying and selling properties. They now have a small holiday rental business, which as Roger explained, keeps the bank manager at bay.

Although Elmore, our cricket loving twenty-three-year-old Jamaican/American friend, and Margaret, the twenty-two-year-old scout leader from Melbourne, had left us in Calcutta, rather than travel the Burma Road. I was very pleased on my return home to have received a letter from Elmore. The following is an extract from that letter:

A letter recently received from Margaret in Australia informing me that you had made it back to England. I want to congratulate you on the accomplishment of your goal and to express my appreciation of your making it possible for me to have accomplished what little I did achieve in making as much of the trip as I did. I do not know if you ever want to as much as hear about us again who ran out on you, but a trip like this, one can never forget, and there are a few of the people whom I would like to see again. I cannot recall that you and I had any quarrels or fights, so I will assume you do not hate my guts in spite of the run-out powder I took.

After Angela left us in New Delhi and had finished her stint there as a kindergarten teacher, she took up another post in Simla for the rest of the year. On her return home to Australia she became an art teacher to young children and was eventually to marry a Swiss guy. She went into business for herself and opened a picture gallery selling high-quality prints. I have been in contact with Angela by phone. She is now retired and lives in New South Wales. During our conversation she reminded me of the occasion when I thought that she was a bit slow in delivering her contribution of jungle rubble to help make a path through a swamp, which prompted me to shout to her, 'Hurry up, Angela, you're like a cow up a rhubarb tree'. Angela never forgot that off the cuff remark and it became an old 'chestnut' throughout the trip. Although she only travelled with us as far as New Delhi, she shared the worst of our mishaps and adventures through Thailand and Burma.

We reluctantly said our goodbyes to Bruce, our New Zealand friend, in Teheran, where he took up a post with the British Council teaching English. I had no further information of him after he left us there, or how long he stayed in the job.

On arriving in the London, John, Lyn and Louise remained there working for some months before returning home to Australia. John returned to the UK a couple of years later for a visit and to cycle round England. He provided the only news I had of the two girls. Louise, when her marriage didn't work out, took the path of religion to become a minister of the church. Lynette worked for an Australian company. Her work involved foreign travel. The last I heard of her she was still single.

Of myself, I soon settled down again to family life, but the lure of the open road was always in my shadow. I formed a small travel company and did three more relatively shorter overland journeys to India and back. One of which was to take me to Calcutta to collect my daughter Carolyn, who was returning home after five years in Australia.

To have attempted to come by way of Thailand and the Burma Road again would have been a dodgy bridge too far.